Per Capita Gross National Product

A CENTURY OF ECONOMIC GROWTH IN THE UNITED STATES

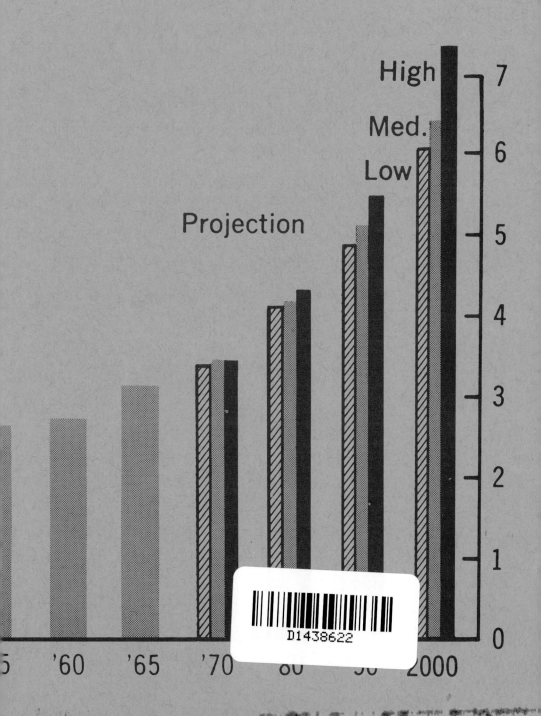

High

Med.

Low

Projection

7

6

5

4

3

2

1

0

'60   '65   '70   '80   '90   2000

The Future of Capitalism

The Future

of Capitalism

a symposium of distinguished comment by

internationally known leaders of industry,

science, government, education, religion,

and the arts delivered at the world convocation

in New York City, September 19-21, 1966,

on the occasion of the Fiftieth Anniversary of

the National Industrial Conference Board

THE MACMILLAN COMPANY · NEW YORK

COLLIER-MACMILLAN LIMITED · LONDON

PHOTO CREDITS:

Mr. Palmer by Fabian Bachrach, New York
Lord Franks by News Chronicle, London
Mr. Grazier by Karsh, Ottawa
Mr. Meany by Fabian Bachrach, New York
Mr. Learson by Karsh, Ottawa
Mr. Moore by Fabian Bachrach, New York
Mr. d'Estaing by AGIP, Robert Cohen, Paris
Mr. Goheen by Gábor Eder, New York
Mr. Helm by Matar Studio, New York
Sir Robson by City Commercial Studio, London
Mr. Twaits by Ashley & Crippen, Toronto
Mr. Martin by Birus & Goldberg, New York
Mr. Fowler by Fabian Bachrach, New York
Mr. Blessing by Edo König, Bonn

Contents

Foreword

I CAN THINK of no more timely subject for study and discussion than "The Future of Capitalism" in these days when the world scene—both economic and political—is shifting so rapidly on every side. The face of our communist competition appears to be changing considerably. It is not quite as red, perhaps, as it used to be. And what about the face of capitalism—or, as I prefer it—the free market economy? As we study its reflection in the mirror of time, what changes shall we find there in the tomorrows to come: Will its basic features remain the same or will the passing years have eroded the personal incentive plan of production, the profit motive, and the absolute right of the customer to determine what shall be produced, and in what quantities at what price?

These questions are more easily asked than answered; and before we seek to peer too deeply into the future it might be well to test check our present position and course, as well as the course and progress of our competition in the communist countries. But how do we make such a test check in this whirling world?

In our market economy we have the statistical means of measuring the relative success of our respective businesses through our profit-and-loss statements. By using widely accepted accounting principles, it is possible to determine how the economic performance of one group of people engaged in an enterprise is measuring up in competition with other groups in other enterprises and industries.

But any statistical attempt to compare the performance of one nation to that of other nations having a different economic system is fraught with frustration; and yields—in the end—more confusions than conclusions. Not only are there inherent difficulties in the data themselves, but there is uncertainty and obscurity in the degree to which various nations reflect the results of one economic system or another; for pure capitalism, like absolute communism, is seldom found. And any combination of them that is found today is likely to change tomorrow, as the recent economic and political events in Brazil, for example, so well illustrate.

An even greater difficulty lies in finding a meaningful basis for statistical measurement. One country may have more bathtubs and television sets than any other. Or it may have more automobiles, more mortgages or more people who can afford to "eat out" when they please. Again it may provide a wider scope of education for a larger percentage of its population. But are any of these criteria—or all of them together—conclusive proof of the advantages of one system over another? And is it certain that the system which provided these economic blessings in one nation will—if transplanted lock, stock and barrel—work similar miracles in some other, geographically remote nation with different customs and traditions of government, levels of education and skills, different climatic conditions and different natural resources?

Currently, it has become popular to compare the economic performances among nations by contrasting the economic growth rate, the rate of capital formation, of personal savings, and of productivity; and to bundle these all together in a statistical comparison of the annual rates of change in the Gross National Product. But in all such comparisons it is well to remember that in a market economy value is determined by market forces, while in a totalitarian society, by contrast, it is arbitrarily fixed by the state. Moreover, these growth rates, of course, are expressed in percentages, and percentages can be notoriously misleading when one is applied to a relatively small base, and another to a much larger base.

So if we turn to available sources for our data, and if we accept them at their face value, it can be asserted that according to this criterion, some communist nations have been enjoying a higher rate of economic progress than have some capitalist countries; and an analyst might thus conclude that Soviet socialism is superior to the market system of the Western world.

But is that a fact or is it merely a statistical mirage? Let's examine these data more closely.

In Russia, for example, we find that during the years 1950 to 1964 the GNP—in real terms—has increased at an average annual rate of 6.3 per cent compared to a rate of only 3.5 per cent in the United States. So on this basis it appears that economic growth in the Soviet Union is 80 per cent faster than in the United States.

But if we measure the actual growth of the GNP of both countries in terms of constant dollars, we find that Russia's has grown by 169 billions during these same fourteen years, while the GNP in the United States—with fewer people—has increased by 242 billions—or about 1½ times as much. And since the necessities and amenities of life can be purchased only with money, and not with per cents, which one of these comparisons provides the most meaningful criterion of measurement?

Another significant measurement of progress—and one which eliminates much of the distortion just mentioned in the use of percentages—concerns the changing trend of growth, over the years, in the two competing economies.

Here we find that the GNP in Russia, from 1950 to 1958, grew at an average annual rate of 7.1 per cent, but in the more recent years, 1958 to 1964, this rate declined to 5.3 per cent. Thus the rate of growth in that country has slowed by 25 per cent between these two periods.

Conversely, in the United States during these same two periods the growth rate rose from 2.9 per cent to 4.4 per cent—a speed-up of 52 per cent. And calculated on a per capita basis, the disparity is even greater, with the decline in Russia being 33 per cent, compared to an increase of 125 per cent in the growth rate of the GNP in the United States.

A similar pattern emerges when we broaden our study to cover the nations of the Free World on the one hand, and the communist nations on the other. Here we find that the per capita growth rate in the free nations, measured in dollars of the same purchasing power, was 8 per cent greater in the years 1960 to 1964 than it was in the 1950s; but that in the communist countries, it was 45 per cent less in the later period than in the earlier one.

So even after allowing for differences in the stage of the business cycles between nations or in this case between systems, a mere statistical analysis yields conflicting results from which diametrically opposite conclusions may be drawn. Nor does it provide much insight into the comparative success of the socialist system in producing heavy industrial goods, armaments and space hardware on the one hand, and consumer goods on the other. Neither does it take into consideration quality, style and usefulness in the consumer goods area—the realization that a pair of shoes in Argentina, for example, may be quite a different thing from a pair of shoes in Outer Mongolia.

Fortunately, however, we have other evidence at hand to help us evaluate the course and the progress of Soviet socialism. There are some who maintain that the most compelling evidence of the failure of communism is to be found in the continuing existence of the Berlin wall and in the iron curtain itself. Why, they ask, is it necessary to string thousands of miles of barbed wire fence, electrify it with lethal voltages, and to erect and maintain watch towers, bristling with armed men, just to prevent the people *inside* the fence escaping from the blessings of the communist system. And in an analysis of the political virtues of communism, this line of reasoning may indeed be persuasive.

But for the purposes of a purely economic appraisal, it seems to me that even more impressive evidence is to be found in what is happening behind the curtain and the wall, as reported in the communist press and—recently—in the report by Gilbert Burck in the July and August issues of *Fortune*.

Certainly no one can discount the tremendous strides that the Marxist-oriented countries have made in production. The first conquerors of space may never be discounted. The nation with the second largest stock of intercontinental missiles may not be disregarded in evaluating productive systems. Yet, on the other hand, standards of living for the average person do count; for in the end any system of production must be measured, I think, by its social usefulness to people as individuals; and it is here that the Soviet socialist system seems to be at its greatest disadvantage.

Despite all the glowing statistics about Russia's economic growth, we read in *Fortune* that the consumption standard of the average Soviet worker is less than that of the average American on relief. We are told that in the Russian Republic and in the Ukraine, in 1962 and 1963, the official inspectors of the Ministry of Trade classified 25 to 33 per cent of the newly produced clothing and shoes as defective. We note that the only laundromat and dry cleaning establishment in Moscow was equipped by a firm in Los Angeles. We learn that the Soviet Government—having decided to quadruple its production of automobiles by 1970—has employed two Western European companies to erect the plants and design the cars. And we know that the USSR—with the greatest land area of any nation in the world—has, in the last two years, had to buy hundreds of millions of bushels of wheat from the free market nations of North America.

Why does a great Marxist nation—able as its people have proved themselves to be—look to the West for know-how in new fertilizer plants, in farm equipment, in food production, and in substantially all the other products that man wears or uses to make its existence more comfortable? Well, perhaps it merely shows that—in the words of a current television commercial—"we must be doing something right." But more probably, it shows that the Soviet Government is recognizing and responding to the mounting disenchantment of the communist consumer with the economic system under which he lives. Indicative of this disenchantment is the translation of an editorial which was published in the January 1965 issue of the Czechoslovak *Chemical Journal;* and which is so frank in its appraisal of the market system that it raises some question as to whether freedom of speech has been suppressed behind the iron curtain to the extent we have been led to believe. The editorial says in part:

"We took over the capitalist technology. It would not occur to any-body to reject the contact process for the production of sulfuric acid on the grounds that it was developed by a capitalist society and that it assisted that society in the accumulation of profits.

"However, we did not take—we rejected—the capitalist principles of commerce which formed the basis for the distribution and consumption of accumulated values. In this manner we gave up their natural effect of regulating the quality and salability of production. We were forced to substitute artificially created regulating mechanisms, which looked beautiful on paper, but failed to perform in practice since they were not supported by any objectively functioning material law."

Then, after discoursing at some length upon the weaknesses of the communist system of production, the editorial goes on to say:

"It is different if the exchange, distribution and consumption (of goods) are controlled by the mechanism of market supply and demand. . . . The necessity of a complicated apparatus is eliminated. The control of productive activity toward the maximization of both its volume and quality becomes automatic by the effect of the marketing mechanism. The customer provides the quality control free of charge . . .

"And it is just these control mechanisms—which represent in socialized production an adequate supplement of a mature technology—that we have disregarded and replaced by a system of artificial prescriptions and supervisions which are closer to orders given to a serf than to the governing principles of a modern industrial civilization."

Now this editorial, of course, expressed only the views of the editors of one publication, in one industry, in one of the Marxist-oriented nations; but it does not seem to be materially at odds with the new economic philosophy which is currently evolving in Russia, where more than ten million people are engaged in compiling data that still fail to supply the basic and vital information that is afforded "free of charge"—as the Czechoslovakian editorial puts it—by the servomechanisms of market pricing in the capitalistic economies of the West.

So it is here, I believe—in the changing economic philosophies of Soviet socialism—that we find the most significant and reliable evidence of the course that this competing system is steering and the changes it is undergoing.

A distinguished professor of economics at Kharkov published an article urging that productive performance be measured primarily by the profitability of capital and that plant managers be allowed to decide for themselves the size of their payrolls, their productivity goals, their costs, capital investment and innovation policies; and he concludes with words that have a strangely familiar ring to Americans:

"What is good for the individual Soviet enterprise," he says, "is good for the Soviet Union."

His writings aroused a storm of protest from Russian "reactionaries" —who, in this case, are the hard core, old line communists; but was the good professor banished to Siberia? To the contrary, he found strong support and agreement in some of the highest government circles, and in the streets and factories of Russia propaganda posters have now appeared bearing messages which might have been penned by the United States Chamber of Commerce or the N.A.M.

One of these depicts a worker holding a package of money labelled "profits"; and the legend under the drawing reads: "The meaning of the word 'profit' is simple and clear: It is—more schools, housing and nurseries. It is—a new upsurge in the great work."

Another propaganda poster in Russian plants depicts the laying of a railroad track upon crossties that are labeled: "profit," "cost account- ing," "material incentives," "credit" and "price"; and the caption reads: "The Soviet people are tirelessly laying tracks where Lenin showed the way."

Beyond that, it is reported that the Soviet government favors more advertising; that it encourages the use of brand names—or "production marks," as they are called in that country—and that it is going in heavily for market research.

So while the Soviets continue to abjure steadfastly the private ownership of production which is the foundation stone of capitalism, they are rapidly adopting from the free market system the principal tools and mechanisms which, under Stalin, they so long denounced as capitalistic evils.

Here in the West there are some who take great satisfaction from this, and who feel that it not only constitutes an admission of the superiority of the free market system, but foreshadows the decline and fall of Soviet socialism. And perhaps they are right. For my part, how- ever, I take a somewhat different view. I do not know how perfectly the automatic mechanisms of our free market system will work in the absence of private ownership of property, private investment, and freedom of pricing in the market place, but I feel sure that to what- ever extent they do work, they will enhance the efficiency and pro- ductiveness of Russia, and thus make the New Communism a much tougher competitor than communism has ever been before.

So it is well, I believe, that we should meet here as we do to con- sult our directional compass and determine the course upon which our own system is heading; for if the countenance of communism is chang- ing apace, so too, indeed, is the face of the free market. It is beginning to show the furrowed lines of worry over welfarism and to reveal the effects of a considerable amount of plastic surgery performed on it by government.

Today there can be no doubt that much of the future of capitalism lies within the purview of government attitudes and government performances. Strong as our free market system is—and great as its accomplishments have been in the past—it is not impregnable. It can be engulfed, even by those with the best of intentions; for many times those who need the superproductiveness of the market system the most seem to understand it the least.

How, for example, can such a sensible people as the British undermine their real interests by nationalizing their steel industry? At a moment when the pound sterling was reeling under the impact of a monetary crisis, why did they decide to burden their beleaguered treasury with the expenditure of hundreds of millions of pounds to transform this industry from a taxpaying to a taxeating enterprise? Why do the hard-working men of government—overburdened as they are with the grave international problems which only they handle—seek to assume all the problems of this industry which can be handled much better by others? And in the hands of these industrially inexperienced and overtaxed men of government, will British steel—and, indeed, the British economy—become noncompetitive in world competition? It is all very mystifying.

Some of you may find it similarly perplexing to see the determined effort in Washington to repeal the investment tax credit on new productive facilities—especially at a time when the competitive position of American industry needs further strengthening by the replacement of billions of dollars' worth of obsolete plants and equipment, and by the addition of capital facilities.

Surely it is obvious that an increased volume of production—through the building of new facilities—will enlarge our national supply of goods in the face of rising demand for these goods, and will thus tend to prevent the bidding up of prices. It is also obvious that replacing this obsolete plant and equipment with modern, highly efficient facilities will yield lower production costs and help offset rising wage costs, thereby not only diminishing the upward pressure on prices, but improving our national competitive position in world markets in aid of our persistent balance of payments deficit.

To discourage capital investment, to retard the growth and efficiency of production, and to weaken the competitive capacity of American industry on the one hand, while enacting minimum wage legislation that will tend to escalate employment costs at every level, and thus to increase production costs and prices on the other, just doesn't make economic sense. And to single out private capital investment—which represents only a very small fraction of the GNP—as the big coal in the fire that is causing the overheating that now disturbs us, doesn't make sense either.

There are many other coals in the fire and the largest and hottest of these, of course, are our rapidly rising governmental expenditures. The National Planning Association estimates that by 1975 American government—at all levels—will be spending 85 billion dollars annually just for welfare payments, health, education and job preparation; and more than half that sum was spent last year on these social needs alone.

Now we Americans are clearly determined that these social needs shall be met; and with the impatience that is characteristic of us we want to meet them yesterday. We deplore, for example, the fact that several million American families have incomes of less than three thousand dollars a year; and we spend billions waging the war on poverty.

But poverty, of course, is a relative term, and to more than half the families on earth today an income equivalent to three thousand dollars a year would represent undreamed-of affluence. So although they are classified as "poor" by government definition, it does not mean that these American families are hungry, homeless or unclothed. In fact, census data show that three out of four of the so-called poor own a television set and the same number own a washing machine; while more than half have both a television and a telephone, 20 per cent own a home freezer and one out of seven bought an automobile last year.

Nevertheless, if we are to have the kind of society to which we aspire, the lot of these people must be greatly improved. They must have access to the kind of education, training and job preparation that will afford them the opportunity to perform a more economically useful and rewarding role in society. The blight that afflicts many of our great metropolitan centers must somehow be overcome. Beyond that, there are many other problems that call for vast expenditures—problems like environmental health—the impurities of air and water which have become an increasing problem largely because of the rapid expansion of the population itself.

All of these social gains are desirable and, in time, indispensable. But if we try to achieve these social goals overnight—if we try to do too much, too fast—we shall load our free market system with a burden of costs that can overwhelm it. To function, the system must throw off enough regenerative results—which we call return on investment or profits—to fuel the system for the future. Burdening it with too heavy a load of social costs simply consumes the fuel which would otherwise keep the system going.

So the delicate task is to determine the optimum speed at which these social needs can be met. To proceed too slowly is to delay unnecessarily the achievement of the goals we seek. To press forward too rapidly is to erode the very source of our wealth-creating process, and thus to impede our economic growth and social progress. It is like administering to a heart patient where a few drops of digitalis may prolong his life greatly while a few too many may end it abruptly.

The late Per Jacobsson, Managing Director of the International Monetary Fund, firmly believed that both the welfare state and a certain degree of government planning were indispensable elements in the proper functioning of the free market system; but, delivering the Jayne Lectures before the American Philosophical Society, he insisted forcefully that "government action must not be arbitrary: it must conform to the basic principles of the market system." And he elaborated upon this statement with Francis Bacon's sagacious reminder that "nature can be commanded only by obeying her."

Thus we recognize that the future of capitalism does not rest with us alone—upon our technological advance, increased efficiency, exhaustive research and an effort to build an ever-stronger competitive position. It rests also in the ability of governments to remain competitive in their tax rates, depreciation laws, trade balances, monetary regulations, buying practices, debt burdens, and the integrity of their currencies. And as the influence of government over business and industry continues to expand, the future of capitalism rests even more importantly upon the extent to which the men of government understand the workings of the free market system and base their decisions upon the natural economic laws which must be obeyed.

The interplay of these decisions, both governmental and private, will be scrutinized here from many differing points of view during these next three days as we seek to assess the future of capitalism; and while in the end we may not succeed in agreeing precisely as to what that future will be, one does not need to be an eternal optimist to believe that capitalism does have a future.

Nor does one have to be an eternal optimist to know that the best way to help people is to teach them to help themselves and to realize that the market economy provides them with the greatest opportunity for self-help yet invented by man.

Teaching the means of providing useful employment, of garnering a growth in personal skills, and of building the wealth of a nation through freedom is not easy. But it can be done and I am confident it will be done.

That confidence, I hope and expect, will be shared by the other contributors to these proceedings. For in gatherings such as this the teachers are taught and the troubled way of man is smoothed—if ever so slightly.

—*Roger M. Blough*
CHAIRMAN, BOARD OF DIRECTORS
UNITED STATES STEEL CORPORATION
CHAIRMAN
NATIONAL INDUSTRIAL CONFERENCE BOARD

Preface

CAPITALISM is still regarded abroad, particularly among the developing countries, as an economic system under which labor is cruelly exploited and wages depressed toward levels of subsistence. The belief also persists that under capitalism profits account for a large, if not the lion's, share of the sales dollar, even though the latest official estimates of the United States Department of Commerce show that after taxes they amount to only 3.3 per cent of all sales. The uninformed still cling to the fiction that under capitalism the preponderance of the national income flows to the owners of capital, particularly in the form of dividends. But, again, official data show that dividends account for 3.4 per cent of national income, while dividends, interest, and rent combined total barely 10 per cent. Income and wealth are both widely believed to be heavily concentrated at the apex of their respective pyramids. In fact, as the Conference Board's studies have recently shown, these pyramids have been almost inverted in recent decades, with the middle classes now receiving the major share of all income through an unparalleled redistribution of income.

Many of these mistaken impressions have been carried over from the era of low national productivity that prevailed when the Conference Board was established. As late as World War I, the pay envelope of a factory employee averaged little more than $10 to $15 for a work week of 50 to 55 hours. True, the dollar then could buy three to four times what it can today. Even so, the contrast is indeed stark when viewed against today's average paycheck of $110 and above. The lean reward to labor under early capitalism, however, was far more a function of the constricted capacity of society to produce and the prevailing low state of science and the arts than of capitalistic exploitation. The size of the total national output pie was then so limited that, if all of our national income had been distributed to labor, it would not have significantly improved the welfare of the masses.

Five decades of the Board's existence have had compounded within them an intensity of change and of economic growth unmatched in world history. This tidal wave of change has left its mark upon the traditional structure and characteristics of capitalism under which the United States and many other members of the Free World organize the production, distribution, and consumption of goods and services for their citizenry. This publication highlights the extent to which the combination of unparalleled technological, political, social, and cultural change has advanced the life, liberty and pursuit of happiness of those who today enjoy the benefits and privileges of modern-day capitalism. In the midst of the new war upon poverty of the lower fifth of our people, it is well to recall that the free market mechanism and the use of the profit incentive have helped raise the remaining four-fifths of this nation's population to levels of living unmatched in history.

As the Board enters its second half century of research into the problems of management in a voluntaristic society, capitalism seems to be entering upon another evolutionary phase, in which its activities and decisions are being increasingly vested with longer-run public purpose, as well as with consideration of short-term profitability. In much the same way that the heightened productivity of the twentieth century has helped industry share its technological gains with employees and customers alike, so, too, is it enabling today's business leaders to devote more of their time and resources toward the constructive resolution of community, regional, and national problems not directly related to the immediate pursuit of profits. The impressive dimensions of industry's contributions to education, to cultural activities, and to philanthropy bear witness to this assumption by business of ever-greater social responsibility. The new generation of business leaders is far more concerned than was its predecessors with the whole broad area of public affairs—with understanding of the external environment under which business operates and, after careful study, with offering constructive solutions consistent with the continuance and preservation of voluntary enterprise to such problems as air and water pollution, the decay of the central city, civil rights, and the effects of automation.

In recognition of this historic expansion in the scope of activities and interest of modern-day industrial management, the Conference Board has on the occasion of this anniversary created a Division of Public Affairs Research and proposes to set aside a growing portion of its resources for studies and conferences in this area. It does so with high hopes that its research activities will help enrich industry's understanding and progress in the area of public affairs, as did its earlier and still continuing half century of research into problems of internal business management and the acceleration of national economic growth.

The central theme for this convocation and its underlying thematic structure was provided by Martin R. Gainbrugh, the Board's Chief Economist, who also edited the proceedings. The mechanics of the convocation were the responsibility of Stuart R. Clarkson, the Board's Conference Director. Donald P. Arrowsmith, the Board's Vice President and Director of Service Extension Division, headed the internal committee charged with planning and promotion of the convocation. The generous help and cooperation is also acknowledged of the Fiftieth Anniversary Observance Committee comprised of the following Trustees of the Board: Rupert C. Thompson, Chairman, Dudley Dowell, Charles E. Eble, Gerald L. Phillippe, and J. R. White.

—H. Bruce Palmer
PRESIDENT
NATIONAL INDUSTRIAL CONFERENCE BOARD

I EVOLUTION OF TWENTIETH-CENTURY CAPITALISM

CHAIRMAN: Roger M. Blough

· *A Welcome to New York, John V. Lindsay*

· *Introduction by Mr. Blough*

· *The Evolution of Twentieth-Century Capitalism,*

Lord Franks

A Welcome to New York

THE HONORABLE

JOHN V. LINDSAY

Mayor, The City of New York

T HIS CITY is not only in effect the international capital of
the world—we have here the United Nations and more consuls-
general than any other city in the world—but it's also the headquarters for international business. And, therefore, it is in a sense
the headquarters of the capitalistic system in the Western community. We think that that is good and to be promoted. We of
the city government here are acutely conscious of our responsibility to see to it that that aspect of a great metropolitan center's
life is recognized, furthered, strengthened. We do all in our
power to see to it that our economy moves forward locally and
nationally by making local government as responsive and as
helpful as possible to those who make the engines of this system
run, and we hope run for the public good.

I have a special interest myself in the thinking that goes on
in this business and my special interest has to do with the future
of cities, in general. I hope that businessmen will devote themselves to making great urban centers really work, to demonstrat-
ing that great, complicated, congested cities can be productive
centers in partnership with the capitalistic system for the public
good as a whole.

3

And if, in fact, that point can't be demonstrated and that is not on the calendar of the agenda of a conference of this kind, well then, something quite important and serious is lacking.

I think that the country did the right thing in its discussions of the Foreign Aid Program and Balance of Payments in providing certain incentives for the capitalistic system to invest in developing areas. I can remember as a Congressman the debates on the floor of the Congress surrounding the foreign aid bills of 1960, 1962 and 1964. Increasingly as this country became concerned about balance of payments, efforts were made on the floor of Congress to write into aspects of the foreign aid bill incentives for private capital to invest abroad—tax and other incentives for capital to invest in developing areas. This was, in effect, an exception from what was at the time an increasing tightening of the provisions that permitted United States industry, for example, to invest in Europe in various forms.

I, myself, think that the same ought to be done for our own country in our great cities in the so-called ghetto areas. I hope that the Congress in its consideration of the administration's request for removal of the 7 per cent tax credit gives serious consideration to an exception for investment in the ghetto areas of the big cities. That is not too difficult of definition. After all, the United States Government in the Department of Housing and Urban Development is increasingly requiring great cities, like New York, to focus their urban renewal funds, which are substantially federal, in the ghetto communities. And, in compliance with that, New York City and all other cities for the present fiscal year will be concentrating the new pipeline money for physical development in those areas as generally defined by the community at large, the government of the locality and by Washington's Department of Housing and Urban Development.

More than anyone realizes, there is strength in these communities for the benefit of the community at large, for the benefit of the residents of those communities, and for the benefit of investors. There is profit, as well as good sense, in connection with such investment.

In New York City, we have the largest untapped labor pool in the country right here in our center, waiting to be used, waiting to be developed. And, I repeat, this can be on such a basis that it will result in a very substantial gain on the part of intelligent investors.

Foundations, which were funded by the great capitalistic strength of this country, are devoting their attention and their studies increasingly to this subject, in example after example on a small scale.

We have seen that those who are beginning to make their investment in developing parts of great cities that need attention will be the ones who will come out ahead a quarter of a century from now, because they will have been there first.

I am pleased to note the number of great corporations that are at the moment considering in the germ stage the possibility of a free enterprise investment, not only for their good, but for the public good as well, in those areas in a big city which need the most attention, both from the point of view of physical renewal and human renewal.

The capitalistic system, business, private enterprise system is the strongest weapon that society has yet devised for developing a society that is advanced, that moves, that changes with the times and is sufficiently flexible to absorb the stresses and strains of changing conditions in populations.

That being the case, this system, it hardly needs repeating, is impressed with the public interest. And, being impressed with the public interest, it has an obligation for its own sake and for the public's sake to see to it that there is a proper partnership between the government and the private sector.

It is the genius, I think, of both sides to recognize where that partnership is, where the balance point is, and how to harness it, so that there is development, growth, employment, housing, schools and profit.

Churchill said, "Democracy is the worst form of government ever invented by the mind of man, except for every other form of government." And, when democracy is able to discover where to find that delicate balance point between the private sector on one hand and the governmental sector on the other hand, then each not only operates as a check upon the other, each uses the best of the other to develop a community for the common good.

I think that the crisis of the big cities the world over—and no country that is a developed country is any exception—is a problem that will have to receive the highest priority attention on the part of the private sector, the free enterprise system and government from now on, for the good of the free system the world over.

And right here in our midst, in the city that is the biggest of all of them, and which has probably the highest concentration of problems because of the diversity of its institutions and its population, right here there can be a demonstration project, I hope, that can show the world at large the importance of the private community, devoting their attentions toward developing the power that is so latent in parts of the city that have been so long neglected.

I AGAIN EXTEND a special welcome to those who have traveled from other countries and from posts of great official responsibility to give us the advantage of their insights and viewpoints that can deepen and broaden our own.

A lesser man than Lord Franks, educator, philosopher, diplomat and banker, doubtless would not have consented so graciously as he to deal as keynoter with the evolution of that complex, adaptable and seemingly still viable organism, Twentieth Century Capitalism.

But, assessing the prospects of capitalism may not have seemed so formidable to Lord Franks in the light of an undertaking in which he has been engaged for some three years. He has been chairman of a very high level commission of inquiry into the evolution, the present circumstances and the future prospects of Oxford University, whose beginnings more than seven centuries ago predate the Industrial Revolution and the publication of The Wealth of Nations by a good 500 years.

Lord Franks is well remembered by a goodly number of us as his country's able ambassador to Washington in early postwar years. That service to his country followed wartime service in the Ministry of Supply that was kept by his appointment as Permanent Secretary of the Ministry during 1945 and 1946. Lord Franks' association with and devotion to Oxford University has extended over practically his adult lifetime.

Following his graduation from Queens College there, he taught philosophy, with one academic year off in the mid-1930s to be a lecturer at our own University of Chicago. During the two years before his appointment as ambassador to Washington, Lord Franks was provost of Queens College and in 1962 was made provost of another college at Oxford, Worcester.

In a field closely allied with the subject matter today, Lord Franks has served since 1962 as a member of the British National Economic Development Council. He has long been a director of Lloyd's Bank, Ltd. and was its chairman from 1954 to 1962.

What finer credentials could a man possess for his current assignment?

— Roger M. Blough

The Evolution of
Twentieth-Century Capitalism

THE RIGHT HONOURABLE

LORD FRANKS

G.C.M.G., K.C.B., C.B.E., F.B.A.

Provost, Worcester College, Oxford

I CONFESS I was daunted when I was asked by Roger Blough to speak on "The Evolution of Twentieth Century Capitalism." He proposed that I should talk about the change from laissez faire capitalism to today's mixed economy and go on to consider the drastically altered relationship between business and government under modern day capitalism.

What a difficult subject! It calls for the knowledge of the historian, the economist and the political scientist, as well as an understanding of business. I am no authority; still less am I a prophet. But I should like, if I may, to offer you some suggestions about the trend of affairs in North American and Western European countries. I shall deal mainly with the relations of government to business and some of the resultant problems; it seems to me that this might serve as an introduction to this great convocation.

I shall illustrate what I want to say by reference to Britain. Not because I consider Britain a pattern for other countries, but because I know it best.

In Britain since the Industrial Revolution there have been three stages in the relations of government to business. The first falls within the period from the publication of *The Wealth of Nations* in 1776, to the great Factory Acts of the 1830s and 1840s. This was the age in Britain of laissez faire. Business was composed of a large number of small enterprises competing against each other in the open market. This freedom of competition had only two limitations: the preservation of private property and freedom of contract. And within these limitations it was thought that the unfettered activity of many individuals in the conduct of their businesses would maximize the general wealth and well-being of the community. In consequence, the role of government was unimportant. In fact, the only important thing was that government should not interfere.

This was all put very simply by Jeremy Bentham in 1793: "The general rule," he said, "is that nothing ought to be done or attempted by government: the motto or watchword of government on these occasions ought to be 'Be quiet.' The request which agriculture, manufacturers and commerce present to government is as modest and as reasonable as that which Diogenes made to Alexander: 'Stand out of my sunshine.'"

The second stage starts from these Factory Acts and lasts, in my view, until the final phase of the Second World War. This, in Britain, is a period of government intervention and of the growth of government intervention. It came to be believed that unless government acted certain objectives of the whole community could not be realized. Under a system of unrestricted competition, the lot of some individuals, it was thought, was so bad that it became a reproach to the community and a political judgment was made that the government must intervene to bring about changes.

Then, too, there were things which the community desired, which were not brought about or not adequately brought about by individual enterprise. For long this had been the case with defense, but now it was judged that education for all fell into this category. So, the government intervened. And, as views changed about the standard of living which should be shared by the citizens, the range of government's intervention extended. What now seem the modest social provisions of liberal administrations before World War I have been enlarged to the full panoply of the welfare state, offering public services of health, education and social benefits to all.

The third stage is, of course, the most interesting to us, for it is contemporary. We have to live with it and it began in Britain in 1944 with the publication of the government White Paper on Employment Policy. That white paper recommended that government should accept responsibility for a high and stable level of employment in the country. Every government elected in Britain in the last twenty years has accepted this proposition as basic to its domestic economic policy. From this acceptance large consequences follow.

No government can maintain a high level of employment unless it can secure the corresponding level of economic activity. Unless government intervenes to achieve this, fluctuations will occur. But such intervention will be blind and haphazard in its timing, unless the government is equipped with adequate information.

The next consequence, therefore, is that the government needs to compile and to possess national income statistics so that its judgment of when, by what means, by how much to intervene may be well informed. National income statistics come into existence year by year and constitute a series. Inevitably, comparisons are made between one year and another. It becomes possible to watch and to measure the growth of the economy. But growth is of the greatest interest to the electorate and to the government, for it carries with it increasing abundance of all the goods and services which men desire. So, equipped with the comparative knowledge given by the series of national income statistics, government becomes preoccupied with growth and seeks appropriate methods of intervening in the economy to promote it.

But the process doesn't stop here. The widening scope of government intervention compels it, so the argument runs, to be concerned with the constituents of growth if its actions are to make practical sense. It is not an accident that government in

Britain has become worried about the levels of prices and incomes and has looked for means of influencing or regulating both. Similarly, the issues of the national balance of payments are brought in. A healthy balance of payments forms a condition without which a desired rate of growth cannot be got and is itself a positive element promoting such growth. Conversely, when the international balance of payments is bad, restrictive action by government becomes inevitable. The economy is stopped from growing.

Further it has seemed reasonable, indeed necessary, to consider the prospects of different sections of the productive economy. Sometimes there are particular reasons, as in the case of agriculture. More generally the process of growth is observed to give rise to bottlenecks. If the desired general level of growth is to be achieved, then particular industries which limit or may limit the general movement fall under consideration. In Britain, the machine tool industry is an instance where government has intervened on these grounds.

At this point, following on what your chairman said, I must make it clear that I am not talking about the socialist doctrine of the public ownership of the means of production. For example, the nationalization of the steel industry in Britain. That doctrine is irrelevant to the trend I am describing. It was a Conservative government in Britain which four years ago accepted the need to work for growth and set up the National Economic Development Council for the purpose. The trend I am concerned with is not toward public ownership or nationalization. It's toward intervention of a particular kind by government in the economic activities of the community. In a word, it is the attempt by government to enter into the general management of the economy.

Such intervention can take many forms and does. It can be anything, from a hint to persuasion; from guidelines of policy to direct action, whether in the field of taxation or through the contracts government places, or by selective executive acts. I am not concerned at the moment with this detail. What I want to emphasize is the radical change of view involved in the third stage of the relations of government to business. It is in principle the change, from intervention ad hoc for particular reasons in aid of particular causes, to intervention inspired and dictated by a general view of the country's economic life as a whole. I would almost say a philosophy of intervention, which looks over the whole field and is practically interested to try to achieve certain overriding objectives, levels of employment and business activity, stability of the economic process and growth of the economy, which as it is held cannot be achieved without the watchful intervention of government.

Now I want to generalize and assert that the trend characteristic of the third stage of British development, the entry of government into a measure of general management of the economy, is evident generally in the countries of Western Europe and North America, but it is not part of my thesis that all these countries went through the same stages of development; still less that the timing was the same.

I happen to think that the three stages can be observed in the history of the United States. I should suppose that the epoch of laissez faire lasted much longer than in Britain, probably till nearly the end of the nineteenth century. The second stage, I think, comes with the Sherman Anti-Trust Act and continues until the end of the Second World War. But in regard to the third stage, the timing in the United States and in Britain seems to me to have been about the same. The British White Paper on Employment Policy is dated 1944. In 1946, the Congress passed the Employment Act which set up the Council of Economic Advisors in the Executive Office of the President. Both are harbingers of the same trend. And as in Britain, so in the United States, it seems to me, the preoccupation of government with the economy as a whole and the attempt to achieve certain overriding objectives have led to major intervention in the economic life of the nation.

I need only mention President Kennedy's dispute with the steel corporations in 1962, the massive tax cuts in 1964-65 when, although business was good, it was judged right to aim at a budget deficit in order further to stimulate the economy and reduce unemployment. And then there has been the long debate this year whether, from the standpoint of the economy as a whole, stabilizing action should be taken by raising taxes. The trend is clear.

These stages in development of capitalism did not occur in the same fashion in Germany or France, nonetheless both France and West Germany show the same trend. What other significance has the stabilization bill proposed by Chancellor Erhard? Its whole design is to counter inflationary pressures thought dangerous to the well-being and progress of the whole economy. Nor do the Germans, acting from the same standpoint, hesitate to use public finance to discriminate in trade and industry, intervening on behalf of those activities which the government thinks should be fostered. And the point is obvious in the case of France. I would only observe that while the British were pushed to their attempts to achieve growth over the longer term by their experience of short-term intervention, the French appear to me to have come to short-term stabilization policies because of their long experience of planning for growth.

My theme then is clear, but I wish it to be equally clear that I do not maintain at all that the scale of intervention is the same in different countries, nor that it is always effected by the same means, nor that it reflects the same degree of acceptance by public opinion. May I add two brief considerations?

The first is that if my general analysis is correct I have been describing fact, the factual relations of government to business. I have not been describing opinion about these relations. I have not asked whether it is generally thought that the present trend is desirable or not desirable. My interest is in the new attitude of government evidenced by what it does in its relations with business.

Secondly, I have been guilty of some oversimplification in my account. The attitudes of governments at any given time are not as clear-cut as my description suggests. I don't refer here to the ingrained political habit of clothing a new departure in familiar, if slightly misleading, terms to make the change more palatable. I mean that in recent years governments have continued to make interventions ad hoc, the interventions characteristic of the second stage. For instance the setting up of the Monopolies Commission and of the Restrictive Practices Court in Britain was mainly due to particular concerns of government with the state of British industry. One way of looking at things had been added to or superimposed on another. There has not been an abrupt transition at a given point in time from one standpoint to a second.

I come back to the trend. Will it persist? I believe it likely to do so. The reason for my statement is that it is originated from value judgments about our communities which have proved politically acceptable in our countries. It is sometimes said that economic science is about means and not ends. And this is a useful abstraction. It enables scholars to explore and understand the nature of economic activity to the benefit of us all, but it remains an abstraction. Once the question of applying the findings of economic thought is raised, then value judgments about the kind of society we want are inevitable. And in my view, the most important judgment of this kind is the view about employment embodied in the British White Paper of 1944 and the American Employment Act of 1946. It is the assertion that employment should not be the variable which chiefly takes the shock of change.

On the contrary, a continuing high level of employment is judged to be an overriding objective, to be accepted and pursued by government, because it expresses the kind of society electorates want. Yet if I am right it is mainly this which has led governments to try to deal with fluctuations, to control inflation and dissipate deflation, as it has also led to preoccupation with growth.

Do you suppose that the political and social values made explicit in this objective are likely soon to be rejected by the voters? I do not. Therefore, I am led to believe that the present relationship of government to business has vitality and won't easily be changed.

Furthermore, governments nowadays are far more able than they were to take action in terms of their general philosophy of the desirable lines of economic activity and development. They have new weapons at their disposal and the greatest of these is the growth of government expenditure, both absolutely and in relation to the Gross National Product. I suppose that in our countries the volume of government expenditure may be anything from a quarter to a third of the Gross National Product. But this vast mass of government expenditure is a very powerful weapon.

First and most simply, as it is increased or decreased it acts to stimulate or depress the economy. The levers of power are there.

But secondly, and this is a fact of increasing importance, it enables the government to intervene in ways which advance the changes it wants to promote. I take an example from Britain. When the Conservatives were in office, before the election of the Labor Government in 1964, Mr. Geoffrey Rippon was Minister of Works. He had contracts to let to the building construction industry worth some 250 million sterling a year. By his control of these contracts, he set out deliberately to induce builders to adopt new methods to raise productivity and save labor. In particular, he introduced "systems building," a method of construction relying on standard factory-made components assembled on the site.

I take a second example from the United States. In June, 1963, the Department of Defense, the Bureau of the Budget, and certain federal agencies jointly issued the Production Evaluation Review Technique guide to management. It says: "Full PERT implementation will be required on many major programs. In addition, the use of PERT will be encouraged, whenever it is applicable, as an effective management technique."

The point I want to make by these two illustrations is that governments today through their large programs of public expenditure have great power over the economy and they use it to get change on the lines they desire. I doubt whether major diminution in the value and size of government expenditure in relation to Gross National Product is a political probability in the foreseeable future.

There is a further consequence of this general position. The extent to which the administrative, speaking English, the executive, speaking American, activities of government have been broadened. The entry of government into some degree of general management of the economy has led not only to more intervention, but intervention of a different kind. We used to think of government laying down general rules within which business was free to get on with its job. It was natural to think this when most intervention by government took the form of monetary measures in one way or another, restricting credit, or making it easier to obtain. But now, more and more there is positive selective intervention by government in relation to particular industries, particular industrial corporations, even individuals.

The willingness of the executive to use its power in this way has grown. My concern is not with justification, but with the fact. For example, it used to be the case that government made a practice of calling for competitive tenders. The specifications were the ground rules. Businesses were free to compete within them. This can be different now. In 1963, Thomas D. Morris, Assistant Secretary of Defense, told the Joint Economic Committee of Congress that "the production of new aircraft and missile systems cannot be economically procured on the basis of price competition, due to the high start-up costs and the deadline required to introduce a new production source after a long period of development." For these reasons, he held government justified in selective executive action in its relation to business.

There has been the affair of the Fairfield Shipping Yard in Britain. This yard found itself unable to continue in business, but the government did not wish it to die. It therefore put pressures of persuasion on particular individuals and organizations to help out and provide additional finance. It was successful. The company was saved. But it was a selective executive action.

At the present time an agency of the British Government, the Monopolies Commission, having had the British detergent industry referred to it by the Board of Trade, has reported its investigations and recommendations to that department. Two great corporations dominate this field—Procter & Gamble and Unilever. The commission recommends and the Board of Trade meets the two corporations this September to discuss implementation that shop prices should be cut by 20 per cent and selling expenditures reduced by 40 per cent. No one doubts that these two corporations compete strenuously with each other, but if the Board of Trade puts these recommendations into force, it will be substituting government executive decisions for decisions of business management in the case of two corporations in active competition with each other. I suppose that the pressures exerted by successive British governments to secure mergers in the airframe and aero-engine industry can be classed under the same general head.

In France too there is a good deal of intervention by government in the affairs of particular industries and particular corporations, employing one method or another of persuasion or of pressure. An instance can be found in the unfinished story of intervention by the French government in the computer industry. It is clear that the more intensively government concerns itself with the economy, the more it will tend to intervene in this way, favoring some business corporations but not others, regulating some but not others.

Once again I do not attack or defend the reasons for these interventions, but I point out the extent to which it has become natural for governments to practice selective executive action, rather than confining themselves to laying down ground rules which are the same for all.

I consider that this changing pattern in the relations of government to business and to the community creates problems both for government and for business, problems of real importance since they can affect the vitality of democratic life. Democracy surely needs many centers of initiative, decision and power. None of them, government included, should overshadow everything else.

Therefore, the present trend raises questions in my mind about the proper limits of government intervention, the proper safeguards to individuals and institutions when it intervenes. I do not think we know how to organize business in the democracy unless there is a large number of business corporations each with much freedom to decide its own affairs and, therefore, in competition with its neighbors. There must be a limit to the substitution of executive decision by government for competition between businesses.

Where is that limit? I do not myself think you can lay down the limit absolutely for all time. I think a judgment has got to be formed from practical experience and good sense. But there are a few general principles which I think can be used to test such a judgment. I should like to mention four.

The first has to do with political leadership. We all know democracy needs a strong executive and the executive has got to do a lot of persuading, since persuasion is the appropriate method most of the time in a free society. But if governments enter into the broad management of the economy with guidelines and overriding objectives, this surely puts a special burden on the political members of the executive. For those who have to give leadership in these matters have normally received no training for the decisions about the direction of the whole economy they have to make. These decisions are neither simple nor obvious. They are highly complex. They involve alternative sets of choices with interrelated consequences and therefore call for expert discrimination. This expertise is necessary if the political executive is to do its work of education and persuasion, creating the consensus required for effective action.

Our different countries today do better or worse in this field according to the political leadership they have. The problem is not that of expert advice. Of course, economists disagree but nonetheless they can produce broad agreement on what the alternative sets of choices are and what are their consequences. The gap emerges when the political leaders consider what they feel they can do. The difficulties are in the political implementation of expert advice received. I doubt whether in any of our countries we know by what methods or through what institutions our political leaders should be trained for this task. At present, what happens is so often too slow and too late; at least I would say this of Britain and I suspect we are not alone.

To my mind these political circumstances should set a limit to the ambitions of government in the general management of the economy.

Secondly, there is the present extension of the range of executive action by government. No doubt it is all done in pursuance of these guidelines and overriding objectives in which government expresses its general philosophy of the economy. But consider cases where the action of government is selective, where it singles out an individual or an individual corporation or a class of individuals or corporations and proceeds to persuade or pressure them to act in a particular way.

The persuasion of government can be heavy. Its efforts can be accompanied by the hint of sanctions, not specific, definable sanctions, but something vaguer though not less real, something amounting to urging that unless the individual or the corporation sees things the way the government sees them, it will be the worse for them. Suppose the individual or the corporation is aggrieved. What recourse have they got? What procedure exists by which they can complain and have their complaints heard? As selective intervention increases and the power of government is used to back it, there arises a real problem affecting both the freedom of business enterprise and the freedom of the individual. There should be, and at present I think there is not, recourse against an overmighty government, a due procedure under law. This is more important, as governments can marshal, beyond their direct powers of persuasion, the larger pressures of public opinion and bring them to bear on those with whom they are dealing.

Thirdly, the extent to which executive intervention in the economic field can erode legislative authority. This happens more easily in Britain with its constitutional arrangements than in the United States with the separation of powers entrenched in the constitution. Yet I think the tendency is general. There is something about intervention by the executive in the economic process, especially when it proceeds from a comprehensive view of the direction and the balance of the whole economy, which makes it difficult for the legislature to keep general control of policy. For the intervention consists of a series of decisions to act in aid of guidelines or objectives the executive itself has adopted. It is sporadic in its incidence: an attempt to prevent a price rise here or to moderate it there; an attempt to influence a wage negotiation here or to settle a strike there. Yet these acts make policy. Just as democracies need a strong executive, so surely that executive should be limited by having to get its broad authority from a legislative assembly, a Parliament or a Congress.

It is in the interest of business as of the community to uphold the legislature. Legislatures can be tiresome, inquisitive and interfering at times. But they are guardians of liberty since they alone authorize, they alone legitimize the broad policies of the executive. How then is this new relationship of the executive to the economy to co-exist with the proper authority of the legislature? Only, I think, if the legislature can purposefully debate the grounds which have led the executive to select one set of choices about the economy with their consequences out of the range offered by its economic advisors. Once again this is easier in the

United States than in Britain. Though expert politicians in most cases, the members of the legislatures are not expert in weighing the quantitative formulae in which economists clothe the alternative views they frame. In the United States, there exist congressional committees with their own expert staffs to advise them. In Britain there are no such standing committees with staffs in this field. In consequence members of Parliament are the more defenseless and the more easily by-passed.

Lastly, I have pointed out that governments, in their efforts to look over the whole field of the economy and set guidelines and objectives for it, are in fact making value judgments. For example, on the desirability of maintaining a high level of employment, or on the advantage of a particular rate of growth to the community.

In my view one result has been that the value judgments inherent in the economic process have seemed to become the preserve of governments and the consequence is that business corporations may be considered as production and marketing machines, uninterested in the values of the society in which they operate. This can have its effects in time, at least in Britain. There the complaint is often heard that too many of the abler young men do not want to go into business. They say it is only about making money, and other activities are more interesting. I have recently read remarks suggesting there are some signs of the same attitude in the United States. I do not know. But if there are, this comes home to the business community itself. Does it think of itself, does it present itself sufficiently as a maker of the good life, the upholder by what it does of the values by which men live? The answer is not just in an increasing production of goods and services. It must be in terms of the kind of society these make possible and what a business itself contributes by its own way of life.

One of the wonders of the age we live in has been the success of modern capitalism. This was not so between the wars. Then many doubted whether the capitalistic system could make a go of it. But in the last twenty years it has been the great engine of prosperity on both sides of the Atlantic. Yet I feel business does not seem to have been altogether successful in convincing people of the value of its role; but this matters. Government ought not to be the sole repository of value judgments about the economy. Those who operate it should have their own and proclaim them. For if there should be limitations on the extent to which government gets into the general management of the economy, and I am sure there should be, then a business community, conscious of the contribution that it makes to the good life of all, is far better placed to gain acceptance of where those limits should be placed than if it were content to appear no more than a sophisticated system for the production and distribution of material civilization.

II LABOR LOOKS AT CAPITALISM

CHAIRMAN: Joseph A. Grazier

· *The Spirit of Equal Opportunity,*

Nelson A. Rockefeller

· *Introduction by Mr. Grazier*

· *Labor Looks at Capitalism, George Meany*

The Spirit of Equal Opportunity

NELSON A. ROCKEFELLER

Governor of New York

SOME thought fifty years ago that capitalism didn't have much future. The Russian Revolution in 1917 was supposed to mark the beginning of the "final conflict." Half a century later our economic system is stronger than ever, for it has brought more people more of life's blessings than any system that mankind has ever known.

Our system is prevailing because it recognizes the appeal to every human being of individual freedom, personal opportunity and incentives to create, to build and to grow.

In the brief time it has been my privilege to be Governor of the State of New York, our average factory worker's paycheck has increased from $83 a week in 1958 to $110 a week this year. Total personal income in this state has risen 42% since 1958 to nearly 60 billion dollars this year. In a very real sense, then, this state is a laboratory of socially responsible capitalism in action, with more people at work under better conditions, with greater protection and at higher pay, than ever before in our history.

We have as a matter of state administration policy taken

steps to encourage industrial research and development by permitting a one year write-off—for state tax purposes—of new research and development facilities. We have created a Science and Technology Foundation to encourage basic and applied research in colleges and universities. And I might say that the leader in this program for the state is one of your guests here at the dais, Mr. Keith McHugh, Commissioner of Commerce, formerly president of the New York Telephone Company and one of the outstanding businessmen of this community, and one who was willing to give up a salary of around $150,000 to take $18,000. Don't ask him why, except I'm awfully grateful. But since then we've done better for him in his salary.

We brought the state into a full-scale partnership with the developing ways of peaceful use of nuclear energy, from nuclear research to nuclear waste disposal facilities, from rocket development to desalting of water. In short, we have sought as a state to be creative and responsive in our approach to industrial growth as the road to greater and equal opportunity for all our people.

That spirit of equal opportunity for all will endure because it projects the human spirit, our fundamental belief in the worth and dignity of each individual, our rejection of the concept that the state is more important than the person.

Fifty years ago any group of businessmen who were considering the future would certainly have recognized organized labor and the general public as groups whose influence in their system was increasing. But they would not have accepted them as genuine and essential partners with capital—nor have foreseen the day when that would be done. That day has long since arrived.

The rise of labor to an equal partnership with capital—and some would say more than equal—quite evidently has not been a solution to at least one public grievance. A half-century ago capitalists were being condemned for having, as one of their leaders so eloquently put it, a "public-be-damned" attitude. Today, labor is having that same charge hurled at it.

In theory, at least, government speaks for the public—and it has been speaking in ever-louder tones. The urgent problem of capitalism in the past has been its relations *with* labor. Now, the urgent problem is the relationship of capital *and* labor with government. The basic interests of labor and capital in our system are identical. Neither can prosper without the other. Neither can be inconsiderate of, or arrogant toward, the interests of the public without involving the other in the backlash. It is not only in the United States that the relationship of capital and labor to government is of great concern. The attention given the matter at the Elsinor Conference earlier this year indicates how truly international the problem is. So, it is more than fitting that today we consider in some detail the viewpoints of labor and the public.

George Meany started his career in the plumbing business—a fact which I can personally attest has not resulted in the plumbing industry's receiving any preferred treatment in union relations. He was born here in New York City in 1894, the son of a plumber who was a staunch trade unionist. He received his journeyman plumber's certificate in 1915, and seven years later—in 1922—was elected business agent of his local. He has devoted himself since that time to union affairs.

In 1934 he was elected president of the New York State Federation of Labor, and in 1939 became treasurer of the American Federation of Labor. He became president of the AF of L in 1952, and three years later was the unanimous choice to become the first president of the combined AFL-CIO. He has been re-elected to that position without opposition at subsequent conventions, and continues today as the number one labor union official in our country.

Occupying positions of influence and responsibility for so many years in such a vital area, Mr. Meany has played significant roles in the development and determination of many economic and social issues in the United States. But he has not restricted his influence to this country. Under his leadership, the American trade union movement has become an important voice internationally. He spearheaded the establishment of the International Confederation of Free Trade Unions, and serves today on the executive board of that organization. He thus is uniquely qualified to speak on the subject, "Labor Looks at Capitalism."

—Joseph A. Grazier
CHAIRMAN OF THE BOARD
AMERICAN RADIATOR AND STANDARD SANITARY CORP.;
CO-CHAIRMAN, NATIONAL INDUSTRIAL CONFERENCE BOARD

Labor Looks at Capitalism

GEORGE MEANY

President, American Federation of Labor

and Congress of Industrial Organizations

I T IS PERHAPS difficult to define an economic system such as ours which is constantly changing and differs greatly from one time and place to another. Our American capitalistic system has changed substantially in the half century since your organization was established. Moreover, despite some similarities our American economic system differs from that of other nations generally regarded as "capitalistic" in character.

Some may attempt to define our system solely in terms of private investment in corporate enterprise, where goods are produced for sale at profit. But as I see it the outstanding feature of our American system that sets it apart from all other so-called capitalistic systems is its emphasis on people, on freedom, on free institutions and on the individual opportunity for betterment. The Bill of Rights, the Constitution and our American educational system are all integral parts of our economic order and in a way more essential to it than the stock exchange or any corporate board.

The founders of the American labor movement saw the great potential for improvement within the system, through the exercise of the right to organize trade unions for collective bargaining and political education. They saw that potential in the dark days of the 1870s and 1880s when wages were miserably low, when poverty was widespread, when Pinkerton agents were experts in breaking unions, when court injunctions were commonly used to break strikes. And they continued to see that potential and continued to work for improvements in the 1920s and 1930s before the Wagner Act established the promotion of collective bargaining as national policy.

The American labor movement had the vision to accept the challenge of America, the opportunity to utilize the constitutional rights of individuals and free institutions to seek and achieve improvements within the basic structure of our society.

In the process, trade unions have in a sense served to humanize the economic system. And in humanizing it, they have made it stronger and more prosperous through the development of broader mass markets for the sale of the products of industry.

It is perhaps useful to recall that only 37 years ago the American economy came close to collapsing. At the lowest point of the Great Depression, about half of our productive capacity was idle. About 25 per cent of the labor force was unemployed and many more were working part time for miserably low wages. Farmers were bankrupt and our banks were closing down.

The seeds of depression were sown in the unbridled prosperity of the 1920s. Profits and dividends had skyrocketed. Speculation had become rampant. The workers' share of national production had declined. The American Federation of Labor, battered by employer attacks, had less than three million members. In that top-heavy, lopsided economy of the 1920s, workers and the consuming public in general had been left behind in the speculative frenzy.

The government's economic policy of that period was stated bluntly by President Calvin Coolidge, when he declared: "The business of government is business." Such a statement caused little surprise at the time. It was just a candid expression of the dominant view in both business and government for most of the previous sixty years.

After three years of economic collapse the New Deal sought to revive the economy by restoring social and economic balance. Most of the New Deal reforms—with their emphasis on people and public welfare—actually should have been undertaken many years before.

I think it's safe to say that history now supports the view that the New Deal, far from undermining the American system, actually saved it, despite the bitter opposition that emanated from the business community. The New Deal redefined the role of government as the protector of the total public interest and it tried to promote the welfare of all the people—workers as well as business.

Its innovations improved and strengthened the economic system. But at each step of the way they were denounced as the wild-eyed ideas of dangerous radicals.

The same kind of resistance has greeted the new programs of the 1960s—Medicare, the war on poverty, aid to education, health and community rehabilitation.

Only recently the AFL-CIO was accused of trying to plant the seeds of communism by espousing Medicare. Thirty years earlier, the same charge was hurled when the trade unions supported the original Social Security and Minimum Wage Laws. And, long ago unions heard the same claim when they dared to seek the eight-hour day and passage of Child Labor, factory-inspection and workmen's compensation laws.

We heard these charges a long time ago. We hear them now and I suppose we'll continue to hear them in the future. However, the AFL-CIO will continue its efforts as a free institution to advance the cause of democracy under freedom. Day by day and year by year we will continue to seek a better life for workers and for the nation as a whole.

Organized labor has long served as the advocate, the lobby, if you please, not only for organized workers, but for those without voice, those without power or privilege who have no effective spokesman in the decision-making process.

Take an old issue, for instance—workmen's compensation. It is on the statute books of every state in the union. It is without question on the statute books because of the work of the trade union movement, and we consider it one of our achievements. But it benefits every person who works for wages, not just union members. There is no doubt that our economic system is stronger for it.

Or take a current issue—minimum wages. The AFL-CIO has been fighting for a much improved federal minimum wage law. It would extend protection to millions of low-wage workers and increase the minimum above $1.25 an hour. This law has passed and undoubtedly will be signed by the President within a few days, increasing the minimum wage as of February, 1968, to $1.60 an hour. But—more important—it will be bringing eight million new workers under the law for the first time.

The members of my union don't need this law. Nor do the auto workers or the steel workers, or the electricians. But there are millions of people who are not members of unions who need the protection of the minimum wage and an increase in the minimum rate. They have no other spokesman to represent them and we're proud to think that we do represent them and that we brought about this most single important step that can be taken at this time in the so-called war on poverty.

Of course, trade unions have other basic functions as well. In tens of thousands of workplaces across the country, they bring democracy to the job. Whenever workers participate in deciding the issues that affect their working lives, a sense of personal dignity is achieved and their regard for freedom is enhanced.

The first-class citizenship on the job, that only unionism confers, helps create first-class producers and makes first-class Americans as well. It is too often forgotten that the reward for most work was little more than a subsistence wage not so many years ago. In prosperous 1929, the average wage in manufacturing in this country was 56 cents an hour. Who then had heard of a standard 40 or 35 hour workweek, overtime pay, shift differentials, paid vacations, health plans, life insurance, pensions and so forth?

Organized labor has played a vital part in helping to lift the living standards of the average American worker to the highest level in the world. And if I read corporate-profit statements correctly, this rise in workers' earnings has not impaired the vitality or affluence of American industry.

Unless the ever-rising tide of goods that American enterprise can produce is matched by the real earnings of workers, these goods cannot be sold. Our mass production system must be matched and supported by mass consumption. The higher take-home pay that unions seek is indispensable to the sustained growth of production, jobs and profits in this evermore productive economy of ours.

Nevertheless, it is claimed that unions are too successful, they are just too strong. To weaken them it has been proposed that collective bargaining be restricted to the local scene—each local union with its local employer—and that any other kind of union activity should be outlawed.

This proposal totally ignores the essential facts of life about collective bargaining in the American economy. Collective bargaining reflects the changing character of the business enterprises with which unions negotiate, the changing nature of the American economy.

Our economy has long since passed the day when the dominant form of enterprise was a small farm or a small local business. Most of our industries are national in scope. They produce for national or at least regional markets. Vast multi-unit corporations increasingly dominate the American economic scene. A recent article in *Fortune* magazine points out that the 500 largest industrial corporations account for 60 per cent of all industrial employment and sales and for 70 per cent of all profits.

In this kind of economy legal restrictions to limit collective bargaining to local unions and local plants would simply undermine, if not destroy, the effectiveness of the collective bargaining system. Possibly this is what some of those who are advocating this proposal want.

But there is really no alternative in a free, industrial society to free unions and collective bargaining. I do not maintain that trade unions have achieved perfection or that the system of collective bargaining is without flaws. No human institutions are in that category. However, I know of no substitute in a free society for the right of workers to belong to trade unions that can bargain effectively with employers. Take free trade unions and free collective bargaining out of the picture and you no longer have the American economic system or a free social order.

There is no uniform way in these United States in which unions and employers bargain. There is no centralized authority on collective bargaining methods and practices.

There are over 14 million members of the AFL-CIO unions, but collective bargaining policies are wholly decided by the 129 autonomous, self-governing national and international unions affiliated with the AFL-CIO and by their 60,000 separate local unions. These 129 national unions and 60,000 local unions bargain with tens of thousands of employers throughout the land and they negotiate about 150,000 collective bargaining agreements.

The large number of agreements is the result of the great diversity in bargaining practices. This variety of collective bargaining methods is largely a mirror of the variety of economic structures in the nation. Each union obviously developed after the establishment of its trade or industry and it has patterned its collective bargaining methods on the facts of life in each different industry.

Just as mass production industries are different from the garment industry and the construction industry, so are the collective bargaining practices and methods of the different unions representing these workers.

There is strength in this variety of bargaining methods and it is strength that many employers undoubtedly appreciate. For through this decentralized procedure each union attempts to develop, jointly with the employers in the industry, workable solutions to the specific problems in the different industries, companies and trades.

At this juncture it is important to keep in mind that the process of collective bargaining between free trade unions and employers very definitely involves the right to strike. Collective bargaining simply means that workers join together to say in effect to the employer, "We don't like the conditions, we don't like the wages, we don't like the hours. We want a better deal." And, if collective bargaining is meaningful it presupposes the right to strike—the right to stop working for the profit of another under conditions which are unsatisfactory. The right to strike is in a sense the heart of the collective bargaining process. Without it there is no free collective bargaining. Moreover, if the government takes away the right to strike, as has been suggested, by forcing free men to work against their will, the government also destroys the basis on which the enterprise or industry operates for the profit of private investors.

No trade union leader worthy of his salt prefers a strike to an orderly and peaceful settlement. And very few workers prefer strikes and the sacrifice of income that is involved. Experience indicates that strikes are almost always a collective bargaining weapon of last resort, when workers and their unions decide that there is no other way.

Let's take a look at the record. In recent years only two per cent of collective bargaining agreements have been affected by strikes and only two-tenths of one per cent of total work time has been lost as the result of work stoppages. Eight times as much has been lost from industrial accidents and illness.

The record proves that 98 per cent of collective bargaining negotiations in recent years result in peaceful settlements. This is not a bad record. Obviously, we should try to improve it, to do a little better. We all want to make the collective bargaining process work better than it does at the present time. But it would be utterly destructive of economic freedom itself to destroy the right to strike.

Does the right to strike and the exercise of that right mean that unions want to put the employer out of business? Obviously, no. Does it mean that we want to do away with profits? Once again, the answer is no. All it means is that unions want a fair share for workers who make their contribution to the economic system. And it means that unions are going to continue to seek a fair share through every legal method, including strikes when necessary.

In other words, we think that the American economic system with its potential for progress works quite well. We see no better system anywhere in the world, today or in the history of the past.

We have no quarrel with the profit system. We have no quarrel with management's right to manage. We have no quarrel with its return for risk capital so that our businesses can expand. But we do say that under the system we have a right to seek what we feel is a fair share of the wealth that is produced by that system for the workers who work with their minds and their hands in producing those results.

May I divert and say, Mr. Chairman, that I think you picked the right speaker today to talk about capitalism, because according to Pravda and Moscow Radio about once every week I am referred to as a lackey of Wall Street. I haven't gone down there to see whether there is any paycheck involved, but at least that's where I stand.

Because we speak so highly of this system doesn't mean that we've reached the millenium here in this country. We have many unresolved problems and I'm quite sure there always will be unresolved problems.

One of these problems today is the continued failure to achieve full employment of the labor force. True, we're doing much better now than in the decade after 1953. Unemployment is lower than it has been in many years. But there is still a hard core of jobless people, particularly among the young, among the unskilled with little if any education or training, and also among our Negro portion of the population.

Moreover, certain trends present a serious threat to the kind of balance required for sustained economic growth. Business investment in new plants and machines is in the third year of a super-boom that cannot possibly continue. The installation of these new and automated plants and machines is increasing productive capacity much faster than the demand for goods and services can grow under ordinary conditions. So the potential for a big gap between the economy's ability to produce and its ability to buy is developing.

In a misguided attempt to slow down this boom, the Federal Reserve's policies have raised interest rates to the highest levels in more than a generation. These rates do not seem to have slowed down business investment in new plants and machines, but they are increasing the cost of loans and they are increasing prices all along the line. They have cut home building down to the lowest level since 1961, at a time when we really need a vast effort, if we're ever going to rebuild our cities.

At the same time the fires that feed this unbalanced capital goods boom continue. From 1960 to 1965 corporate profits rose 52 per cent before taxes and 67 per cent after taxes while total wage, salary and fringe benefit payments increased only 33 per cent.

An improved balance in the economy—between wages, prices, profits and investment—is clearly needed. But attempts to achieve such balance through still-higher interest rates and further reduction of labor's share of the value of production can only further aggravate the problem.

Another group of problems arises from the rapid and radical changes that are taking place all around us—in technology, in the growth of metropolitan areas, in race relations.

With the spread of automation, productivity is rising at a very rapid pace—50 per cent faster in postwar years than in the period between the two world wars. The technological revolution is reducing manpower requirements, changing the location of industries and the character of the work-force.

In the first half of this year there were 2.2 million fewer people working on American farms than in 1953, only 13 years ago. In the wake of the technological revolution, hundreds of thousands of farmers, farm workers and their families left the rural areas to seek homes and jobs in the cities, at a time when automation was reducing labor requirements in other key parts of the economy. Many of them were Negroes with poor education and confronted by discrimination in housing and employment. So, our metropolitan areas expanded rapidly, with growing pockets of poverty and unemployment.

At the same time, mining and railroad employment fell sharply. The number of soft coal miners has dropped almost 160,000 since 1953—a drop of over 50 per cent. Railroad employment has declined almost 50 per cent, or close to 600,000 lost jobs.

After 1953, factory employment also declined. The sharp pickup of industrial production in the past three years has, however, brought a substantial improvement and in recent months factory employment has finally bounced back to where it was 13 years ago.

This is only a small part of the story. It leaves out the changes in skills and materials, the upgrading of some jobs and downgrading of others. It also leaves out the continuing spread of automation at a fast pace, while the number of youngsters entering the labor force is greater than ever before.

We are also confronted by the vast growth of metropolitan areas and the pressing need to rebuild our cities. Each year the population increases by 2½ million or more, the size of a very large city. And each year tens of thousands of people move off the farms out of the rural areas into the cities.

In 1955, less than 60 per cent of the population lived in the 212 major metropolitan areas, occupying less than 10 per cent of the land area of the country. Today that figure is about 70 per cent. By 1985, it is expected to reach 80 per cent of a far greater population.

By 1985, almost one-half of all Americans will live in three super-metropolitan regions of the country—between Boston and Washington, between Buffalo and Milwaukee, and between San Diego and San Francisco.

The major political, social and economic problems of the United States are, to an ever-increasing degree, urban problems. The problems of people living, working and trying to raise their families in crowded cities and teeming slums.

The need for housing, schools, mass transit, clean air and water, recreation and other facilities and services demands progressive legislation and far heavier public expenditures for such facilities and services than have ever been provided for in the past. We of organized labor insist that such massive efforts are a vital, necessary public investment in the future of America and its people.

The Negro citizens of our country are also demanding their full civil rights—to enter the mainstream of American society and share fully in the abundance that the economy can produce. Decades of neglect, prejudice and discrimination have left a massive problem, particularly when automation is wiping out large numbers of unskilled and semiskilled jobs in farming and industry.

The Civil Rights Act of 1964 and the Voting Rights Act of 1965 are giant steps in the struggle for true democracy and for the redemption of America from the shame of discrimination and injustice. The right of every citizen regardless of creed or color to equal access to public accommodations, equal opportunity for employment and the equal exercise of voting rights, free of intimidation or evasive devices, is now the law of the land.

I am proud to say that the AFL-CIO was in the forefront of the campaign to secure enactment of these laws and is today in the forefront of the effort to enact the new civil rights bill of 1966. The AFL-CIO will stay in the front of the fight to improve and perfect those laws and to insure that they are fully and vigorously enforced.

Adjustments to these social and economic changes—and achievement of full employment, as well as a better balance in the economy—are needed if we are to preserve the American system. In the world of the 1960s we cannot afford to sit and wait for a crisis to compel us to do what should be done now. But no one group alone can meet these problems. Government action and cooperative efforts of all sectors of the population are required.

The successes of the past indicate the continued great potential of the American system. I am convinced that organized labor, with all of its weaknesses, imperfections and mistakes, has contributed much to the flexibility and strength of this system.

However, we have to move ahead. There is no canned ideology—communist, fascist or any other—that can give us a workable solution within a free society to the problems of today and tomorrow.

I have faith and confidence that these challenges can be met successfully through the exercise of our liberties, our free institutions, our wisdom and our hopefully growing mutual tolerance.

III THE PUBLIC LOOKS AT LABOR

CHAIRMAN: Joseph A. Grazier

· *Introduction by Mr. Grazier*

· *The Public Looks at Labor, Mr. Erwin Canham*

Our other speaker in this colloquy is to take a look at labor from the point of view of the public—and it would be difficult to find a more qualified man to do it.

Erwin Canham has made a career of looking at things, and reporting on what he sees. He has been a firsthand observer at many of the gatherings and events which have shaped recent history.

For more than 35 years he has been associated with one of the world's greatest newspapers—the *Christian Science Monitor*. He covered the London Naval Conference for the paper in 1930 and then began service as the paper's Geneva correspondent. From 1932 to 1939 he was chief of the Monitor's Washington bureau. Since then he has been, successively, general news editor, managing editor, editor and, since 1964, editor-in-chief. He won great renown as a journalist, has been an advisor to many leaders in public life, and has served on many commissions and boards by presidential appointment.

He has written or edited a number of books, including a most perceptive appraisal of capitalism entitled, *New Frontiers for Freedom*.

Throughout his writings there is great appreciation of the dynamic revolutionary power of our capitalistic system which, he says, is based on its dedication to individual man, his rights and his unfoldment.

Mr. Canham is chairman of the National Manpower Council, a past president of the American Society of Newspaper Editors, and a past president of the National Chamber of Commerce of the United States. It would be difficult indeed to find an area of society with which he is unfamiliar.

—Joseph A. Grazier

The Public Looks at Labor

ERWIN D. CANHAM

Editor-in-Chief

The Christian Science Monitor

You WILL understand, of course, that I do not know what the public thinks of labor. I do not believe anybody knows. There are many publics. Union members and their families make up about 75,000,000 of the American public, and I suspect Mr. Meany will agree that there are many differences among them. But they are friends and participants in the movement.

You have asked me to talk about some of the unresolved problems that today endanger the collective bargaining process. But first, as the title suggests, let us briefly take a broader view of labor.

I believe most of you will agree that if labor unions did not exist in the United States somebody would have to create them. We can be grateful that is no longer necessary. The organizing phase is the toughest, the most violent, the most provocative of the worst in both sides. When or if the unorganized majority of American workers will be organized I do not know. The labor movement has been declining rather than growing in membership in recent years. Its power and strength are great but, in the view of some labor specialists, not so great as they have been at some times in the past, nor as great as labor leaders themselves (and sometimes business leaders) would have us think.

The American economy needs labor unions. Their contribution to the development of a balanced and a productive national life was and is vital. We can all be enormously grateful for the almost uniquely good things about the American labor movement. It is not a movement based on class struggle. It is not striving to bring down the national system. It is not essentially a political movement but an economic movement. Indeed, the leaders of American labor, it seems to me, often display precisely the same attributes as do the leaders of American business management or capital.

Sometimes I have a little mischievously suggested that some leaders of American labor remind me of some leaders of American capital as they were in about 1900. But this is not a point I will press with Mr. Meany.

Both kinds of leaders—management and labor—are representatives: one set is responsible to members and the other set to stockholders. They are no longer free-wheeling titans. Sometimes their relationship to their constituency is precarious. Quite often they fall from authority and are replaced.

And I believe that leaders of labor and of management are growing more and more alike, especially since unions have become custodians of very large accumulations of capital, which they must invest partially at least in productive enterprise. They are both thoroughgoing capitalists, one set representing money-capital and management, and the other set representing labor-force-capital and a considerable degree of management as well.

I suppose it is inevitable that the relationship which exists between these two sets of capitalists is an adversary relationship. Yet such an adversary relationship does not exist in quite the same way as between other elements in the competitive economy. Men and companies can be stiff competitors and yet not quite be adversaries. Labor and management ought not to be mere adversaries. They should more nearly resemble buyers and sellers. Customers and clients. A stern battle can take place over price, quality, and other conditions between buyers and sellers. They bargain together but they need not oppose or damage one another's real best interests.

Could we in time introduce into the collective bargaining process more of the atmosphere of the encounter between buyer and seller? The great virtue—the protective element—of the buyer-seller relationship is that normally and usually in an economy like ours both buyer and seller have alternatives. If the buyer does not like the price or the product he can often shop around elsewhere. When he cannot, there may be trouble. Competition among several sellers creates the safeguarding condition which keeps the price down under most circumstances.

Unfortunately, in the buyer-seller bargaining between labor and management a monopoly situation largely prevails. Or almost prevails. The buyer cannot turn elsewhere for a competitive product except to the limited degree that he can work out increased mechanization and the reduction of labor. So the bargain that has to be struck between the management and the union is one in which the ultimate sanction, instead of competition and choice between sellers, is the strike. That's the trouble. Because the strike, while probably an inevitable ultimate weapon, is often a destructive and occasionally a suicidal weapon. It is costly in a sense that nothing else needs to be costly in our economic system.

Would there be any other way than the strike of enforcing the best and fairest bargaining terms? Could there be a better way of making sure that the three constituents of the enterprise —the worker, the stockholder, and the customer—each gets his fair share?

I have no ready-made alternative to suggest. I do feel, however, that many better ways can and must be attempted to bring labor and its representatives more closely into the framework of the enterprise. Labor has a right to know more than it now does about the state of the enterprise and its balance sheets. The most effective employers in their dealings with labor have been those who were frankest and fullest in their information to labor.

In a corporation with stockholders able to buy shares on the open market, there are theoretically few secrets. The management stands accountable at the annual meeting. I know that this process of economic democracy, so-called, has many shortcomings. I know, too, that a corporation has a right to protect itself against information that would be used to its disadvantage by competitors. But even so, stockholders are entitled to a great deal of information.

I believe that the labor force and its delegates should also be entitled to a great deal of information.

Sooner or later, the two kinds of capitalists who control the elements of American production need to cooperate on the basis of ultimate mutuality of interest.

The co-determination system which prevails in certain German industries is doubtless no panacea. A few years ago when I talked to responsible leaders of German labor unions and German industries, I found both warm in their praise of the co-determination system by which labor as well as capital had representatives on the boards of directors of the companies. One labor leader described to me the board on which he sat with ten representatives of the union, ten of the management, and an eleventh man who was to be the arbiter in the event of disagreement. My friend told me the eleventh man had never had to cast his vote. I am not so naive as to think the situation is as simple as all that. But it does suggest that the more labor leaders know of the actual financial picture and operational problems of the business, the more likely they are to bargain with the well-being of the enterprise in mind.

You would probably ride me out of here on a rail if I suggested that it might be helpful if organized labor had an open and direct share in deciding the levels of profits, of reserves and re-investment, and of pricing, though of course they have such a share right now. You will say that it would be inviting the wolf into the parlor to suggest consultation. Well, I am not so sure. And I am not so sure Mr. Meany would accept an invitation to sit on a company board of directors. He might regard it as a slick device to take him into camp. He might think his constituents would denounce him as a turncoat, as some of them certainly would.

But, looking down the road, let us not close our minds to a closer relationship between those who manage capital and those who manage labor. The committees set up in the steel industry, and in various others, seem to head in this direction. Their failure to make greater progress is generally attributed to circumstances surrounding the change in leadership of the steel union. I am not passing judgment. But I am sure that all those intimately involved in the well-being and prosperity of an enterprise ought to be informed, consulted, and have a share in deciding its vital issues. They participate now, but in an adversary posture. We could do better.

It is quite apparent that the process of collective bargaining in the United States is right now in serious trouble. It has failed miserably in several recent trials. I think it is fair to say—though I do not expect Mr. Meany to agree on the causes but perhaps he would on the results—that it failed in the airline machinists' strike. It failed in the New York transit strike. It failed in the New York newspaper strikes. If, in the big bargaining struggles that lie ahead of us now, it also fails, then I believe the nation and its legislators will demand some changes. They will not put all the blame on labor. They will not put all the blame on management. They will not put all the blame on government.

But none of these three groups will escape. Again I do not expect Mr. Meany to agree with my opinion that public criticism of the role of organized labor in these recent failures will be far greater than public criticism of management or of government. If I were a labor leader today, I would be deeply concerned about the future of the movement. I know that many of them are, for various reasons.

I do not believe that the failure of labor to grow is healthy for labor. I do not believe it is healthy for labor to drive management into more and more automation, though it may have some value for the economy as a whole. I do not believe it is good for labor to exert its political influence in favor of ever-higher minimum wages. I do not believe this is the way to improve wages, and especially the lowest wages. Higher minimum wages cut off job opportunities for the members of our work force who sociologically need jobs most. Ill-educated, racially discriminated, poorly equipped labor—especially youth—are hit hardest by higher minimum wages. It is not inconsistent to believe firmly in the necessity of higher wages and also to believe there should be latitude to hire at the lower edge of the labor scale some of those who are not really worth more, and who are most readily displaced by automation.

Increasingly in the future, collective bargaining will be preoccupied with work rules and job security. American labor has reason to be proud of much in its record toward technological change, especially in recent years. There are glaring exceptions, where bitter resistance to change has greatly damaged the enterprise, as in the case of newspapers. There is the attitude of the railroad brotherhoods, fighting a rear guard action with the aid of a featherbed.

Though management has usually had to pay a heavy price for work rules, it has thereby gained greater control over its working force than it could have had in any other feasible way. The value of such agreements is not to be underestimated. Moreover, labor is increasingly aware of the importance of improved productivity, especially where wage gains are linked to production increases. The pressure of unions through work rules and wage demands has often forced management to more efficient methods.

If the collective bargaining process regarding work rules can be spread out through yearlong consultations and committees, it can turn into a well-informed and productive relationship. Indeed, the degree to which the bargaining is a steady, quiet, informative process rather than a battle just preceding and following the contract expiration date, the more effective it becomes.

It is very much in the interest of both sides to make the collective bargaining process work more effectively. Its failure is likely to lead to a greater intervention of government. Such intervention is harmful to both sides. It interposes government in the market process. Government has no business in the market process. It does not have enough information or judgment to take sides in the market process. It does not know what the price of labor ought to be any more than it knows what the price of pork ought to be. Still less does it know what work rules and conditions are suitable and effective in a given industry at a given period under given market conditions. All these things vary. They can only be tested and set by market facts, and collective bargaining is the process which should bring out the market facts and make the stark realities of economic life prevail.

For thirty years, the Wagner Act has set up conditions which actively placed government on the side of labor, whatever else it may have accomplished in achieving greater social justice for labor. The Taft-Hartley Law partly redressed the balance. At present the weight of government still leans favorably to labor, through the pressure of partisan politics. Everybody is aware of the general alliance between organized labor and the Democratic

Party. The power of labor at the polls is practical and great, though often far from decisive.

When Mr. Meany told members of the House of Representatives that if they voted for the airlines bill they would regret it the rest of their lives, a good many of them had ample reason to believe him. And for various reasons. There were those who justifiably feared labor's reprisal at the polls, of which Mr. Meany has never made any secret. There were those who justifiably feared Congress' intervention in a collective bargaining struggle which had gone wrong but should have been solvable on its own terms. On balance, it seems to me that labor and the Congress and the President suffered as a result of the episode. American travelers and five airlines and widespread elements of business also suffered. We all paid a high price, an unnecessarily high price. The ultimate decision, I suppose, was produced by the threat of Congressional action and the continuous power of federal regulation. The airlines are heavily dependent on government.

It is to avoid such fiascos in future that collective bargaining must be rescued and improved as an institution. It sounds vague and altruistic, perhaps, but I believe what we need most are mutual information, trust, and reasonableness. I do not believe these qualities will come by law, but by closer contact and awareness of the great need for improving the process.

We will not and we need not eliminate strikes. They are sometimes a healthy catharsis. But some strikes raise terrible questions of public well-being. It is these concerning which President Johnson promised last January to submit legislation, which is still to come. But there are other strikes which go far beyond the bounds of catharsis, or of the legitimate market process of struggle between seller and buyer. There are agreements which cripple rather than free the productive process. There are costs too high to pay, sometimes almost collusively high, which result in managed prices penalizing the consumer.

How can we get more rationality in the collective bargaining process? Well, I suppose one way is to have Mr. Meany at more meetings like this one. But then, Mr. Meany has always been a very reasonable man. He knows the score. The dialogue between the managers of labor and the managers of capital enterprise is today a good deal clearer and better than ever before. Yet the crisis of collective bargaining and of trade unionism is with us. We are all riding the tiger of a more-or-less managed economy. We must get as free as possible from this fateful ride, or we may both end up inside the tiger—as Mr. Meany said a few weeks ago —with socialism.

Frankly, I think that both management and labor have a great responsibility to make their interaction more fruitful, effective, productive, beneficial, just. The seller and the buyer require one another. They are not essential adversaries, but in that tritest of clichés, they are partners.

We must help make American enterprise and American life worthy of our role in the modern world. It is our mandate to weld together freedom and responsibility so that the delusions of socialism and the snares of the police state do not overwhelm mankind. We must not be—in a vivid phrase applied to atomic war—two scorpions in a barrel. An increasing awareness of our respective roles and our inextricable interaction has come into being. Let us not lose but let us nurture our common interest.

IV TECHNOLOGICAL CHANGE AND CAPITALISM

CHAIRMAN: T. Vincent Learson

· *Introduction by Mr. Learson*

· *Technological Change and Capitalism,*

  Dr. Lee A. DuBridge

THE GREATEST strength of capitalism has been the freedom it gives the individual to create things that people want, and the rewards given the individual for his creativity. Under capitalism individual creativity has flourished, technology has progressed rapidly and standards of living have risen tremendously.

Change is one of the bench marks of man in this latter half of the twentieth century. Today one's approach must differ significantly from the attitude of the keynoter in the annual meeting of the National Association of Carriage Builders held early in this century.

May I quote from the keynoter's speech:

> Eighty-five per cent of the horse-drawn vehicle industry of the country is untouched by the automobile. In proof of the foregoing permit me to say that in 1906-7 and coincident with an enormous demand for automobiles, the demand for buggies reached the highest tide of its history. The demand during the present season was a capacity one. The man who predicts the downfall of the automobile is a fool; the man who denies its great necessity and general adoption for many uses is a bigger fool; and the man who predicts the general annihilation of the horse and his vehicle is the greatest fool of all.

Such "head in the sand" attitude is completely alien to our times.

If Adam Smith or Isaac Newton were suddenly to materialize in this hall today, they probably wouldn't understand half of what we are talking about. Both might very well take violent exception to what we say, for changes, both in economic theory and in science, to put it mildly, have been very dramatic.

The economics that I studied some 30 years ago under Taussig were more closely related to Adam Smith's theory than are the economics that are taught in our universities today.

Although the expression "controlled economy" came from the socialists over a hundred years ago, it wasn't until the mid-1930s that this concept was applied in the capitalistic environment, and then, as you all remember, they were considered very naughty words. The changes in capitalism up to that time were mostly reactions against excesses, real or imaginary. We then began to take a more creative, as opposed to a reactive, approach to changes in our economic system. We flatly rejected socialism but found we could significantly improve the management of our economy. Our ability to do this has continued to this date. And today's newspapers are filled with requests for the government to exercise control which would affect capital investments, the supply and demand of money, and, indeed, even the supply and demand of consumer products.

Why are all these changes more acceptable today? Because during the past 30-odd years, technology and capitalism have developed methods to identify, to measure, and to predict the influence of the multitude of variables that play a part in our capitalist structure. Leontiev, for example, began his work with his Input/Output Tables in the mid-1930s. Today econometric models are accepted, not only as a necessary tool for the understanding and improved general control of the national economy, but for the understanding and improved general control of individual product markets.

No longer do we need to allow the "natural forces" of economics to run unchecked, for now we have models which permit us, through simulation techniques, to anticipate the havoc that might result. And, perhaps, even more important, we have methods to predict the effect of counterforces which might be brought into play to control or off-set disruptive factors. One of the major benefits of the technological revolution of the last 30 years has been this ability which is now in the hands of economists, government planners, and the businessman himself.

Our task in the years ahead is to understand better the use of these tools and to be responsive to their predictions. They will be helpful to all of us in the planning and control of our individual businesses.

In dramatic contrast to just 30 years ago, it might well be said that the prized possession of capitalism is its ability to manage a national economy so that it improves the lot of all its people.

I can think of no one who is better able to teach us about technological change and its great significance for capitalism than Dr. Lee DuBridge, president of the California Institute of Technology.

Dr. DuBridge has had one of the most singularly eminent careers in American science and education. And if history is any guide, I feel safe in predicting he's only starting to get warmed up.

At the age of 25, Dr. DuBridge was named a National Research Council Fellow at Cal Tech.

From that time until today there has never been any possibility of slowing him down. But unlike many very busy men, he's got a lot to show for all that activity. Among other things:

He taught physics at Washington University in St. Louis.

He served as dean of the Faculty of Arts & Sciences at the University of Rochester.

He did pioneering research work on the electronic and nuclear properties of matter which has been universally acclaimed.

Aside from these achievements, Dr. DuBridge has other claims to fame. Among them, one is particularly exciting.

Let me quote for just a minute from the remarks of Dr. Detlev Bronk when he presented Dr. DuBridge with the honorary degree of Doctor of Science in 1965.

Dr. Bronk said, in a tribute that I suspect needs no elaboration, that Dr. DuBridge has added significantly to the greatness of Cal Tech, "by resisting the glamor of numbers for the satisfaction of excellence."

—T. Vincent Learson
PRESIDENT
INTERNATIONAL BUSINESS MACHINES CORP.

Technological Change and Capitalism

LEE A. DU BRIDGE

President

California Institute of Technology

I HAVE FOUND it a puzzling problem to know just how to approach the topic of "Technological Change and Capitalism." Should I explore how capitalism either encourages or hinders technological change? Or how technology helps or hinders capitalism? Or should I contrast a capitalistic versus a communistic society as far as technology is concerned?

Unfortunately, I am not competent to answer any one of these questions in any definitive way—for I am not an economist or a political scientist. In fact, I am not even a technologist. All I can really do is to examine the nature and role of technology in the one kind of society—a free society—in which I have always lived.

I think, however, we should begin by recognizing that technology is a product of human inventiveness—and human inventiveness can be found in any kind of society—from the most primitive tribe to the most sophisticated, industrialized, modern nation—capitalist or socialist. It is just one thing that happens to characterize the animal species which we call *homo sapiens;* that he continually invents new tools and techniques to do more

53

easily and more effectively the things that he has to do to survive, or that he wants to do to have a better life. It could be argued that it took as great a leap in human imagination to develop the first club or boomerang or spear as to develop the first gun—or the first atomic bomb. The first wheel or the first sailing vessel may have been as great an intellectual *tour de force* as the steam engine or nuclear submarine. The invention of the alphabet and the number system were as great breakthroughs as the computer.

Furthermore, every form of society—the tribe, the kingdom, the empire, or the modern nation—has used its technological inventions to defend itself against enemies, to improve its competitive economic position or to improve the welfare of its people —or for whatever other purpose seemed advantageous to the people or their rulers.

So while—throughout human history and in various forms of human societies—there has been a marked continuity of technological inventiveness, one must also recognize that in the past 300 years there has been a marked change in the rate of technological invention and also in the contrasting ways in which various societies have been able to encourage, stimulate, and use new technological developments. Technology in America is thus a vastly different thing from technology in central Africa. And the technology in America and Europe today is vastly different from what it was 200 years ago—or even 30 years ago.

Now I am not enough of a sociologist to be able to explain why the beginnings of modern scientific technology took place about 300 years ago in Europe rather than in Asia or Africa or America. But the fact is that they did. The nations of Europe where these beginnings took place could not at that time be called either democratic or capitalistic in the modern sense. One king or emperor might be a friend or patron of scientists or inventors; another one, their enemy.

And yet the seeds of the idea of human freedom were being sown in Europe during the Renaissance period—and it was then and there that Copernicus and Galileo and Kepler and Newton did their work—and the world has never been the same since. Those men demonstrated conclusively the enormous potentialities of the unfettered human mind—though Copernicus and Galileo encountered their troubles in trying to express their new ideas.

However, I think it was no accident that after Newton's revolutionary work the idea of the *intellectually* free human being grew and thrived in parallel with the idea of the politically free individual.

Now Galileo and Newton were not technologists; they were scientists. They were not trying to invent new tools or new devices; they were trying to understand nature. They would surely have been surprised if they could have seen—200 years later, say—how the tools of theory and experiment which they invented in order to understand nature had not only have led to such enormous success in that enterprise, but had also given rise to such spectacular technological developments.

The difference between the technology of primitive and of modern peoples is that the former comes from trial-and-error type of invention while the latter stems from guiding principles based on a knowledge of nature. Modern technology is based on science. And modern science stems from the discovery by Galileo and Newton and others that nature can be studied, can be understood, in a systematic, thoroughgoing way.

Such a discovery could hardly have been made in a primitive society where all the attention of all people had to be focused on the problem of survival. This discovery was, strangely enough, not even made by the sophisticated philosophers of ancient Greece. The Greeks *thought* deeply about the nature of the world and of life. But they did no experiments. Hence, it was only accidental whether their speculations happened to turn out to be right or wrong. However, when the great power of experiment combined with theory was demonstrated, modern science and technology were born. And the underlying assumption of modern science and technology is that knowledge and understanding can be systematically pursued. An organized society thus can encourage and support scientific discovery, can thus accelerate the progress of science, and can accelerate putting the new knowledge to practical use.

The technologically advanced nations of today—and therefore the economically prosperous ones—are those that have found the ways and means to encourage scientific discovery and to encourage *and use* technological development.

Today America leads the world in these endeavors. Why?

The story is long and complex. But the fact that it is long and complex—that many factors were involved—helps explain why many underdeveloped countries are finding it impossible to attain overnight a high degree of industrial and technological development. It is a slow, complex process. And technological sophistication is *not* easily exportable.

Admittedly America was lucky.

America was born as a free country. The freedom of each individual to think and speak and act as he chose (within the law) was a paramount tenet of the American Revolution.

America was a rich country. Its enormous resources of land, water, minerals, forests, and moderate climate meant that men, by exploiting these resources energetically, could not only survive—they could prosper.

Nevertheless, the resources of America were not easy to exploit. It took sturdy and determined and resourceful pioneers to tame the wilderness, to establish agriculture, to find, remove, and use the minerals, to develop transportation. Resourcefulness and inventiveness were necessary—and they paid off.

They paid off! That was the key fact. The inventive farmer, or artisan or manufacturer or businessman could profit from his efforts. The profits were not confiscated by the king or by the state.

But the early Americans were not only ruggedly practical and resourceful. They were also, paradoxically, idealists. They were devoted to freedom; they were devoted to their families, their friends, their community. They founded churches and schools and colleges almost before the wilderness was cleared. They had a passionate belief in the life of the mind and of the spirit.

All these and many other things helped America to develop the essentials of a prosperous society. The great farms grew enough food to do more than feed the family—enough to sell to the nearby city and feed also those engaged in manufacturing, in transportation, in teaching, and in preaching—and eventually those in a host of service operations and professions.

Yes, America was lucky. It had a sound base of resources, incentives, and ideas on which to build a scientific-technological society.

Historically, America was lucky, too. The colonists were just getting well-settled here at the time of Galileo and Newton. The steam engine was developed in Europe just after the American Revolution—and it soon became literally the driving force behind the new nation—powering its factories, its railroads, its ships, and its agricultural machinery.

Thus, in the nineteenth century Americans became aware of the enormous values inherent in new discoveries, new inventions, new scientific knowledge.

As early as 1802 the United States government established the nation's first engineering college—the United States Military Academy—which trained the army engineers who played so critical a role in surveying the new country, laying out its highways and waterways. In 1824 a civilian engineering school—Rensselaer Polytechnic—was founded, and its graduates, plus those of West Point, were the backbone of the engineering skills required to build the factories and machines which laid the base of modern industry.

The devotion to education was surely a mainspring of American life and American progress. Harvard was founded in 1636, and by 1776 eight other colleges were operating in the 13 colonies. These, and their many successors, served as the channel which fed the surging intellectual revolution of Europe directly into American life. As early as 1787 the Northwest Ordinance—the charter of the great West—stated emphatically: "Religion, morality and knowledge being necessary to good government and to the happiness of mankind, schools and the means of education shall forever be encouraged." (Our founding fathers separated the state from the church—but not from religion. They did not want to suppress religion, but to elevate it—to make it free and dynamic. Do we sometimes forget that?)

Education, then, was a keystone of the new America—including engineering education. The Morrill Land-Grant College Act of 1862 established our system of state universities—charging them first with the study of agriculture and the mechanic arts. This move was a radical break with the European university tradition which then—and for many years later—ignored the "vulgar" practical type of learning and investigation. (The École Militaire of Paris was an exception. It was the model on which West Point was based.)

Yet it was a bit strange and contradictory that these burgeoning schools of engineering and agriculture so long ignored the study of science itself. We left that to Europe—and even up until the 1930s European universities far excelled the American universities in study and research in sciences. America produced great inventors: Robert Fulton, Cyrus McCormick, Alexander Graham Bell, Thomas Edison. Europe produced the great scientists—Helmholtz, Maxwell, Rutherford, and many more.

That imbalance, of course, has been dramatically reversed in the past 30 years—to the vast benefit of America and of the whole free world. One hates to think of what the outcome of World War II might have been had America been as weak, scientifically, in 1941 as it was in 1918. Today the majority of the Nobel prizes in science come to America.

I need not review what has happened to America in these past 30 years. In spite of all our troubles and tragedies—at home and abroad—it is a fabulous story.

The fabulous part of it—so far as our present subject of discussion is concerned—is the remarkable three-way partnership that has developed between education, business and government. It has been the keystone of our economic development, of our security—and of our determination vastly to improve our society and the living conditions for all our people.

This three-way collaboration first proved itself, of course, in World War II, during which the scientific resources of the universities, plus the colossal engineering and production potential of American industry, were combined under government leadership into building a tremendous military machine. Why should this system not be turned to peacetime pursuits? It could be—and it was.

World War II, contrary to popular belief—was not an era of rapid advance in *science*. Science indeed was stopped so that scientific knowledge and talents could be turned to urgent problems of military technology. But some of these new technologies, it was quickly evident, could be turned back to scientific pursuits after the war and they could immeasurably accelerate scientific progress. The techniques of radar, electronics, atomic energy, propulsion, rockets, etc. which the war produced, gave new tools of unimagined power to the scientist. But they were expensive tools. Was there any way of making them available to the university scientist—who had helped develop them and who knew how to use them? There was a way—the federal government could help. It did. And the fabulous advances in our understanding of the nature of matter and energy, of the properties of new materials, of the nature of chemical reactions and of biological processes— and now of outer space—have been the result.

The war technologies had other uses, too—new airplanes, missiles, computers, transistors, also new materials and processes —a host of things emerged. They were developed and brought to practical use by American industry—often again with federal assistance.

The partnership between science and technology—as between the university, government, and industry—which the war proved so productive, has continued. Industry has multiplied its own basic scientific research, has made it a point to have its scientists keep in close touch with university scientists, has helped the universities to improve their scientific and their educational programs. And wherever you turn in modern America you see the results of the collaboration. Whether you look at computers and automation, at new plastics and alloys, at new techniques of measurement and control, at new pharmaceuticals and medical practices, at supersonic airplanes and spacecraft traveling to the moon and Mars—you see the fruits of science and technology, working together and interacting.

It goes without saying that much of this could, and did, result from private enterprise. It is equally apparent that much did not and could not happen without government sponsorship. There are those who decry the latter situation—the large expenditures of government funds. But, by and large, the instrument to which the government has turned—the instrument that has made possible the vast technological enterprises the government has financed— is private enterprise—our privately owned industrial establishments, the private and state universities.

Paradoxically, modern technology and modern science require so much capital that old style capitalism could not possibly supply it. So, in those areas where science and technology lead demonstrably to a national benefit—or, as in the case of defense, to a national necessity—large investments of government capital have been made. And they are going to pay off.

There have been plenty of headaches which have developed

in this process—as we are all aware. Often new technologies—by virtue of their great success—lead to unexpected problems: air pollution, water pollution, and traffic congestion, for example. Often government sponsorship means undue bureaucratic control and interference, and frequently leads to wasted efforts and wasteful expenditures.

But America's modern free enterprise, technological-industrial system is surely a booming economic success. It is a social success, too—compared with any other system in the world. None of us would minimize the remaining inequities—nor will we fail to accelerate our efforts to cure them. But we have, to put it mildly—and looking at the whole picture—done moderately well.

The end, of course, is not yet in sight. We have indeed seen only the beginning—both of the successes and of the headaches. We know now that the physical universe is a vast and a vastly complex thing. We know that for centuries to come we can be learning new things—and facing new puzzles. But we have the tools and the experience to proceed. Knowledge of the physical world and of ourselves will surely grow apace.

We know now also how to use our knowledge. We can use our present knowledge to solve many technological problems, to create new technologies. As new knowledge accumulates, we shall use that too—and the world of 2000 A.D. will be very different from the world of 1966. Will it be a better world? That, of course, is up to us. I think it will be!

But as we pursue science and technology ever more energetically there are other problems to which we must also turn our attention. Our growing technology and our growing population have created new problems: air and water pollution, congested highways and airports, city slums, high accident rates, a dependence on our power and transport facilities to the extent that a breakdown of either can be a calamity. There are many industries which new technology has hardly touched. And finally we find that to have prosperity at home and poverty abroad is not a situation in which we find ourselves either comfortable or safe.

How do we tackle *these* problems? Some of them require new technological inventions. But most of them require new social, economic or political inventions. Can we be as ingenious in finding these as we have in technology? The problems are much tougher than our technical problems. The scientific method—as such—is not applicable. But human ingenuity *is* applicable. And the problems cry out for ingenious answers. To discover answers—to get new ideas—is not primarily a matter of money. Exploiting and using the ideas may be. It is a prime challenge to private enterprise in this country—business, industry and education—to find mechanisms for focusing the intelligence of our best and most imaginative people on these problems.

V THE FUTURE OF CAPITALISM IN THE DEVELOPING COUNTRIES

CHAIRMAN: George S. Moore

· *Introduction by Mr. Moore*

· *The Future of Capitalism in the Developing*

Countries, Dr. Alberto Lleras Camargo

It seems redundant for the president of the Citibank and equally high-placed corporate leaders to say that capitalism is a good thing, and that it has a rosy future!

But none of us is satisfied with the present status of the dialogue. We know that multitudes are confused by their problems and the labels on proposed solutions. This is especially true in Latin America. What we need is a realistic evaluation of the problems capitalism is having around the world, and why, and what we can and should be doing about them. If some tangible action flows from these discussions, it will have been worth our while.

First we must define the word "capitalism." It is not a good word in English, and probably a less satisfactory label in translation. I am afraid that to many the word capitalism, and its translations, connotes entrenched economic power, with suspicion about its social and economic impact. To me the word "capitalism" means a free competitive economic and social system, with the right to work, produce, sell, and enjoy the fruits therefrom. The rules of the game are different everywhere and constantly changing. "People's capitalism" is a somewhat better label.

I suspect that when history evaluates this twentieth century, its most important social accomplishment will have been its discovery that dictatorship or totalitarianism in all its many forms, from communism to fascism, is an economic as well as a social failure; its discovery by trial and error that an evolving, free competitive system is the most effective road to the satisfaction of human needs and aspirations. I suspect this discovery will rival the century's scientific achievements in its impact on the human race.

The obsolete view that capitalism is an exploitive private property device is nevertheless widely held by many people of many nations. For example, there is an appalling degree of misunderstanding among the less developed countries, as well as in the United States, of how income is divided between investors and employees of major U. S. corporations.

Seventy-five per cent of the people of Caracas believe that the owners of United States corporations receive the larger share of corporate income. In Rio the figure is 70 per cent; in Mexico City it is 66 per cent.

The facts, of course, are that the net profit margin of U. S. manufacturing corporations was only 4.3 per cent of gross income in 1965. More than half of this was plowed back into the business to produce jobs. Putting it another way, last year, 76 cents of every dollar of gross

64

income of manufacturing corporations was paid as compensation to employees.

And so the problem is:

1) To clarify the label of capitalism.

2) To get this message over to the confused multitudes who need leadership.

3) To get an action program under way to make capitalism work more effectively.

Let us examine the problem briefly, "East/West" and "North/South."

We are having plenty of problems in the developed world— "East/West" for short—but they are basically minor compared with the "North/South" problem. Naturally, we are concerned with the form of British and EFTA association with the Common Market, with the outcome of the Kennedy Round, with NATO's problems, and the problems of the key currencies, and the world's monetary system. But these "East/West" problems seem solvable and are in fact being solved. Even the cold war has cooled. There is a good prospect that evolutionary changes in the Soviet Union and Eastern Europe will enable us to live with the iron curtain, and that it will be eroded in time by trade and travel and investment and the changes they will bring. Growth and progress are continuing; human needs are being reasonably met.

Our real problem, the challenge to capitalism, or let's better say, to our free competitive system, therefore, lies primarily in closing the gap between the developing nations which tend to lie south of a northern tier of affluence that stretches from Japan across North America and Europe.

To the north, we find incredible prosperity with a total GNP of over $1⅓ trillion among noncommunist, developed countries; to the south, instability and poverty and a total GNP barely a quarter as large. In 1965, for example, the United States added $56 billion to its GNP. That is just about twice the total GNP for all of Africa and nearly twice the figure for both the Near East and also for the Far East, excluding Japan.

Yet there are nearly three times as many people to the south and the disparity in population levels increases daily. Just to stay abreast of the growing population, economies in the southern countries need to grow at a rate of 2.4 per cent annually which, if you recall, is somewhat better than the United States rate over the past 50 years.

The forward look is little better unless present trends change. It has been estimated, for example, that per capita income in the United

States in constant dollars will increase some $1,500 by the year 2000. Among the less developed countries, the increase is expected to be about $50. One reason for this enormous disparity is that such large percentages of the population still remain outside the money economy despite the billions of aid, as well as investment and credit, the northern nations have pumped into the developing countries in the last 15 years.

Under these circumstances, it is no wonder that many question the future of capitalism in the developing countries.

Our single answer is that capitalism, or competitive enterprise, is their only future. But we must enlist broader support and it must be made to work.

The old clichés about capitalism are obsolete.

Today's free competitive societies have achieved man's dream in which the broad masses enjoy the fruits of production and ownership.

The Marxian systems have not done this.

The question of exploitation is irrelevant in this framework of development. Nor is there any longer a question of the fair division of society's production. The only real answer is increased productivity, and the steps necessary to achieve that goal.

And we have learned from the billions of aid and credit that neither philanthropy nor technology will do the job unless the conditions essential to savings, investment, and growth in productivity are created.

In short, we need more stability, economically and politically, in the area.

1. This means better fiscal and monetary policies.
2. It means realistic attitudes toward investment, both domestic and foreign.
3. It means practical trade policies; in Latin America, for example, that economic integration, LAFTA, must move forward, and be more than a dream.
4. It means that some policies of the developed countries must be revised, or alternatives developed. For example, European discriminations against Latin American primary products must disappear in the Kennedy Round review, or the United States must surrender its favored-nations policy and give intermediate preference to Latin America to compensate for these discriminations, as long as they last.
5. It means that the IMF, the developed nations, must find an answer to the periodic terms-of-trade squeezes, which sharp declines in prices of primary products cause, and which are in good part beyond the control of the victims. I don't think re-

strictive agreements are the whole answer, but they have a place—and I believe the IMF compensatory financing program meets the problem partially, too.

Now I think all these matters are becoming better recognized; many of them are on the road to achievement in Latin America.

Many of us have analyzed these problems in detail. The CED and the Inter-American Council for Production and Industry (CICYP), representing the businessmen of Latin America, have just completed the best joint study of these matters I have yet seen. I commend it to your attention when it is released.

What we need, then, is a more effective campaign to broadcast the need for these essential ingredients of social and economic progress.

The church and all those who mold public opinion—the press, educators, political leaders—must be brought into the act.

The Council for Latin America, headed by David Rockefeller and Bill Barlow, of *Vision*, representing United States business interests in the area, has recognized this and has a good program under way. CICYP, with which this council is affiliated, is, of course, participating, and also has programs in individual countries.

But the job is too big for businessmen alone.

I am especially heartened by the increasing evidence that church leaders are realizing that these matters are also vital to their interests, and are joining in, as you can see from the presence on this program of His Eminence Cardinal Marella from Rome.

I believe Latin America has the human and material resources to achieve the necessary expansion in production. This will take care of most of the reforms we hear so much about.

We are fortunate in having as our principal speaker a man who understands these problems, and is a demonstrated leader and molder of public opinion.

The optimism I have repeatedly expressed with respect to Latin America's destiny, and which is reflected in my own organization's 50 years of increasing participation there, is based on our confidence in leaders like Dr. Alberto Lleras Camargo.

A statesman of note, a writer of acute perception, a friend and adviser to many presidents, a dedicated man of peace and freedom, Dr. Lleras is a citizen of all the Americas, not just Colombia.

Twice he has been president of his native Colombia; now he writes a signed column for the Latin American magazine, *Vision*, and is chairman of its editorial board. In between, he has served his own country and the Latin American world with distinction.

During the course of his political career, he was congressman, speaker of the Colombian house, minister of government, minister of foreign affairs, and ambassador to the United States.

As director general of the Pan-American Union, Dr. Lleras was instrumental in its restructuring into the Organization of American States. He has been an adviser to the Alliance for Progress: he is credited with the authorship of the Treaty of Rio.

–*George S. Moore*
PRESIDENT
FIRST NATIONAL CITY BANK

The Future of Capitalism in the Developing Countries

THE HONORABLE

DR. ALBERTO LLERAS CAMARGO

Former President of Colombia;

Chairman, Editorial Board, Vision *Magazine*

I MUST CONFESS that I have rarely been as perplexed as during these past weeks in which I have been thinking about the awesome theme of: *The Future of Capitalism in the Developing Countries.* I accepted this invitation in the hope that I might shed some light on the problem. I realize that your disappointment will at least equal mine in discovering that the question cannot be fully answered. For one thing, what I am expected to do is to stab bodily into the realm of the future, which is, and always will be, beyond our ken. What is more, capitalism in the underdeveloped countries is, and will remain, closely linked to the destiny of capitalism in the rich and highly industrialized countries, about the future of which we know very little. Finally, among all systems of productive and social organization none is more vague and subject to change than that known as "capitalism."

But after thinking about it a little more I found a way out of the impasse. We can be sure that capitalism is, and will be, part

69

of the future of the developing countries. But what kind of capitalism will it be? What will be its shape and its frame of reference? Will it be of the type that is now beginning to develop in the Soviet Union? Or will it be the kind that exists in the United States? Or will it be the capitalism that prevailed here and in Europe in those far-off, fabulous days of the Industrial Revolution? This is the question about which it is difficult to make predictions. In the last five years alone, the capitalist system in this country—the cradle and stronghold of capitalism around the world—has undergone such dizzying change that only a few doctrinaire and out-of-date communists still bother to discuss it in terms of the ideas and words of Karl Marx; as if anything of what Marx saw and dealt with still existed!

During my lifetime, which is contemporaneous both with man's first attempts to leave the ground and with his latest attempts to reach the planets, capitalism has changed enormously. Because of its flexibility, its amorphousness, and its capacity to adapt itself to the most adverse conditions, it has lost the very characteristics of a *system*. Today capitalism is saturated down to its marrow with ideas that a bare 66 years ago, at the dawn of the century (not to mention the 60 previous years), would have been regarded as unacceptable socialism.

Furthermore, in the course of the long ideological struggle between capitalism and communism, we have witnessed a process of mutual absorption of influence and ideas. Unlike those superficial students of Marxism who limit their reading to propaganda brochures, the people who studied Marxism in the perspective of its Hegelian antecedents could have foreseen this development. But I am afraid that out of this coexistence has come a synthesis in our day which is no less dogmatic than the unrestrained capitalism of the early days of the Industrial Revolution, or the communism of the terrorist era of Stalin. The synthesis I have in mind is the technocracy of our time. Here, in its bureaucratic structure of the second half of the twentieth century, we find the expression and the development of characteristics common to both systems. The technocrats that administer the state-run factories and enterprises of the Soviet Union and that run public and, in a certain way, private enterprise in the United States have more in common than many people realize.

Both are creatures of modern technology; and the behavior of both is governed by the statistics of production and consumption and by the economic doctrines which feed on these statistics. Both are fanatically addicted to the figures documenting the growth of the Gross National Product. And both are always on the lookout against any fall-off or weakening of consumption, investment and wages, as well as against any harbingers of inflation or of any sort of economic trouble. Most importantly, both respond in similar ways to a wide range of issues—fiscal and monetary problems, incentives to productivity, stimulation or throttling of consumption, investment for expansion and development. In fact, both act and react in patterns which could, with equal ease, be applied to a market economy and to a centrally planned system.

Naturally, many of you may indignantly reject the notion that there is any similarity between the American system and the state-run Soviet economy. On the other side of the fence, I am quite sure that the insults which the Chinese are flinging at Moscow are designed to point out capitalistic and bourgeois deviations in the policies of Khrushchev, Kosygin and Brezhnev. Why this hypersensitivity on both sides of the disintegrating iron curtain? Perhaps because—in line with Hegelian theory, the clash of contrasting ideas—in which this country and the Soviet Union were caught up in a now-bygone period—has produced this synthesis. It has thus also staked out the lines along which the dialectical process will develop in the future. The assimilation of the opponent's ideas is a well known historical phenomenon. The farther apart the two ideologies are at the outset, the more quickly do the clash and the ensuing process of assimilation set in.

Countries outside the mainstream of world events may still live under primitive and crude forms of capitalism or under the savage and rigid type of communism such as that we hear raging in China. But in the advanced countries the assimilating process is moving ahead at a rapid pace. This does not mean that these more modern countries will automatically live in peace with each other. After all, countries do not strengthen themselves or adopt the ideas, methods and systems of their chief adversaries merely to surrender in the end. They are doing it in order to be better prepared for the decisive battle that lies ahead. This may well have happened in mankind's infancy when the Egyptians adopted the famous chariot equipped with sharp iron blades that protruded from the axle—a Hittite invention most recently employed by James Bond. In so doing, the Egyptians were not submitting to any technical superiority of the enemy. On the contrary, they were using the enemy's own weapon system in order to turn it against him.

Still, it is rather comforting to conclude—as I am doing now at the end of a long public life—that in 40 years of political activity I have passionately advocated or opposed many different concepts which have been shifting back and forth over such wide areas so rapidly, and at the same time so subtly, that I have never known whether I was a heretic, or a conformist, ahead of my time or behind it. This experience has taught me that in the field of political ideas we have no choice but to follow the wisdom of Montaigne. This gentle French moralist in discussing his thesis that different roads lead to the same or similar destinations reached the conclusion that: "Certes, c'est un sujet merveilleusement vain, divers, et ondoyant, que l'homme." "Man in sooth is a marvelous, vain, fickle and unstable subject."

It is my conviction that capitalism is far less important as a productive technique than as the fruit of a political system which will have a far more decisive effect on the shape of things to come than any economic doctrine. Of late, due to what might be called "the Marxist complex," people have paid more attention to capitalism as an economic process than to the capsule of principles that produced it. The issue is not simply one of a free market economy against a planned economy. It is one of the relative degree of freedom granted by the political systems under which these economic systems develop. It is clear to me that there can be central control—and a good deal of it—within a liberal political regime. I have seen this proved time and again within American society. It can be said without causing a scandal that this country's economy—doubtless more liberal and democratic than those of other Western countries—is also more deeply and thoroughly directed in some of its sectors. But the control is by liberal procedures based on consent, and its purpose is not the achievement of some arbitrary goal, but the desire to avoid accidents in the congested, speeding traffic of a modern economy.

Nobody wants the economy of this country to be subordinated

to a given doctrine or some politically predetermined purpose or concept. Anyone can oppose the policies of the administration or of an arrogant and highly expert technocracy without incurring retribution; anyone is free to ask for public rejection of those policies. This essential freedom continues to be more important than protection against interference from government agencies or immunity from laws designed to restrict abuses by powerful interests. Americans accept these many interferences and curbs on private enterprise. They realize that most were requested by private businessmen who felt threatened with extinction by the growing pressure of giant concerns. If government is omnipresent in the economic sphere—more so than in any other parts of the world, save the communist countries—if we find government giving advice and establishing standards, fixing prices, making subsidies and regulating just about everything, it is because this kind of activity has been demanded in large part by spokesmen for private enterprise—those who were afraid of the activity of more powerful interests.

In other Western nations these problems have been solved in different ways. Privileged monopolies have been established to which governments have informally entrusted what amounts to representation of national interests. Americans would consider this kind of economy as heavily laced with intervention and discriminatory practices, and they are probably right. But when the Europeans in turn look at the United States and see the forms capitalism assumes here, they are surprised to find that private enterprise is so subject to intervention, checking and government control. All of which proves that there are many forms of capitalism and that it would be idle to speculate which particular type will come to predominate in the underdeveloped countries. A further complication is the great variety to be found in the underdeveloped countries themselves, shaped as they are by the colonial regimes from which they have recently emerged, or by the feudal or tribal traditions of the past.

International capitalism, which represents the sublimation of different national capitalisms, would, alas, many a time and oft, like to have in the underdeveloped third world, virgin territory in which to experiment under conditions which the capitalists of our time have never enjoyed anywhere in the industrialized world, but which nevertheless arouse in them an overwhelming sense of nostalgia.

But this is not possible. Conditions in these underdeveloped countries—and I shall now be speaking of those I know best, the Latin American nations—are not always favorable to the untrammeled development of private enterprise. Some of the essential prerequisites are missing. For example, it is obvious that competition is a requirement in any system of private enterprise—free, aggressive and tough competition. Recently, however, economists have noted that the governments of the industrial nations, in their eagerness to increase the predictability of economic trends, have been putting less emphasis on the kind of ferocious competition that could upset projected patterns of production and consumption. The underlying principle is, however, that the many different productive forces should find the way open to compete with each other, that costs should be cut, quality improved and prices to consumers progressively reduced.

None of this has been observable in Latin America since its Industrial Revolution began at the turn of the century. It is probably not an exaggeration to state that Latin America's industry is the product of extraordinary public sacrifice. This sacrifice originated in superprotective tariffs and in an agreement among producers to eliminate the risks of competition. This in turn has brought about the development of small national markets which make life relatively easy for the manufacturer but which are characterized by low productivity and by prices spiraling to the endurance limits of the consumer. The American industrialists would consider such market conditions in the United States as contrary to the nature of things. Nevertheless, when some of these same industrialists do business in the underdeveloped world, all too often they look upon these same conditions as indispensable. When the government in one of these countries attempts to improve the situation, it is regarded with alarm and denounced as an enemy of private enterprise. One must defend oneself against this camaraderie which so easily develops among those who bask in the fading splendors of the past, like brothers in some international order of buffalo hunters.

I believe we must recognize that capitalism in the underdeveloped countries—and this holds true particularly for the Latin American countries—will develop within a framework of government planning, much the same as in Britain, France, Italy and the Scandinavian countries (but perhaps less so than will be the case in North America in the years to come). The reason for this is quite simple. The developing nations will have to carry out simultaneously an economic revolution and a social transformation. If such an almost superhuman endeavor is to be undertaken with any chance of success, it must take place under a system of strict priorities and carefully projected investments.

It is utopian to think that the Latin American nations might develop in the traditional European or American manner, which left it entirely up to private enterprise to create a better life for the people. We need only to look at the indices of population growth to realize that rapid economic development is impossible under the pressure of massive unemployment, growing misery, unmet needs and general disorder. Many people may say that all that needs to be done is to introduce birth control measures to relieve this pressure. But who will apply these measures? Will persuasion alone be enough? Will illiterate masses who have traditionally looked upon procreation as a religious, patriotic and family duty—will these masses suddenly make a 360-degree turn without any kind of government intervention? Obviously not, you say. But if the government is to intervene in these most delicate and personal of problems, should it not then be allowed to intervene in the economic sphere to guard against possible distortions and damaging developments which the unrestrained exercise of private initiative may entail?

As the United States itself realized at the very start of the Alliance for Progress, without economic planning there will be no development. Nor will there be that limited degree of social well-being which permits and guarantees conditions of political stability without which the underdeveloped countries will stagger from revolt to dictatorship and through successive coups d'état to a social revolution totally alien to our concepts of existence.

The kind of planning of which I speak will probably be no more vigorous or effective than other kinds which are already being applied around the world. I am aware that there are still those who believe that to plan is to socialize and to act contrary to the interests of private enterprise. But right now there are national plans in France, Belgium, England, Italy, Sweden, Holland, Norway and Austria. If there is no planning in Latin America, our region's economies will not become healthy. Only planning can provide for our countries what they most badly need: consistency of policy; timely action to avoid monetary breakdowns; the strength to resist improvisation and the capacity to make commitments which give our creditors an adequate sense of security. The huge tasks these governments have to achieve must be part of a plan. Underdeveloped countries are so, principally, because they have not completed their basic infrastructure. Private enterprise cannot take the place of government in this effort, since it must be carried out in the absence of profits, the chief incentive of the private entrepreneur.

I have no doubt that private business will thrive in these countries. There will be ample opportunities for profit. And contrary to what many people may think, I am sure that once the economic facts of life are better understood, governments will be under diminishing pressure to expropriate enterprises producing maximum public benefits consonant with a fair return to the private businessman. But it must be understood that in Latin America, as in the rest of the world, there are no more virgin or half-discovered territories available to private experimentation. Nor should there be any. It would serve nobody's interest, least of all the interests of capitalism in the industrial world. As it was the achievement of capitalism in the past to enrich the largest number of workers and to create a broad middle class, in sharp contrast to the communist thesis which anticipated the gradual impoverishment of the proletariat, now it is the task of capitalism to help create a better life in the underdeveloped countries, whose plight, in a much smaller and interrelated world, constitutes the greatest menace to free enterprise.

I have no doubt that this is what will happen. If capitalism has demonstrated anything in this century, it is intelligence, effectiveness and a sense of responsibility for the development of a world of abundance and the preservation of a system of fundamental liberties. But now the challenge is much greater than in the past. Millions of human beings—the overwhelming majority of mankind—live in conditions of underdevelopment. In their struggle against the baffling obstacles which bar the road to a better life, they are locked in poverty and stagnation and their destiny is misery and despair. This situation directly affects the capitalist as well as the communist system, as represented by the two large nations which are the main exponents of these two approaches to the organization of society. Within the past months we have witnessed the most unbelievable dislocations in that vast belt of underdeveloped countries. We are now becoming aware of a phenomenon unparalleled in history, with the exception of Hungary under Bela Kuhn at the end of the First World War: a people controlled by communism, or deeply infiltrated by communism, throwing off that system and changing sides abruptly. Indonesia and Ghana are cases in point.

If capitalism does not want to lose a great opportunity to continue developing in the underdeveloped world in a great variety of patterns, just as it has done in the industrial world, then it must not be regarded as a rigid philosophical theory, which it is not; nor as a religion, which it is not; nor as a nation, which it is not. Those who believe in the capitalist system as the best system should put primary emphasis on the fact that it is the natural product of political freedom, not the other way around. The innumerable friends of freedom throughout the world will not be disturbed. But if it presents itself as a rigid form of control of the means of production to which the political organization of society is subordinated, capitalism is sure to engender resistance— at least in the developing world, and surely in Latin America.

Finally, there is one factor which will be decisive in the quest of capitalism to win out in the underdeveloped world, and especially in Latin America. It will be very difficult for this productive system to operate with maximum effectiveness in the context of a large number of small national markets. In some cases these are simply the hunting grounds of those who control both the political power and the means of production. But the tendency of the underdeveloped world to carve itself up into small independent units and to shout the defiant slogans of narrow nationalism will have to change if reason is to guide mankind's course. And reason does guide our course, even though at times it may not seem that way.

In Latin America, for example, one or two customs unions

and the steady growth of economic integration will lead to the development of one vast economic area and a single broad market. When this happens, indigenous capitalism in Latin America will have as great a potential as American capitalism had in its initial phase. The best climate for free enterprise to unfold its strength is one in which national barriers fall—barriers which have created an industry that in some cases is absolutely artificial and deformed. Those, like the people of this country, who have put their faith in the capitalist system, should applaud its evolution and modernization in Latin America and its acceptance by the Latin American masses who, in a market that could not become dominated by selfishness, avarice, sloth or injustice, would be enjoying for the first time the benefits of abundant production and increased employment.

VI FREE ENTERPRISE AND THE INDIVIDUAL

CHAIRMAN: General Lauris Norstad

· *Introduction by General Norstad*

· *Free Enterprise and the Individual,*

The Honorable V. Giscard d'Estaing

To me and my fellow countrymen, the words "Free Enterprise and the Individual" have a particularly American ring. But surely they are as familiar to the Scandinavian or the Italian, the English or the German, or other nationalities represented here—certainly to the French. This, it seems to me, is one of the strongest cords binding us together, this respect for the individual, for his freedom, for his rights.

Free enterprise is a reflection from one of the facets of individual freedom. In the simplest and most elementary terms, it has meant over the years the opportunity to direct one's talents, energies and resources to any useful purpose, freely, restrained only by consideration of the safety and well-being of others who may be concerned. The private, individual nature of free enterprise is pretty much a constant factor; the variable—the big variable—is the continuously expanding restraint imposed in the name of the public interest.

In the complex society in which we live, the individual can no longer maintain his freedom by his own hands alone. To secure the liberty we enjoy, the state must preserve order. This means the power to raise armies, to take a man's substance in taxes, to punish him if he violates the law; in short, it means the power to compel. Thus government, by its very nature, is coercive in many if not most of its fields of activity. How to reconcile freedom and good order and discipline has been a question over the centuries. Lincoln spoke of the problem of a democracy as the need to be strong enough to preserve the nation in time of crisis and yet weak enough to satisfy the desire of the people for liberty.

Perhaps it is inevitable that the pendulum of government influence may seem at times to overswing. In this country, for instance, the catalogue of federal powers is all but endless. Scarcely a single area of our life remains untouched by the hand of government. Wage-price guidelines, price rollbacks under government pressure, "voluntary" curbs on private investment abroad and expansion at home, investment credit,—these words and subjects and many more of the same nature now compete with news of an expanding war in the Far East for the interest and attention of the public. It is not for me to conclude that what has been done in the public interest is excessive; it is for all of us, however, to recognize the danger of excess.

We might recall what Benjamin Franklin once said: "They that give up essential liberty to obtain a little temporary safety deserve neither liberty *nor* safety."

The Honorable Valery Giscard d'Estaing is certainly one of the most outstanding men in public life. From a distinguished family, he has added distinction to his name by volunteer service as a boy of

18 in World War II; by an impressive record at the École Polytechnique and the National School of Administration, the remarkable educational system by which France trains talented young men for public service; by service as a deputy to the National Assembly and in various cabinets as secretary of state for finance, minister of finance and minister of financial economic affairs. No longer in the government, he is a leader of the small but influential conservative independent Republican Party.

And we Americans will recall that an admiral of his name first brought effective assistance to this country during our war of independence. It was a fleet under Admiral d'Estaing which assisted the American forces in gaining control of the city of Philadelphia in 1778.

—General Lauris Norstad
PRESIDENT
OWENS CORNING FIBERGLAS CORP.

Free Enterprise and the Individual

THE HONORABLE

V. GISCARD D'ESTAING

Former French Minister of Finance

Frist i must say that I am very pleased to be introduced
by General Lauris Norstad, who helped with determination and
comprehension to insure the security of the Western world at a
critical time. I thank him, too, for his very kind words. But I
must correct one adjective. He has said that the (Republican)
Party is an "influential" one. I will not correct this, but it's a
"small" one. Well, it has 35 congressmen and 21 senators, which
is not so bad for a baby just four years old.

I want too to compliment the organizers of this convocation
for the versatility of their tastes. I think it is not possible to offer
you more contrasting brands of the English language. The purest
one was practiced by Lord Franks and the original one I will
now use. But, I noticed that when Lord Franks said the only
two French words in his remarkable lecture, words which were
"laissez-faire," he pronounced them with a characteristically Oxford accent. So I will now, with your permission, pronounce the
few English words of my lecture with a pure French accent.

I come to my subject which is "Free Enterprise and the Individual." I think that the two basic features of the free enterprise
economic society in which we live are size and competition.

Compared to the ever-growing size of the business firm, the individual looks like a speck of dust.

Compared to the ever-increasing competition and the adaptations it necessarily entails, the individual looks like a piece of slag.

And yet it is in consideration of that dust and of that piece of slag that we must build our economic system and make it work, since its real purpose is to satisfy the needs of the individual.

This predominance of the individual is due to the fact that, as General Norstad expressed it, our common civilization stands at the crossroads of two trends of thought; that of Christian humanism, and that of political freedom for which the eighteenth-century French philosophers laid the groundwork and the American war of independence served as an illustration.

Free enterprise emerged from the economic expression of the rights of the individual. In the opposite direction, the free play of economic laws exercises certain constraints on the individual and the question is, what is the proper balance to be established between these two opposite trends?

It is not, of course, the job of economists to make men happy. Happiness will not be the goal, either of science or of technology, for a long time to come. I do, however, recognize two paramount roles of economists:

The first role concerns the present. In a given state of society, with its technical level, its social structures, its customs, it is to insure the individual the best value in goods and services as opposed to the minimum hardship and constraint. This is an enormous task in which great progress has been made for half a century, but the practice of which is still very imperfect.

The second role concerns the future. It is to develop the outside social factors—technology (by incentives for research and investment) and customs (for example, by voluntary changes in income distribution)—so as to raise levels of production and consumption and to reduce both man's hardships and his feeling of dependence.

The economist therefore considers the human being as an end. But he is also a means—truly, the basic means of progress.

This raises a permanent contradiction between the satisfactions given the individual and the hardships asked of him, between the effort of the producer and the value of the goods and services available to the consumer—a continuous debate over the intensity of the sacrifices man asks of himself or his fellowmen in order to gain greater wealth more quickly for himself or for them.

In this field, the long-term progress of the major industrial countries is substantial. Despite a rapid population increase, everywhere each man is now working shorter hours than in the last century. His work is done in highly improved conditions of democracy, freedom and relative independence. He enjoys considerably larger resources in the form of goods and services.

What I would like to do now is to comment on the most outstanding trends witnessed since the last war and to give my opinion on how to make the swiftest progress in the future.

First, what do we see for the last twenty years? Over the last twenty years, substantial progress has been made, and yet, decisive progress remains to be made.

Some of the practical progress made is well known. This has been emphasized earlier and includes the sizable increase in goods and services that the individual has at his disposal. It also includes the overall advance in living standards and the decrease in man's hardship, in the economic world.

But, in my view, the main achievement is the victory over recession. Let us return to the prewar era, which was a time of periodic and unexplained crises. Classical economic theory made no provision for crises, or rather led us to believe that they could not occur. This same theory led to the conclusion that there could not be underemployment.

Deflation, recession and unemployment were, if I may say so, clearly inexplicable. Keynes made it possible to gain a clearer insight into them. The economic policies followed since the end of World War II show that we know how to avert recession. This is really a major event in economic history and does honor to Western economists.

Today, it can be said that if this progress in thought and action had not been made or had been made only a half-century later, it is probable that a great many states would have become Marxist in the interim. For almost everywhere and especially in Europe, the workers would, perhaps mistakenly, have preferred a collectivist system to the cyclical unemployment of the 1930s.

But, of course, there are many serious deficiencies, which means that we must continue to go forward.

First of all, and we heard an expression of this earlier, it is clear that our economic civilization is still at the awkward, adolescent age: sprawling, noisy, polluted cities; a civilization which is still the civilization of the internal combustion engine and the gadget.

From the economic standpoint, the danger is no longer deflation, but inflation, which is apparently more bearable and more accepted, but is also more pernicious and eats through the economic fabric. It is a kind of creeping cancer of the modern economy. That is why it is vital for Western economists to achieve the same progress in the struggle against inflation that they have made in the struggle against recession. And for them to develop a clear doctrine of growth without inflation and with almost full employment.

Only when an economy is equipped with two symmetrical systems—one to struggle against recession, which exists; the other to eliminate inflation, which remains to be created—can we confidently look forward to continuing growth.

Social justice on the second hand is not yet adequate. To be more precise, there is still no adequate correlation, whatever the difficulty to establish it, between the services each man renders to the collectivity and the level of his remuneration. In certain sectors or areas, structural unemployment remains too high.

The individual's dependence has undoubtedly decreased, but more probably it has changed in form. The growing importance of large-sized bodies—big businesses, unions, government—makes the individual who is not a part of the "machine" to a large extent alien to his society and a minor voice in its decisions.

Those are the results gained in twenty years. I shall now speak about the future.

The future fate of the mutual relations between free enterprises on the one hand and the individuals on the other can be estimated only by working from a vision of the future that is still bound by much uncertainty.

The vision I will try to submit to you seems—I will not say the surest—but at least the most probable.

Two major trends with opposite consequences will continue and even grow sharper in the years to come: These are the trend toward decentralization of decision-making and the trend toward concentration of power.

As regards the first point, the society toward which we are moving will require a growing complexity in the tasks of production, increasingly sophisticated and complicated techniques and technicians with more and more training.

The necessary improvement of technology in the firm and alongside in the cultural level of the individuals who take part in production bears two highly important practical consequences: uneducated societies are condemned to a rapid decline; educated societies are destined for a decentralized and, therefore, democratic and liberal type of management.

In this sense, it is possible to assert that economic progress unfailingly condemns the systems of centralized management practiced by the countries of the East. Their present worries, that I personally know very well, are proof of it.

An educated society actually means human, social and economic relations that are not controlled, but based on growing decentralization of decision-making.

In the internal relations of each nation, or of each large firm, the central power can no longer be exercised in detail over the basic acts of management. The decentralization of an ever-increasing number of decisions is both desirable and inevitable. This is true on the level of the states. I am thinking particularly of the European states and of our own. This is also true of very large firms. I am thinking particularly of the large firms in your country.

In external relations with the rest of the world, a similar trend is foreseeable. There can be no state of lasting dependence between large groups of industrial nations. I am going to give you an example of this which is not yet an actuality, but could be in a few years. Six Western European countries have come together in a common market. This is a difficult and courageous task in a Europe divided by a long history, but there is no turning back on the decision from now on.

The Common Market will be an important economic entity

in the world of 1980. American firms understood this well and many of them have chosen to make a place for themselves there. But, it is clear that if the important management decisions, the "noble" work in these firms, were reserved to the executives of this country, European technicians and executives would not fail, regardless of their wages, to feel deprived of a part of their full responsibilities. And you know that either politically or economically these situations do not last long.

A society based on qualified manpower should, therefore, be very decentralized. Similarly, it is inevitably a liberal society, for free competition in the market remains the only effective instrument we know that can keep decentralized decisions compatible and coherent. American business leaders will certainly not deny this.

That is the first trend. The second, like the first, derives from a technological progress, but it bears consequences for the management of industrial societies, for the lives of business firms and for individuals that are contrary to decentralization. It is a trend toward concentration.

Of course, in all countries, there are still a great many prosperous business firms in which the owner is also the main producer. These individual businesses are highly effective in their fields. The sociological reason for this is that the owner experiences no feelings of dependence and without putting a price on either his trouble, his working time or his imagination, works for the success of the business of which he will be the main and sometimes the only beneficiary. But the role of these individual businesses is confined to the sectors in which production techniques necessitate no large scale investment.

Everywhere else concentration can be seen. It carries a whole chain of consequences. First it both favors and conditions technological progress. It is, in itself, therefore, a healthy phenomenon.

Secondly, contrary to what is often maintained, at least in Europe, it favors democracy to a certain extent, for it fosters ownership of the means of production. The development of large companies actually spreads out ownership over a growing number of stockholders. But at the same time concentration upsets the normal working of economic life.

Markets perform their function badly when only a limited

number of large firms remain. The investments of these firms, which are inevitably discontinued, have a multiplier effect on the national economy and push it to a breakneck pace.

The errors in forecasting or, further, the incompatibility between the plans of these various firms can cause crises and can seriously affect full employment. Concentration of power tends to run counter to decentralization of decision-making and in the final analysis increases the individual's dependence.

So, what consequences should we draw from these two contradictory requirements? They involve management by the state, management by business; first separately and then together. And each of them exerts a direct influence on the fate of the individual.

So, I will speak briefly of the consequences for the state, the consequences for the business and the consequences for both.

As regards the state, whether the state should intervene in economic life is really not the problem at all. The debate has long been settled by the facts. The problem is whether, how, and how intensively it should intervene.

The future trends that we have just seen logically lead us to define, objectively and dispassionately, the sphere of influence of public power. In the light of the distinctions made by Lord Franks, which distinguished three stages, I will say that this brings us to look for a fourth stage, a stage in which the state intervention will be more restricted, since the state will refrain from substituting itself for the specific economic decisions. But on the other hand the state's own responsibility to maintain the major economic balances will be fully exercised.

First, to facilitate the decentralization of decision-making the policy is actually not to intervene or at least to intervene in order to re-establish equal opportunity. For instance, to foster competition when it is distorted, to supervise combinations, to prevent advertising abuses, to establish the most neutral tax laws possible, to open frontiers, to reduce tariffs, etc.

It is also to insure the smooth operation of the market by improving the knowledge and the circulation of information, since an exact knowledge and a very short delay in the producer's reaction to a variation in demand can carry important improvement. It is also to insure public knowledge of the state's economic intentions with respect to its own buying, spending and investing plans. The plan as it is conceived of in France today is an excellent five-year market study.

But it should be stressed that these actions are not intervention in the classical sense; that is, they do not tend to substitute a central state decision for the responsibilities of the business firms. The experience of recent years has convinced me that on the contrary it is to our interest to leave the maximum of management decision making to the firms themselves. The vision of a Doctor Faustus deciding for the whole universe proves cumbersome, paralyzing and sterilizing. At a time when schools and universities are educating and will educate millions of Doctor Faustuses each year, the decision-making power should be broken down and divided among them.

Intervention aimed at insuring the proper play of the economy is not moreover the easiest or the least effective intervention. It is not the easiest for, quite often, in our countries certain economic sectors besiege the state to get it to intervene to cut and distort competition in their favor from inside or from outside.

It is not the least effective, for there is no more decisive tool of progress and growth than economic selection based on competition. We have practically verified this over the first eight years of the Common Market's operation. And this is the path that France, after quite a different past, chose when she began opening wide her economic frontiers in 1958.

The second type of state intervention is not strictly speaking "intervention," which means interfering in the affairs of others. It is, in fact, simply the exercise of the state's normal and modern responsibilities. This action is necessary in the contemporary economy in order to guarantee three results:

The first result is to insure the major economic balances and to protect the country against inflation and recession. These balances include stability of price levels, full employment, balance between investments and nonmonetary savings and equilibrium of the balance of payment. This task can be done only by the state. It assumes no shift of responsibilities, but adequate use of the state's traditional action; that is, public expenditure in its bulk and its composition, taxation and the conditions of creation of currency. All progress made in this direction insures the business firm and the individual against crises and insecurity.

The second result is to cultivate the seeds of growth. For example, by aid to scientific research and to advanced technology, and by occupational training and education.

The third is to protect the weak from the disparities resulting from economic development. As you know, economic expansion alone does not create social justice. Numerous segments of the population have resources that are linked only indirectly to economic activity and, on the other hand, productivity gains do not develop at the same rate in different sectors.

This is for the state. Now as regards business, the problem is actually of the same nature. It is basically for the largest firms to develop a sort of democracy within themselves. In our time the freedom of the consumer is almost fully insured—at least if advertising is not abusive and if the development of consumer credit does not exceed the limit beyond which it enslaves its beneficiaries.

In contrast, the freedom of the producer within the firm raises a more complex problem. It is necessary to make it so that the man who wishes to work, to invent, to advance, is not kept within too narrow bounds and even finds his reward there, either in the form of wages or in the form of increased responsibility.

Here we have a technical problem of organization and management that should be treated as such, methodically and calmly, as is automation or marketing. It is being raised in Europe in public and private enterprise alike. Sociologists and psychologists must collaborate to solve it. Everything indicates that tremendous progress can still be made to allay the feelings of alienation, which will grow increasingly strong in social behavior as raising the standard of living frees man from his immediate needs and as economic concentration gives him the feeling of living in a world beyond his grasp.

But the state and business also have responsibilities toward the individual to exercise together. They include mainly all those whose purpose is to mitigate the consequences, at the individual level, of economic and technical transformation that necessitates abrupt job changes.

Paradoxically, this is the area in which, to speak like Lord Franks, the law of "laissez faire," or to be more precise the law of "laissez tout faire," still persists to a great extent. Confronted with sudden transformations, for example, the new energy sources, the appearance of textile industries in the underdeveloped countries or the severing of economic ties born during the colonial period have imposed on different types of industries in Europe, one has too often the impression that the repercussions of these transformations on the individual level are being treated with an attitude that is expressed in a familiar slogan of today's French youth and probably in American youth, too: "Goodbye and thanks for everything."

In a society tailored to the individual, the changes that technological developments impose on employment should be attenuated by three types of action in which the state and business exercise their responsibilities together:

First, forecasting changes long in advance, so as to soften the repercussions by an appropriate policy of recruitment and normal retirement.

Two, constant adaptation of vocational training along with the foreseeable evaluation of needs and automatic retraining of adults, whatever their age, to new requirements.

And third, proper financial compensation for expenses incurred by those with modest resources because of changes in residence or sizable losses in wages.

A modern society built for man must meet two conditions: It must guarantee the maximum economic development and the maximum improvement in living standards, in keeping with existing resources and technological advances. But it must see also that its machinery respects the fundamental requirements of the individual, which are freedom, the exercise of responsibilities, and the feeling of being a full participant in his times.

The free enterprise system, or rather what I will call the free enterprise-conscious system, seems indeed the best suited to this requirement. First, because freedom is its mainspring. Second, because it has, in the past, shown its remarkable flexibility.

But as in any human endeavor, consciousness must be added to this system. Otherwise it would be perhaps the best possible machine, but a machine with neither faith nor soul.

Consciousness, in this field, is the clear and constant perception of the quality of the action undertaken, which in fact is, through increased production and lasting expansion, to satisfy more widely and more fairly the material aspirations of the individual.

We here are wondering about the future chances of a system based on free enterprise. If it succeeds in combining effectively the two fundamental requirements of man, which are freedom and consciousness, this system is not only guaranteed to last—which, after all, is not the essential thing—but this system will have been and will be an instrument for the advancement and liberation of man. That and that alone is what counts.

VII CAPITALISM, EDUCATION, AND THE MANAGERIAL DISCIPLINE

CHAIRMAN: Dr. Robert F. Goheen

· *Introduction by Dr. Goheen*

· *Capitalism, Education, and the Managerial*

Discipline, Monroe E. Spaght

An OLD STORY comes to mind and though some of you undoubtedly know it, I'm going to tell it anyhow because in some ways it's appropriate. The setting is an amusement park with many games of chance and tests of skill. In particular, there is a machine where you grab a handle, and as you squeeze it a mark goes up on a rod, measuring your strength. If you're really strong, when you squeeze the mark goes all the way up and rings a bell, and you get a prize. This day many people had tried the machine and none had rung the bell—indeed nobody had rung it for weeks—when a nondescript little man walked up, calmly seized the handle, squeezed it, the mark shot up, and the bell really clanged. The manager was astounded and said, "Well sir, how can it be, that a little fellow like you has such a grip? What in the world do you do for a living?" The man said, "Oh well, it's very simple. You see, I'm a college president. I spend most of my time with my fists tightly clenched on the college budget and the rest of the time I'm out shaking hands with potential donors." And then he added, "But you really ought to see my brother's grip. He's a *university* president."

In the modern world the interlocking, interdependent interests of capitalism, education and the managerial discipline are no laughing matter, and I am sure that Mr. Spaght is going to deal with rather different aspects of these three elements of our topic than those suggested in my story.

There can be no doubt at all that over the past fifty years in America we have been evolving a kind of scientifically invigorated, technologically potent society that now possesses an almost insatiable appetite for highly trained forms of manpower, in a wide variety of professions and callings. The country's position of great power in the world, our involvements in affairs the globe over, extend and enlarge these requirements for advanced education. So, very importantly, do our national domestic commitments to a large measure of pluralism, to personal enterprise, and to individual freedom combined with equal rights. Coupled to these requirements and these commitments, there is good reason to believe, the vigorous expansion and upgrading of educational opportunities in this country in the past two decades have had great instrumental force in helping to release the tremendous productive energy which our country currently displays.

To probe into these interrelationships, to share his thoughts about them with us this morning, we could have no more qualified an observer than Mr. Monroe E. Spaght, formerly president of the Shell Oil Company of United States, currently a managing director of the Royal Dutch/Shell Group.

Mr. Spaght is a graduate of Stanford University, where he also earned a Ph.D. in physical chemistry in 1933. Almost immediately thereafter he entered the business world as a research scientist, but for some thirty years now he has been in management, displaying great vision and effectiveness along the course of a brilliant career to larger and larger responsibilities. Alongside a very active business career, he has for quite a number of years carried devoted service as a trustee of Stanford University and for a number of years now he has been an active and valued member of the Committee for Corporate Support of American Universities, which he also chaired at one period. A great many more instances of Mr. Spaght's thoughtful and able involvement with higher education and with science could be cited. He is the author of *The Bright Key*, a book of essays on the relation of education and business. And he is a man, who in John Gardner's words, "takes a really large view of the leadership assignment."

—Dr. Robert F. Goheen

PRESIDENT
PRINCETON UNIVERSITY

Capitalism, Education, and the Managerial Discipline

MONROE E. SPAGHT

Chairman, Board of Directors

Shell Oil Company

THEY TELL A STORY at Princeton about a mother who cornered the president of the university and talked about what she wanted Princeton to do for her son. The president listened as long as he could, and then said, "Madam, we guarantee results or we return the boy."

So you see—Princeton presidents know a free market principle when they see one. Not that Dr. Goheen is a stranger to the business world, because he occupies many important offices on the American business scene.

In the next few minutes Dr. Goheen, I, a businessman, am going to speak for education. If I don't get results, you may return me to capitalism.

In this September week of the year 1966 we come together in the largest city of America to consider the status of one of our society's main institutions, the economic system of capitalism. We find it to be not only a vigorous component, and a remarkably successful one, but we see that its basic philosophical concept is at the highest level of development ever. It has never before flowered so extensively.

If we were called together to consider the status not of capitalism, but of education, as an institution of our society, I would want to use almost the identical expressions. I would declare this component to be accepted, vigorous, and to be the highest development yet seen of the concept of broad, general education.

It is my pleasant duty today to relate these two institutions. While we will consider the place of the managerial discipline, which is in our assigned title, I believe my task to be primarily the relating of capitalism with education. Indeed, the relationship turns out to be most significant and meaningful.

Allow me to speak primarily in an American context. In observing that both capitalism and education are at all-time peaks of vitality and acceptance, this is no light comment. For while such a society as this does seem to produce the most and biggest ever of many things, this is not true of everything. For example, the world has seen big government before, it has seen relatively larger war machines, and it has seen greater attention to the arts.

Why did these two particular concepts, capitalism and education, thrive in the American environment and come at the same time to their new high states of development? Neither institution is peculiar to this society. They have been seen before in many lands and at many times. It can hardly be happenstance that they succeeded simultaneously and so well. If you will think with me about this subject for a few minutes, I suggest that we will find good reasons why they have thrived together. Perhaps we could begin by considering how education developed in the American scene.

There was attention to education from our very beginning. In the year 1636, the general court of the Massachusetts Bay Colony agreed to give £400—a quarter of the colony's tax levy for the year—"towards a schoale or colledge . . . dreading," as they said, "to leave an illiterate ministry to the churches." Not long afterward, a young Puritan minister died and left all his books and half his estate to the college. (Thus public funds worked hand in hand with private contributions to produce, incidentally, what is probably the first matching grant in the history of American education.) This young man's name was John Harvard and the college was named after him.

Then there was the American Constitution, prescribing rights and privileges and freedoms. And not the least of these guarantees was the right of free inquiry. This was of mighty importance to the story of education that followed. The Constitution is undoubtedly a very great document. It was described by Gladstone as "the most remarkable work to have been produced by the human intellect. . . ."

As the country developed, education became an ever-growing concern. Abraham Lincoln signed the first "Morrill Act" in 1862, donating public lands to states. Proceeds of the sale of land were to be used as a perpetual fund, the interest of which was to be appropriated for the support of at least one college where the leading object should be "to teach branches of learning . . . in order to promote liberal and practical education in the several pursuits and professions of life."

Of course, the Constitution did not come out of a vacuum, nor did our history of regard for education. To understand we should observe rather the character of our people, from the days of the Massachusetts Bay Colony, and notice too the environment in which they have lived.

Our country has been populated from the beginning by people in search of freedom and opportunity. There has been a continuing infusion of the blood of the discontented, the oppressed, and the venturesome. As the geographical frontier was pushed back, and ended on another ocean, the ensuing generations used new avenues for their quest of freedom and opportunity. That education should flourish at this time in the American story would seem logical, even predictable.

If you will pardon a personal reference, I grew up in a rather remote region of northern California accessible only via a small harbor. I was ten years old before a railroad reached the region. It was a lumbering community populated by New-Englanders and newly arrived northern Europeans, largely Scandinavians. This was an American pioneer community—and in our time! The charge we received on our mother's knee was to "get out and make something of yourself." Believe me, there was no reference to Social Security! And while make work wasn't in their vocabulary, education was. This was the pioneer community, in which freedom of opportunity prevailed, and where education and hard work were acknowledged tools by which one could realize his ambitions. As one was free to risk, so was one free to learn as a means to excel.

The appeal of education to American youth has always had a practical bias. The American boy has never found it demeaning to admit that he is getting an education in order to have a better chance! Yes—for as practical a reason as to get a better job! This is the environment too in which study can be directed proudly to practical ends, where knowledge that is *useful* is not for that reason bad or unclean.

The backdrop of American education continues as ever to be one of freedom, of freedom to inquire, to question, to disagree. In this one country today it is difficult to think of a single area of ignorance that is not being subjected to the scrutiny of organized research. There is no human institution that is not under continuing dissection, analysis and re-evaluation.

Whatever our shortcomings—this is still the land of freedom. In it has developed this most remarkable educational establishment. It is a wonderfully heterogeneous system in which diversity is a cardinal strength. It has produced, by this year 1966, a system of such acceptance that over forty per cent of all high school graduates go on to higher education. In one state, California, this fraction has reached the remarkable level of seventy-nine per cent. I am not suggesting that the job is done, but there could be in sight now that goal of everyone being educated to the limit of his ability. In this nation there are twenty million people who have had some exposure to higher education; ten million who have earned a college degree.

In the United States, the percentage of the total population that is engaged in higher education is seventy per cent above that in Russia, our nearest competitor and, regretfully, four to six times higher than it is in the countries of Western Europe. The likelihood of a young person in England finishing high school is the same as of a young American obtaining a college degree.

I can anticipate that there is in the minds of some of you certain doubt about the quality of American education, and not only at the college level. One university president illustrates the point in saying "In the U.S., all higher education is not of the same height." This we all know and you may discount it as you wish, but there is a great deal of very fine education at all levels and in all parts of this land and the quality of American education has never received so much constructive thought from so many.

There can be no doubt that America is on its way to becoming the first generally educated people in history. This is a strength and a potential that have never before existed. The capacity of such a people is not yet tested; it may well be quite beyond what we have ever imagined. A generally educated people may be able to stay virile and useful, to avoid the degenerative diseases of civilizations. It may be able to prevent democracy from failing due to what some describe as "the seeds of destruction inherent in the concept."

There is one prediction about the future of America's education that I would wish to make. It is that it will continue to thrive and develop only in an environment of freedom, in an atmosphere of free inquiry.

I say *continue* to thrive. You may be thinking that it is doing pretty well in some parts of the world where there isn't much freedom. But I wonder whether education can long thrive in such environments. It would seem more likely that in time either education will create a society of greater freedom, or the continuing lack of free inquiry will sterilize education.

I have wanted to say then that I believe education here is inextricably bound up with the concept of freedom, and to contend that the system will survive only so long as an atmosphere of freedom prevails.

Does capitalism fit into such a system? I believe that it does indeed, and in a fashion that should give us courage and optimism.

I would believe that the pioneer story of America was one that could accommodate only capitalism as its economic philosophy. The liberties and freedoms that so characterized our history, that gave rise to the system of education we have just discussed, was a setting ideally suited to a system of free enterprise. The freedom to risk, to venture, to lose, to prosper, is the only imaginable economic system of pioneer America.

Of course, since we are free to inquire, a review of capitalism in America produces some sordid chapters. Just as in the bad old days of the Industrial Revolution in England when children were chained to their machines for sixteen hours a day, the story of the sweat shops of Boston and New York doesn't make comfortable reading. But capitalism evolved, through chapters of strife and regulation, to the modern time when we see it socially accepted and with a civic conscience. What we want to consider here, however, is whether capitalism is consonant with modern America, and how it now relates to education and free inquiry.

You and I are participants in this economic system of capitalism, and many of us have been involved in some measure in the evolution to its present most remarkable state. We are proud to be participants because we see it to be singularly productive and useful. It just "seems to work" in a fashion unequalled by any other economic system around.

Indeed, at this point in time, capitalism can fairly lay claim to having *proved* itself as the *best economic system yet devised!* Yet its success does not guarantee it immunity from debate and analysis. This we must expect, for here is the working of free inquiry. Capitalism or any other institution will survive in a free society only as long as the continuing analysis so dictates. We are strong as long as we merit the support of an inquiring society. We will survive only as long as we stand approved by free, truthful analysis. We could never hope for survival based on ignorance or suppression of the truth.

The great hope of any institution such as capitalism is that the inquiring society is able. It needs most urgently, then, an enlightened society; in other words, one that is educated!

When I say inquiring society, I mean to include, of course, all elements that have the power to influence capitalism directly. This is government, both executive and legislative, and also the voices of the people who, in this fashion or that, have an inordinate weight in influencing society's views. In these people one hopes for the day when their judgments are based on a good knowledge of history, with an accompanying understanding of the current society, including the economic system that makes it all go.

But in order to thrive and contribute, capitalism needs more from its society than merely to be understood and fairly judged—valuable as those are.

Here, for instance, is another need—the machinery may be able to produce, but capitalism needs customers. It needs a population of individuals with purchasing power. The ability of a population to purchase, to consume, is highly variable throughout the world. The wealth of a nation does not seem to depend upon some of the more obvious or commonplace variables.

What does determine a nation's wealth? Well, for example, if endowment with natural resources were the determining criterion, Japan and Norway would be poor, which they are not, while Brazil and Indonesia would be rich, which they are not. If, as some of the opponents of foreign investment allege, "colonial exploitation" were the stumbling block to progress, Thailand and Abyssinia would be rich, which they are not, while Canada and Australia would be poor, which they are not. If lack of heavy industry is the handicap, then Denmark and New Zealand, where agriculture predominates, would be poor, which they are not. If high population density drags down living standards, the Netherlands and Japan should be poor, which they are not. If capital for investment is the required ingredient, then Kuwait and Venezuela would be rich, which they are not.

Could a main factor in the wealth of a nation be a high level of education spread widely over the population? If it is, the United States should be very rich, which it is; Western Europe should be fairly rich, which it is; Latin America should be fairly poor, which it is, and Africa should be very poor, which it is. I am not leading you to conclude that education is the one and only prerequisite for an affluent society. But it is most certainly a prime one, for widespread ignorance and prosperity just aren't found together.

If, as it seems, the success of capitalist private enterprise is related to the existence of an educated populace, here then is another reason for the health of the education system to be of prime concern to the business community.

The dependence of capitalism on the enlightened society doesn't end there. Business lives on an endless supply of trained people, ever more so as the technical complexity of our production machine increases. Have you ever considered what the plight of business would be if the college graduating class of next spring were the same in number and training as the class of fifty years ago? The dependence of capitalism on the trained mind becomes ever greater and more sophisticated. But this is quite well understood throughout our society today and needs no elaboration here.

By the way, with all the opportunities that capitalism provides the young, educated person, and its record of service and productivity, it is disquieting to hear that there is a revulsion against business on the American college campus. Not that we should worry about the continuing analysis of what we are and how we perform, but it would be worrisome if we are indeed being judged as *unworthy* of the efforts of an outstanding young trained person. I have tried to learn something about the facts behind this report. The advice from a good cross section of American universities is that the noises come largely from a small strident fringe, that by no means does it represent a broad or serious disaffection with business. We are told not to be too concerned about it. I suggest though that it be kept in mind. Help with facts and the truth whenever you can. It is important that the truth be available, for it would certainly seem that American business deserves no decrease in regard on the American campus.

I say it is important that the facts be told. Of course, we are repeatedly reminded that capitalism needs to do more in telling its story, which is a good one and one which can be proudly defended. It is a proper admonition and you and I must accept it. It isn't that we fail completely, but rather that the job is never done and if it ever were it wouldn't remain done. Like the pursuit of virtue, it is never ending and in allocating your efforts in this crusade, may I suggest that educational institutions are very good places to tell the story and argue for it.

Among the many needs of industry for trained and talented people, there is one that receives considerable special notoriety today, and that is the manager. It was in our assigned title today, perhaps because I have been so careless as to join the many who have been speaking and writing about what comprises the good American manager. Much is being said about the development, selection, and training of managers, and they are indeed vital to capitalism. Perhaps we could spend a minute or two on this special link between education and business.

One hears the argument that American industry is what it is in large measure due to the quality of its management. It is maintained that its managers are the best in the field, and that their excellence is related to the educational system from which they came.

Indeed, the good manager *has* been a great asset to capitalism. Each decade has brought forth new names on the American scene of men who have capably and courageously led business through times of evolution and change. What sort of person is this top management man in American business?

No two people can seem to agree entirely on what qualities are the most needed, but I join those who gravitate into the following general area:

He must indeed be reasonably well educated, and the more the better. He may benefit by being especially well grounded in one discipline, but this is not absolutely required. He also needs in substantial measure all the human virtues. But he needs something more—or at least some things in special measure. For example, he needs great vitality and an insatiable urge to succeed.

There is a recurring view—incidentally one that I hear with increasing frequency in Europe—that the American manager is outstanding because of the existence here of schools of management, particularly the graduate schools of business. It would seem to me that this specific contention can be questioned. I wonder whether the outstanding manager of anything—corporation, university, or community—can be produced by formal instruction.

He works and accomplishes through people rather than things. His ways may be subtle. They are varied, depending on the scene. He is more of the artist than the writer of contracts or the chemical analyst. In that sense he is born rather than made. This is the regard in which one questions whether the most important distinguishing qualities of the manager can be taught at all.

I need hardly say that this observation implies no disregard whatsoever for our fine graduate schools of business, which contribute so greatly to the fabric of American business.

I suggest, nevertheless, that there *is* something that we can do to insure a *continuing supply* of good managers. It is the same theme—to encourage the education of everyone to the limit of his ability so that all potential born managers get what is certainly one needed ingredient, an education. Thereafter, we need only supply a business environment in which a young person can grow.

And as to what will characterize that environment, let me use just once more that same old homely word freedom. It will be an environment, within a company or group, in which an individual can use his full talents and reap his commensurate reward.

Here then was a third reason for capitalism's concern for education; the supply of trained people, including the manager.

I may have appeared to be relating capitalism and education as though they were unknown to each other. These two vital constructive elements of our society are not strangers. One of the hallmarks of our time, I would think, is the emergence of the university from cloistered isolation, taking a place now as an active, integral part of the total society. This is a new role for the university. With this emergence, the capitalistic business community participates as never before in the affairs of the university and, I believe, in capacities and attitudes generally approved by the university. There is, of course, the tangible financial support with which you are well acquainted. The contribution of the American business community to higher education is now over $300 million per year and is expected to increase to $500 million by 1970. But less well recorded is the involvement of thousands of our leading businessmen on boards of trustees, on advising and visiting committees, as counselors and on fund raising committees. At the same time, university people from presidents to professors contribute most vitally to American business as directors, consultants, and research administrators. A very fine and wholesome working rapport has developed between these two segments of our society—a relationship which can, and does, do much good for both parties.

I apologize for talking mainly in an American context. For these considerations we have been assured are equally valid elsewhere. In thinking of the many less-developed lands, we think painfully of the long road ahead before those peoples can come to judge economic systems, before informed peoples of all lands can lift themselves up the economic scale, before peoples can supply the millions of trained minds that will be needed to duplicate the Western capitalistic machine. The task is enormous, the one key is education.

In summary, I suggest that the American story brought forth a system of general education which first fed on freedom and now sustains it. That same environment was one conducive to the development of modern capitalism. Now capitalism finds education its greatest strength and its constant ally. Freedom, with the right to risk and the right to inquire, has enabled this flowering of both mind and material.

As businessmen we have understandable pride in being a part of this great scene. But we know too that every society would not give us the same opportunity to succeed and for that blessing may I finally point out one responsibility which I believe falls on us. It is that capitalism should support education, support it and work with it because capitalism needs education. Support education as if your businesses depended upon it, because they do.

It is in an environment of maximum freedom that capitalism will thrive best. And no better contribution can be made to the maintenance of freedom than the unqualified support of education. In such favored lands, capitalism and education can *continue* to thrive, side by side. Both have great and proud roles to play in the *best social system* yet devised by man.

VIII BUSINESS SIZE AND NATIONAL ECONOMIC GROWTH

CHAIRMAN: Harold H. Helm

· *Introduction by Mr. Helm*

· *Text by Nicholas deB. Katzenbach*

· *Introduction by Mr. Helm*

· *Text by Sir Thomas B. Robson*

THE THEME of "Business Size and National Economic Growth" deals with one of the most important and complex and often heated issues of our day. I shall resist the temptation to have a go at it myself as I have some rather strong opinions. Our Attorney General doesn't miss many of them. He is, of course, very close to the antitrust division which has shown some interest in the subject. That may qualify as one of the understatements of the day.

Nicholas deB. Katzenbach was nominated as Attorney General by President Lyndon B. Johnson January 28, 1965 and was confirmed by the Senate February 10. He took the oath of office as Attorney General in a ceremony at the White House February 13, at the beginning of his fifth year in the Department of Justice. He came to the Department February 1961, as Assistant Attorney General in charge of the office of legal counsel and was elevated to the position of Deputy Attorney General on May 3, 1962 succeeding Byron White, who was appointed to the Supreme Court of the United States.

Mr. Katzenbach was born in Philadelphia January 17, 1922 and is a native of Trenton, New Jersey, where he grew up. His late father served as Attorney General of New Jersey. His mother retired recently as President of the New Jersey Board of Education. After graduating from Phillips Exeter Academy, where he was goalie on the hockey team, in 1939 he enrolled at Princeton University—one of his first good decisions—where he majored in public and international affairs.

Shortly after Pearl Harbor Mr. Katzenbach left college to join the Army Air Force. He was commissioned a second lieutenant and became a navigator. In October 1943 Mr. Katzenbach was in action over the Mediterranean Sea when his plane was struck by enemy fire. After twenty hours in the water, an Italian seaplane picked up the crew members. They were made prisoners of war, but Mr. Katzenbach escaped twice. On the second try he was captured by the Germans and was committed to a German POW Camp where he remained until VE day.

He read sufficiently in the prison camp's YMCA library to be able, when he returned to Princeton, to complete his last two years and win his degree by taking examinations and writing a thesis. He was graduated with honors, and moved on to Yale Law School where he was Editor-in-Chief of the Yale Law Journal, where he also won a cum laude degree. He then won a Rhodes scholarship to Oxford University in England.

Mr. Katzenbach entered private law practice in Trenton, New Jersey as an associate in the firm of Katzenbach, Guilday and Rudner. Two years later he went to the Pentagon to serve as Attorney, Advisor and Consultant in the office of the General Counsel to the Secretary of the Air Force. After serving as an associate professor at the Yale Law School, Mr. Katzenbach moved to the University of Chicago as a full professor, teaching international law, trial practice and commercial law.

In 1960 he won a Ford Foundation fellowship for a project in international law in Geneva, Switzerland. Before finishing the project, he was summoned home by Attorney General Robert Kennedy and offered the position of Assistant Attorney General in the new administration. After his selection as Deputy Attorney General upon the promotion of Mr. White, Mr. Katzenbach handled a variety of assignments dealing with every facet of the Department of Justice operations. He was the principal drafter of legislation establishing Communications Satellite Corporation, drew up a lengthy brief in support of the decision to blockade Cuba during the 1962 missile crisis, and played an important role in drafting the Civil Rights Act of 1964 and securing its enactment. He was the department official in command on the scene during the desegregation incidents at the University of Mississippi and the University of Alabama.

Mr. Katzenbach is a member of the bar in New Jersey and Connecticut, a member of the American Law Institute and the American Bar Association. He is the recipient of numerous honorary degrees: from Rutgers, Northeastern University, Doctor of Laws from Seton Hall, and an LLD. from his alma mater in 1966. In 1965 he was chosen as the recipient of the Woodrow Wilson award conferred on the Princeton alumnus who in the preceding year made the most significant contribution to the nation and public welfare. He received the Human Rights Award of the Anti-Defamation League in New York City April 14, 1966.

—Harold H. Helm
CHAIRMAN, EXECUTIVE COMMITTEE
CHEMICAL BANK NEW YORK TRUST COMPANY

Business Size and
National Economic Growth

THE HONORABLE

NICHOLAS DEB. KATZENBACH

Attorney General

U.S. Department of Justice

I HOPE that none of you anticipate a great debate in either the traditions of the United States Senate or the Oxford Union. The harsh truth is that this fight is fixed. The terms of debate are collusive. And the restraint of competition between Sir Thomas and myself is deliberate.

The authorities are enviable stage managers. In selecting Sir Thomas they have chosen a voice of reason as well as a man of exceptional foresight. Sir Thomas sent me his address six weeks ago. I hardly did as well by him, but my words will not come as a complete surprise to him either. I doubt, therefore, that you will find any gladiatorial overtones in our remarks. Indeed the program announces this as a "colloquy."

I must depart in only one particular from the careful brief I was given by the management. Sir Thomas and I were cautioned not to be splenetic or antagonistic—advice easy to follow—but we were also entreated to cleanse our language and avoid as much as possible such emotive terms as "antitrust."

I fear that as Attorney General this would require excessive self-abnegation. For to discuss business size and national economic growth involves centrally an appraisal of our antitrust policy. I will promise, however, to avoid legalisms which would only lose you—and me—in a trackless jungle.

I.

I think it fair to say that a strong antitrust policy has not won universal acceptance among leaders of our business community. The president of the United States Chamber of Commerce has recently called the antitrust laws "outmoded" and added that present policy "works at cross purposes with economic objectives of maximum growth and efficiency."[1]

Fortune Magazine argues that our attempt to prevent undue concentration in a market "frustrates the natural tendency of business to adjust to changes in technology, merchandising, finance, and corporate organization by growing bigger and by merging." The net effect, according to *Fortune,* is to impede innovation and progress.[2]

Others have argued that to prevent mergers that unduly increase market shares of the merging firms may discourage firms from growing in size, and this may impede technological progress.

The editors of *Fortune* are heirs to a distinguished bloodline of economic scholarship. I am sure, for example, that their views were bolstered by a magisterial text, *Recent Economic Changes,* by Professor David Wells of Harvard, who wrote:

> Society has practically abandoned—and from the very necessity of the case has got to abandon, unless it proposes to war against progress and civilization—the prohibition of industrial concentrations and combinations. The world demands abundance of commodities, and demands them cheaply; and experience shows that it can have them only by the employment of great capital upon the most extensive scale.[3]

1. *New York Times,* Sept. 9, 1966, p. 65.
2. *Fortune,* March 1966, p. 128.
3. Wells, "Recent Economic Changes" (1889), p. 74.

Professor Wells likely would agree, too, with the observation by George Gunton that "the concentration of production capital" is "the most effective, if not the only means of remedying . . . [a] constant social calamity."[4]

What Professor Wells wrote—in 1889, and what Mr. Gunton wrote—in 1899, obviously lack no adherents today. But it must be admitted, at least, that the enforcement of our antitrust laws has been less than a "constant social calamity."

This enforcement has not prevented what, by any historical test, has been an astonishing record of economic progress. We may rightfully suspect that antitrust has made an affirmative contribution to this progress.

To say this does not, of course, dispose of the argument. There have indeed been drastic changes in our economy since the Sherman Act was passed seventy-five years ago:

—Our national income in terms of current prices has grown twelve times.

—The businessman of today is far more perceptive, knowledgeable, and sensitive to the public interest than his predecessors.

—Throughout the managerial community, the economic role of innovation and the introduction of new processes and products is much more fully appreciated.

In short, the traditional arguments against a strong anticoncentration policy have been shown to be wrong when laid against economic patterns of the past. But surely it is rational now to ask whether the reincarnations of the old arguments might not have *new* relevance, against the greatly changed economic patterns of the present. Is it not possible that the arguments have thus acquired a new, persuasive, respectability?

Respectable they surely are. Persuasive, in my opinion, they are not. And I would like to spend a few minutes telling you why I believe concentration cannot be justified any better now than it was seventy years ago. Then I would like to explain why I believe not only that these *positive* justifications are false, but that concentration has a *negative* impact on economic growth.

4. Gunton, "Large Aggregations of Capital," *Trusts and the Public*, pp. 78-79, (1899).

II.

There seem to me to be five principal arguments in the modern case for concentration. Let me consider each of them.

1. *Efficiency.*

First, it is argued that mergers, by producing bigger companies, produce more efficient companies. "Remember Henry Ford and the assembly line" one hears. A merger, it is claimed, like a marriage, allows two to live more cheaply than one. Thus, by preventing mergers when they increase concentration substantially, the antitrust laws obstruct the provision of cheaper goods to the American public.

The trouble with this argument is that it does not square with the facts. What economic evidence there is on the subject[5] suggests that many firms in concentrated industries are far larger than necessary to produce goods at the lowest possible costs.

In other words, most industries can easily sustain many competing firms, each using assembly line production techniques. American markets tend to be large enough to allow firms to enjoy all important efficiencies of size, without dangerously restricting the number of competitors.

If economies of scale ascended in proportion to size, one would expect to find large firms enjoying higher profits. And yet one study shows that, in general, profit rates of medium-sized firms are as large as those of giant firms.[6] There is little, if any, evidence justifying concentrated markets on the grounds of economic efficiency.

---

5. Among the most significant of these studies is one done by Professor Bain. He measured the extent of scale economies within twenty leading manufacturing industries. In this manner he attempted to determine the minimum plant size which is sufficiently large to realize all of the cost savings associated with mass production. On the basis of this analysis, he examined whether the extent of existing concentration was greater or less than the level which was required for economic efficiency. He concluded that "referring to the first four firms in each of our industries, it appears that concentration by the large firms is, in every case but one, greater than required by single-plant economies, and in more than half of the cases very substantially greater." Joe S. Bain, *Barriers to New Competition*, p. 111. See also J. Johnston, *Statistical Cost Analysis.*

6. Sidney S. Alexander, "The Effect of Size of Manufacturing Corporation on the Distribution of the Rate of Return," *Review of Economics and Statistics,* Vol. XXXI, No. 3, August 1949, pp. 229-235.

Moreover, we should keep in mind that while the antitrust laws do indeed prohibit some mergers, they do not prohibit any firms from growing internally. This route is explicitly left open to insure that firms can achieve those economies and efficiencies they may find in large size. It is difficult to believe that significant economies will long go unrealized because a particular merger has been prohibited.

2. Research and Development.

A second argument for concentration is the frequent plausible claim that large firm size and monopoly are necessary to support creative and efficient research.

We are told that today's inventor no longer lives in a basement or wears a green eye shade. Rather, he is the well-trained, efficient scientist—a member of a research team working in the laboratory of a large corporation.

Paying him and his colleagues to look for new plastics or electronic devices, or to turn a drawing board idea into a marketed product, is an expensive business. Thus a corporation must be large indeed, it is added, to pay for the steady research underlying Schumpeter's "gale of creative destruction" which represents the pinnacle of modern capitalism's achievement.

Statistical evidence supports the view that small firms are less likely to engage in research than large firms.[7] But most markets in this country are big enough to support many large competing firms—they can even support several giants. Since markets are likely to become concentrated only when large firms are replaced by giants—or giants by supergiants—the crucial question is not whether large firms conduct more or better research than small firms, but how large firms compare with giants and with supergiants.[8]

The best evidence strongly suggests that firms simply do not need to be immense to support an adequate research establishment.

When Edwin Land developed his revolutionary camera, the Polaroid Corporation was not an industrial giant with vast re-

7. Jacob Schmookler, "Technological Progress and the Modern American Corporation" in Mason, *The Corporation in Modern Society* (1960), p. 162.

8. Carl Kaysen and Donald F. Turner, *Antitrust Policy* (1959), pp. 84-85.

search facilities. It was a million-and-a-half dollar firm specializing in sunglasses.

The Xerox Corporation is not founded on the products of extensive laboratories. Rather, its success began with a gamble made in 1955 by a small Rochester, New York firm on the invention developed by Frank Carlson in his New York City apartment.

And the oxygen converter—a pathbreaking advance in steel manufacturing—was not promoted by one of the steel giants. It was first put to use in a very small company and then adopted in two of the smaller steel corporations.

Indeed, it has been found in repeated studies that among firms which undertake research, the laboratories of the smaller firms tend to be as large and productive as those of their larger rivals.[9] In fact, a recent study of the drug industry concludes that once drug firms grow past a moderate size, their research techniques seem to become more cumbersome, for their research and development has proved less efficient and fruitful.[10]

In the chemical, petroleum, and steel industries, too, there is great evidence that the inventive output per dollar of R&D expenditure generally is lower in the largest firms than in large and medium-sized firms.[11]

9. In a recent study Professor Worley found that among firms which support research establishments smaller firms tend to spend proportionately as much as their larger rivals. J. S. Worley, "Industrial Research and the New Competition," *Journal of Political Economy*, April, 1961. Another interesting study shows that between 1899 and 1937 industries in which labor productivity increased most sharply were those in which concentration declined. George J. Stigler, "Industrial Organization and Economic Progress," as reprinted in Harry J. Levin, Editor, *Business Organization and Public Policy*, pp. 131-133. A third study examined the rate of innovation within manufacturing industries as measured by the number of patents issued to firms within these industries. This study concludes that "Inventive output (as measured by patents granted) increased with firm sales but generally at less than a proportionate rate." F. M. Scherer, "Firm Size and Patented Inventions," *American Economic Review*, December 1965, pp. 1097-1125. A fourth study examined the relative efficiency of large and small research laboratories in the pharmaceutical industry. On the basis of a statistical investigation the author concluded that "in the pharmaceutical industry, there are substantial diseconomies of scale in research and development; and that these disadvantages are encountered even by moderately sized firms." W. S. Comanor, "Research and Technical Change in the Pharmaceutical Industry," *Review of Economics and Statistics*, May 1965, p. 190.

10. Comanor, "Research and Technical Change in the Pharmaceutical Industry," *Review of Economics and Statistics*, May 1965, p. 190.

11. Edwin Mansfield, "Industrial Research and Development Expenditures: Determinants, Prospects, and Relation to Size of Firm and Inventive Output," *Journal of Political Economy*, August 1964, Vol. 72, p. 336.

The popular belief that we must pay the price of increased concentration and reduced competition in order to buy effective research appears to be almost weightless.

3. *Managerial Scarcity.*

A third modern justification for concentration is the claim that mergers put to their most efficient use at least one very important ingredient in the production of each and every product—managerial brains.

As you gentlemen well know, talent is scarce, and a talented manager should not go unused. The large size of this audience, however, which itself is only representative of a much larger array of talent, strengthens the view that good management is not so scarce. Surely it is not so scarce that it can only be achieved by permitting levels of concentration well beyond what other economies of scale would dictate.

If one of the firms in a proposed merger has bad management, its salvation most obviously lies in seeking new executives. I suspect it is the rare situation in which the only way to buy good management is to buy a competing company. The Yankees, for example, didn't merge with the Twins; they fired Johnny Keane (and discovered their problem wasn't management at all).

Even if there were shortages in managerial talent, we have plainly entered into a generation of superb managerial training, not only in the splendid schools of business administration, but also in the growing array of sabbatical and mid-career programs being conducted around the country. (Indeed, some businessmen are even willing to concede the educational benefits that accrue from working for a time in the government.)

4. *Improved Competition.*

As the fourth argument on behalf of concentration, we often hear two companies contend that if they are allowed to merge they will be able to compete better with the industry leader.

This argument is frequently made and sometimes it has merit. There are occasions, for example, when a manufacturer can demonstrate overriding advantages of a conglomerate merger with a large enterprise.

It surely is not the policy of the Department of Justice to oppose all mergers. Indeed, we go to court to oppose only about twenty of the more than one thousand mergers consummated each year, some of them involving very large companies indeed.

Generally, however, when the major justification raised by merging companies is that they would be able to compete better against an industry leader if they merge, it does not withstand analysis.

If the two firms are basically inefficient, it is difficult to see how a merger can cure their problems. Second, as I have already suggested, if the merger is so substantial as to be anti-competitive, it also would exceed economies of scale, and only rarely would it be necessary to achieve savings in production costs.

Third, if we allow the second and third firms in an industry to combine in order to compete better with the largest firm, we should also have to allow the fourth, fifth and sixth largest firms to combine to do the same, and so on. We might soon discover that a competitive industry containing twenty firms had been turned into a noncompetitive one containing only two or three.

5. Saving the Community.

The fifth and final argument on behalf of concentration is that a merger with competitors will bring great benefits to the community concerned. The argument usually takes the following form:

Company A, which is in a weak or failing condition, would like to sell out to a large competitor, B. Company A, and the community in which A is located, argue that the sale should be allowed, even if it lessens competition, for sale to B provides the strongest possibility that A will not be shut down with a consequent loss of jobs and general hardship to the community.

I believe that we should reject this argument for several reasons. First, if A is actually failing, the antitrust laws do not forbid its sale, though they might require A's owner to try to sell to other firms before he sells to A's largest competitor.

Second, the sale of a weak but not failing company to a large firm in the same industry might not, after all, save the jobs of A's employees. If A were in such rocky condition, the buying company might well decide to close down the plant.

Finally, if fear of unemployment justifies an anticompetitive merger in one community, it justifies such mergers in all similar communities. To accept such a justification therefore may well reduce competition—and employment—throughout the country.

In the short run as well as in the long run, a reduction in competition tends to produce higher prices, *lower* sales, and thus lower employment for the industries concerned. It makes little sense to pay so high a price for so uncertain and unlikely a reward.

To summarize my response to all five arguments, then, in the United States an easy acquiescence in mergers which significantly increase concentration is not necessary to economic efficiency or to a lively rate of technological innovation and progress.

III.

A harder test of antitrust policy is the specific one raised by the title of this colloquy. Does a strong policy against concentration in fact actively *promote* economic growth and progress?

There are traditional reasons for believing that this is so. There are also, I suggest, some newer patterns in our economy which suggest the continued, perhaps even increased, validity of the type of anticoncentration policy we are pursuing.

The traditional premise of our policy is that competition leads to an economic system more efficient and productive than any other. Both theory and experience teach us that when a market becomes highly concentrated, the intensity and effectiveness of competition are reduced.[12] Thus, by preventing the development of concentrated markets, we expect by and large to achieve better market performance.

12. That significant increases in concentration in the production of particular products will normally lead to less competition is strongly supported by empirical evidence. Professor Caves has pointed out: "We would expect from economic theory that high concentration . . . would tend to produce high profit rates . . . by giving firms a chance to garner some of the potential monopoly profits. . . ." "This prediction," adds Professor Caves, "turn[s] out to be accurate." Richard Caves, *American Industry: Structure, Conduct, Performance* (1964), p. 104. A study by Professor Bain on the relation of profit rates to industry concentration in forty industries defined more or less along traditional product lines shows a significant correlation between higher than average profits and high concentration. Joe S. Bain, "Relation of Profit Rate to Industry Concentration: American Manufacturing, 1936-1940," in the *Quarterly Journal of Economics,* Vol. LXV (August, 1951) pp. 293-324. A more recent study shows that among industries with medium entry barriers (again defined along traditional product lines), the industry that is more highly concentrated shows higher profits. Joe S. Bain, *Barriers to New Competition,* Ch. 7, pp. 182-204.

The fact that lack of competition produces lazy industries, just as lack of exercise produces flabby executives, can be easily observed.

A recent study has examined the popularly held belief that American firms are more productive than their European counterparts because they enjoy better technology. It concludes, however, that "in most industries the best British firms equal the best American in efficiency. The real difference between the two nations' industries is in the average firm. The average American firm is usually much closer to the best commercial practice than is the average British firm."[13]

The author of this study goes on to suggest that a major reason for this difference may be that American firms are likely to be more competitive than those in Britain, and inefficient American firms are more likely to get pushed to the wall. He concludes that "in America the prevalence of competitive behavior tends to make industrial research compulsory for all once it gets a foothold in an industry. In consequence, corporate research is far more common in America."[14]

I do not mean to suggest that all unconcentrated industries are more competitive than all concentrated industries. Some industries remain competitive despite the presence of only a handful of firms. I do mean to suggest that, as a general rule, increased concentration tends to remove the competitive goad to industrial vitality.

Antitrust law, like all law, to be workable and tolerable must operate by means of general rules. The benefits of a general rule prohibiting mergers that significantly increase concentration heavily outweigh, in my opinion, any inhibitions, any injuries that such a rule might impose in exceptional cases.

So much for the traditional appraisal of the evils of concentration. There is, in addition, a less traditional argument for a strong antitrust policy against concentration—that such a policy helps to promote economic growth by making inflation easier to control.

In essence, the argument is, first, that concentration may add

13. Schmookler, *op. cit. supra* at p. 148.
14. Ibid.

to inflationary pressures because of the power of concentrated industries to set prices relatively independent of market factors and second, that by making inflation more difficult to control, concentration can interfere with full employment and rapid economic growth.

If industries in our economy are concentrated or tend to become concentrated, inflationary pressures may be increased in several ways. Firms in concentrated industries tend to cooperate in exercising shared monopoly power, and this enables them to push up prices even when costs are stable and demand does not exceed supply.[15] Increasing concentration in an industry thus may well be accompanied by increasing prices even when excess demand does not generally exist.

Further, the fact that an industry is concentrated can act as a brake on any tendency for prices to fall. For example, increased productivity or other factors may well lead to lower costs. But these do not then as readily result in lowered prices as in non-concentrated firms.

There is, finally, some reason to believe that the higher profits earned by firms in concentrated industries become a target for labor wage demands higher than increases in productivity may justify. It is easier, at the same time, for firms in concentrated industries to pass on the costs of wage increases to the public.[16] And these wage increases have a broader effect because of the pressures they create for the leaders of other unions, in non-concentrated industries, to seek parallel gains.

Concentrated markets are not the major factor responsible for inflation in the American economy. I do believe, however, that they play a significant, if complex, role in almost all modern inflations—a role that promises to become increasingly important.

In so far as concentration contributes to inflation, it tends to retard economic growth. Costly experience has taught us that the environment most conducive to rapid economic progress is not characterized either as inflationary or deflationary—it is one free

---

15. *The Annual Report of the Council of Economic Advisors,* January 1965, p. 107.

16. Segal, "The Relation Between Union Wage Impact and Market Structure," in *Quarterly Journal of Economics,* February 1964; Eckstein & Wilson, "The Determination of Money Wages in American Industry," in *Quarterly Journal of Economics,* August 1962.

of both significant unemployment and rapidly rising prices. The dislocations caused by inflation and any excessively deflationary reactions that it may provoke can well restrict the rate at which our economy expands.

There is then no question but that inflation must be controlled. As President Johnson observed in his recent message to Congress, "Inflation imposes a cruel and unjust tax on all of the people . . . when total spending rises more rapidly than the economy can accommodate—when business investment creates undue pressures —when armed conflict overseas imposes new burdens on government—then we must be willing to shift into lower gear and reduce inflationary pressures."

The President's recommendations to defer and to reduce federal expenditures and to suspend temporarily the investment tax credit are designed to distribute the burden of anti-inflationary measures more equitably. And they are designed to control inflation while at the same time maintaining an economy which operates at full capacity. In short, these recommendations seek to combat the harm that inflation can cause individual Americans and the nation as a whole in our search for rapid and orderly economic progress.

The case I am making is the case for antitrust and for our attentive policy concerning mergers. I submit that the task of controlling inflations is easier and will be easier in the future if, through persistent efforts to deal with the problems of market power in the Antitrust Division, we continue to contribute to the reduction of conditions of concentration.

My conclusion is simply that as our nation's economy expands and as technological progress becomes increasingly important, we have more need than ever to adhere to the 75-year-old, still salutory, principles embodied in our antitrust laws.

Sɪʀ Tʜᴏᴍᴀs Rᴏʙsᴏɴ is a gentleman for whom I feel considerable awe. It is quite possible that British accountants know more about the inside of world business affairs than anyone else. After all, they have been watching what has been going on for something like 300 years. I'm sure that all companies operating internationally have a great respect for them.

In my own memory I go back to the time when a team of accountants from London, from Sir Thomas' firm I believe, went to Stockholm to check Ivor Krueger, International Match Company. That was the end of his far extended empire. And it was the end of Mr. Krueger as he dived out of a plane into the English Channel, when he learned that those auditors were on to him. I don't know whether Sir Thomas himself was in on that rundown but the reputation of British accounting and auditing is well known.

From his wide experience in business in many countries, Sir Thomas gives us his views on bigness and smallness and how they affect a nation's economic growth. I asked him a while ago if he believed in mergers. He replied: "Yes, if they are the right kind."

Sir Thomas Robson became a chartered accountant in England in 1923 and was admitted in 1934 into partnership in the United Kingdom firm of Price, Waterhouse and Company of which he is a present senior partner. A member of the council of the Institute of Chartered Accountants in England and Wales since 1941, Sir Thomas was president of that body in 1952-53. He was knighted by Queen Elizabeth in 1954. He is also a member of the Institute of Accountants in several other countries and for 1963-64 he was vice-president of the European Union of Expert Accountants in Economics and Finances. In the United Kingdom he has appeared as a witness before or acted as chairman of a number of government committees. His current appointments include that of Chairman of the Economic Development Committee for the Paper and Board Industry under the National Economic Development Counsel.

—Harold H. Helm

Business Size and
National Economic Growth

SIR THOMAS B. ROBSON,

M.B.E., F.C.A.

Past President, Institute of Chartered

Accountants in England and Wales

In COMING from England to address this convocation and to endeavour to complement the address of Attorney General Katzenbach on the subject allotted to us, I felt as some of the Pilgrim Fathers must have as they set out on their historic voyage to this country. A mixture of faith and hope was my portion, faith that you would be kind about my inadequacies and hope that a British point of view on Business Size might be of interest.

Perhaps I should start by saying that your objectives of high economic growth, full employment and price stability would find a ready response from those concerned with business affairs in the United Kingdom. Those of us who had personal experience of the conditions which prevailed in the United States and the United Kingdom in the depression of the early 1930s or of the appalling consequences of the currency devaluations in other countries which followed the first and second World Wars will not relinquish readily the hope that means may be found of moving closer to your three objectives. I trust that this conference may be a step forward towards realizing this hope.

You may like to have some factual background about British business as a preliminary to an attempt on my part to discuss our subject further. What evidence can I give about Britain for this short address which might be useful?

First of all, I should remind you that the population of the United Kingdom is about 54 millions or under one-third of that of the United States, and is concentrated in an area less than 3 per cent of the size of your country. Much of our food and raw materials has to be imported and we are largely dependent upon exports for our livelihood. In 1965 British exports totalled nearly £5 billions, or £5,000 millions as we would say in England, where the billion means a million millions, not a thousand millions as it does here.

This was an increase of 7 per cent in value and over 5 per cent in volume compared with 1964 and of about 60 per cent in value compared with 1955.

Business in the United Kingdom is carried on mainly, as it is here, by individuals, private firms, and companies, but differs from the United States in that some of our major industries have been nationalized.

Companies, of which there are over half a million, carry on a vast part of the business of the country. On December 31, 1965, 15,000 of these companies were "public" companies, that is companies which had over fifty shareholders or had raised share or loan capital from the public. The remainder were private companies, probably about 80 per cent of which are family or similar concerns which are little more than private businesses in company form.

On March 31, 1965 the securities of 4,400 companies were quoted on the Stock Exchange, London, and had at that time a market value of about £57 billions. Of these about 3,000 were industrial or commercial concerns other than iron and steel undertakings. I believe that the number of securities of all kinds (that is company and other securities) quoted in London is about three times that of the securities quoted in New York, but that in terms of market value this comparison may well be reversed because of the relatively larger size of a substantial proportion of the companies whose securities are quoted on the New York Exchange.

Within the list of 3,000 industrial companies great disparities of size are apparent. Not more than about 300 of them have capital employed of over £12 millions, each; some are greatly under that amount. Of those which exceed £12 millions less than fifty have capital employed of £100 millions or more each, only three of them employing a billion pounds or more. The total capital employed by the 300 is about £20 billions.

In their latest financial years the 300 companies made aggregate profits of £2½ billions of which the first fifty made about £1½ billions, the three largest of them making together over half a billion pounds. Only five of the 300 companies showed losses for their latest years; these losses were not significant in relation to the aggregate profits of the other 295 companies.

Twenty-two of the companies are wholly-owned subsidiaries of other corporations and their equity capitals are, therefore, not quoted on a stock exchange. The equity capitals of the other 278 companies had a market value on the London Exchange of about £17 billions, of which the first 47 accounted for £10 billions, and the first three for £3½ billions.

As the equity capitals of all the companies whose securities are quoted on the exchange had a market value slightly over £50 billions the importance of the place of the large industrial companies in the national economy will be apparent.

This is not to denigrate the importance of the activities of the vast number of smaller concerns which carry on business in the United Kingdom. That is very great indeed but, unfortunately, I do not have any useful statistics which I can give you about them. Nor does it ignore the importance of the banks and insurance companies and the nationalized industries.

Our banks are of the greatest importance, particularly in the provision of short-term finance for industry and for financing foreign trade. Unlike those in the United States, banks in the United Kingdom are permitted to have branches outside the city where they were first established; three of them have each over 2,000 branches spread over the country and two others have each about 1,500. These five banks have total deposits of £8½ billions. The big insurance companies are also important, particularly as material contributors of permanent capital for other businesses. The largest of the life companies itself has funds of £1½ billions, whilst those of fourteen others aggregate £4½ billions. Such banks and insurance companies are themselves large businesses which make an important contribution to the economy of the country and its growth.

Large-scale business is also carried on by the nationalized industries and by other undertakings owned by public authorities. With some exceptions these activities are in the public utility industries and are statutory monopolies. The capital employed in the major nationalized industries amounts to £8 billions, the largest amount being in the electricity industry, which employs capital not far short of the aggregate employed by the three largest industrial companies taken together. In their latest years the major nationalized industries showed aggregate profits of about £400 millions, less losses of about £72 millions which were incurred mainly in the railways. On the completion of the projected re-nationalization of the fourteen major steel companies with an aggregate annual production capacity of 28 million tons of crude steel, equivalent to 94 per cent of the British steel industry's capacity, these nationalized industries will employ a total of more than two million persons, or nearly 9 per cent of the total working population of the United Kingdom. Five of the nationalized industries will each employ a greater number of persons than any industrial company; the Coal Board itself employs about three times as many as the largest company employer. The part played by the nationalized industries as big businesses in the national economy is, therefore, of great importance.

Such then is a broad-brush picture of the part played by large businesses in British industry and of their financial importance. An indication of the way in which growth has been taking place in large businesses relatively to the industries in which they operate may be inferred from the results shown by the Census of Production.

Concentration ratios measuring the share of a particular industry's labour force or net output taken by the three largest firms in it have been derived from the statistics. These show the relative weight of the largest firms, and are a rough and ready measure of the likelihood of the presence of monopoly power. The statistics indicate that whereas in 1951 industries in the most concentrated group were responsible for 5.6 per cent of manufacturing net output and 4.4 per cent of employment in manufacturing, the corresponding 1958 percentages were much larger, namely, 14.2 per cent and 12.4 per cent. Out of seventy-three industries forty-nine had increases in concentration ratios between 1951 and 1958, thirteen showed decreases, and eleven remained unchanged. These figures indicate a striking rate of growth in business concentration between 1951 and 1958. It is unfortunate that later figures are not yet available, but there is no reason to think that the growth rate has diminished in subsequent years.

Before leaving statistics for the next part of these remarks I should perhaps add that whilst several of the figures which I have given are nothing more than rough estimates based on information prepared for other purposes, they appear, nevertheless, to justify the conclusions at which I have arrived.

How useful is British experience in a study of our subject? To what extent has the size of businesses been a relevant consideration in relation to national economic growth in Britain and to what extent and in what form has it been necessary to impose controls on the size of businesses or on the behaviour of large businesses in order that economic growth may be healthy and beneficial from the national standpoint?

Experience in the United Kingdom suggests that the large business can often reap the benefit of economies which are not available to its smaller competitors. This does not mean that size by itself implies efficiency or success. Whether it does so depends also on whether efficient, enterprising and wise management is present. The management which lacks these qualities and relies on mere size of its business as a guarantee of development is doomed to disappointment. Britain has seen, as you must have done here, businesses fall on evil days because they were expanded in directions in which their management lacked competence and failed to make adequate assessments of potentialities and prospects. Such occurrences have militated against national economic growth as they did against the interests of the owners of the businesses concerned. Competent managerial leadership and control are a first essential in guiding and controlling business expansion; without them the attainment of size can be and has been a danger to economic health.

Given, however, the right management and right decisions as

to how, when and where expansion should occur, there is real scope for obtaining advantages which are available only to large businesses. Figures given to me recently in respect of 137 British companies illustrate this. The companies are engaged in five groups of industries, namely, aircraft construction, electrical engineering, light electrical production, mechanical engineering, and the automobile industry. Over the last four years the fourteen largest of the companies, i.e., those which have a turnover of £100 millions or more, had an overall rate of growth in value as indicated by the prices of their securities in the capital market of about 1¾ times that of the average rate of growth for the 137 companies taken group by group.

It is in fact true to say that, given good management, the economies of scale, whether these be related to production or distribution or to both, accrue only to businesses of an appropriate substantial size. Specialization, standardization and long production runs become possible; mass production methods and machines can be employed, the individual worker can be engaged increasingly on maintaining a group of automatic or semi-automatic machines in efficient condition and operation instead of operating a single machine or making a product by hand. Substantial economies in the use of manpower can be obtained.

Generally it is possible for the large business to raise money more economically than the small business can obtain it. This applies both to short-term borrowing and the raising of share and loan capital. It is thus easier for the large business with a good record to finance its further growth and make an increased contribution to the national economy than for its smaller competitor which has not these advantages.

In research and development and in establishing and expanding its export trade too, the large business has advantages. Some types of product research and of advertising schemes for launching new products and the exploitation in some businesses of overseas markets require the expenditure of large sums of money. If successful they bring a rich harvest. The small company cannot afford to embark on the scale of expenditure required, but the large concern, by the allocation of what may even be a relatively modest proportion of its resources to this work, may achieve outstanding results which accrue in terms of growth to the national economy as well as to its own benefit.

The advent of trade depression is not easy for any business. With a proper management structure and the right people to run it, however, and given adequate forecasting and planning with a sound system of budgetary control, there is no reason why the organization of the large business should be so inflexible that it cannot be adjusted to meet the needs of a changing situation. Moreover, apart from world-wide depressions, the large business often finds that a recession in one part of its trade or in one area of its activities is accompanied by improvement in others. If so, this can be a source of strength to the national economy.

If, owing to benefits reaped by the business in profitable periods it has built up substantial reserves, these are available to it in difficult times and the security which the assets representing them affords is a factor in maintaining the confidence of bankers and others whose help may be required until the earning capacity of the business is re-established.

This is not to suggest that a large company which is engaged in an industry whose world-wide prospects have changed permanently for the worse can be immune from the running-down process. A readiness to recognize in time the facts of business life is essential for the big business as for the small; whether to wind it up or to take steps to develop or intensify efforts to develop in other directions is a question for which the management in such a company must find an answer. This will clearly depend upon the circumstances of the particular company.

In general, however, the advantages which can properly be claimed for the large business as a benefit to the national economy are considerable, provided always that it has and maintains a dynamic and competent management and that the size of the business is such as to enable that management to bring to the business the economies to which I have briefly referred. What is the optimum size which will bring these advantages to the greatest extent for any particular company depends on its own circumstances and I do not attempt to define them here.

You may wonder about the attitude in Britain towards political expenditure by large businesses. As far as I know there is nothing specific in the statute law of the United Kingdom to pro-hibit a company from incurring such expenditure provided that it is made in the interests of the company or its business. In one industry which was expecting to be nationalized after the Second World War the leading company embarked on a heavy publicity campaign designed to protect itself against this fate. The cost of its campaign was not only regarded as a proper expense for the company but after a battle in the courts was allowed as a deduct-ible expense for taxation purposes. A small company could not have afforded to defend itself in this way. Hitherto political ex-penditure has not had to be disclosed in a company's report or accounts, but this seems likely to become a requirement when parliamentary time can be found for a new Companies Bill. I should add that I have no reason to think that large companies are any more prone than small to incur political expenditure in normal circumstances; I have only mentioned this matter because the size of the company which fought against its nationalization enabled it to protect itself where a smaller concern would have been unable to do so.

Let us now turn for a time to examine the attitude of the au-thorities in the United Kingdom toward expansion of businesses into large concerns. As a generalization it may be said that suc-cessive governments have taken broadly the same favourable view. As long ago as 1927 Parliament recognized the need for en-couraging the amalgamation of companies. In that year relief from stamp duties was granted on acquisitions where either the undertaking of a company or at least 90 per cent of its share capital was acquired and where not less than 90 per cent of the consideration consisted of the issue of shares by the acquiring company to the shareholders in the company whose business or shares were acquired.

The same attitude was exhibited more explicitly in a govern-ment White Paper published in January, 1966, as the following extracts will show:

> The need for more concentration and rationalisation to pro-mote the greater efficiency and international competitiveness of British industry . . . is now widely recognised. . . . Many industries have already substantially altered their structure

and organisation through mergers, acquisitions and regroupings. . . . Nevertheless, the pace and scale of change do not yet match the needs of the national economy. Many of the production units in this country are small by comparison with the most successful companies in international trade, whose operations are often based on a much larger market. In some sectors the typical company in Britain is too small to achieve long production runs; to take advantage of economies of scale, to undertake effective research and development; to support specialist departments for design and marketing; to install the most modern equipment or to attract the best qualified management . . .

This view of successive United Kingdom governments, that increases in the size of the business unit are desirable from the standpoint of the national economy, is accompanied by a recognition that they may need to be accompanied by controls in the public interest to prevent countervailing disadvantages from outweighing them. We have recognized this in Britain to a greater extent since the Second World War than previously, though not to the extent to which, I gather, anti-trust legislation has imposed restrictions in the United States.

As I have already indicated, some of the nationalized industries are among the largest businesses in Britain. In theory, they are under the autonomous direction of their own boards, but they are not free from controls in the interest of the public. Whilst they are not subject, as are privately owned undertakings, to review by the Monopolies Commission to which I will refer shortly, they conduct their affairs under a considerable measure of supervision by the Select Committee on Nationalised Industries of the House of Commons and are subject to directions on certain matters by their sponsoring government departments. Finance for their activities is provided in the main by the United Kingdom Treasury and they are expected so to conduct their affairs as to earn a profit which, taking one year with another, is at a rate prescribed by the government on their capital employed.

In private industry, direct government intervention has taken place in certain industries with a view to promoting groupings into larger units. Some years ago this occurred in the cotton textile industry, but the governmental efforts there were not success-ful; take-over bids by a few large companies in that industry have recently brought about voluntary groupings, the long-term out-come of which is being watched with the greatest interest. In the last few years the aircraft construction industry has been reduced under government pressure to a small number of groups of large units designed to secure greater strength in the face of curtail-ment of sales and financial difficulties. Pressure is also now being exercised on shipbuilders to seek the benefits of larger scale organ-ization by grouping themselves into area mergers, with govern-ment financial help.

An initiative intended to have a more general effect has re-cently been taken by the government, which is establishing a corporation with substantial capital to undertake the task of searching out opportunities for the promotion of rationalization schemes which could yield substantial benefits to the economy. As in the case of the nationalized industries, mergers effected as a result of the activities of this corporation will not be subject to review by the Monopolies Commission to which I must now refer.

The Monopolies Commission was established by law in 1948 and is the principal mechanism of control over private businesses in regard to monopolies and mergers which are deemed to be or may be contrary to the public interest. It is an investigating body whose *raison d'être* is indicated by the following extract from a White Paper which also reiterates the governmental view on the advantages of large business size and rejection of the view that monopoly is necessarily undesirable:

> Optimum efficiency of operation may demand large plants, costly research and highly developed marketing arrangements. Units must be large enough to raise the necessary capital to take risks. Large-scale production may be necessary in order to compete in international trade. Thus there may sometimes be room only for one or two large firms in an industry." It went on to say: "The Government therefore reaffirm their view that it would be wrong to introduce into the law any presumption that monopoly is in itself undesirable, without regard to the conditions in which it operates, or to the manner in which it conducts its business. It follows from this basic approach that judgment should only be reached on a particular monopoly

after investigation into the way in which it is in fact operating. Such inquiries can best be carried out by an investigating body like the Monopolies Commission.

The Board of Trade, which is the United Kingdom equivalent of a ministry of commerce, has the responsibility for deciding whether an inquiry by the Commission is required in a particular case. This applies to investigations both of individual businesses and of proposed or recently effected mergers. In an investigation of a single concern the function of the Commission is to investigate and report (i) whether monopoly conditions are present and (ii) whether the monopoly conditions operate or may be expected to operate against the public interest; and it may make recommendations.

Monopoly conditions are deemed to exist where a concern (including its subsidiaries) supplies (or buys) at least one-third of the particular goods or services in question in the United Kingdom or any substantial part of the United Kingdom. It is thus not the *absolute* size of the firm that matters, but its size relative to its industry in the United Kingdom. Bigness as such is not subject to investigation. In practice so far the single-firm monopolies investigated by the Commission have generally exceeded the one-third fraction by a wide margin.

The circumstances in which a merger or proposed merger may be referred to the Commission by the Board of Trade are at the latter's complete discretion but must be such that either (i) monopoly conditions which I have just described would prevail in the merged undertaking, or (ii) the value of the assets taken over exceeds £5 millions. The latter alternative, it may be noted, allows a merger to be investigated where the resulting company would be large without necessarily being in a monopoly situation.

Where the Board exercises its powers in relation to a proposed or recent merger it may require an investigation and report by the Commission. The Board may order the impending merger to be suspended until after the Commission has reported, and it can, in consequence of a report, prevent a proposed merger or unscramble a merger recently effected.

The function of the Commission in regard to both single-firm monopolies and to mergers is that of an adviser to the Board of Trade, executive action being the preserve of the Board: the latter need not accept the recommendations made to it by the Commission, though with a few exceptions it has in practice done so. The Board of Trade itself has powers to issue statutory orders to implement the remedial measures which it thinks fit in relation to monopolies. It has even been able since 1965 to order the breaking-up of a monopoly firm, provided, however, that for such an order to be effective it must have the specific approval of Parliament.

Since 1948 the Monopolies Commission has issued nine reports on single-firm monopolies. None of these reports has concluded that the firm investigated was inefficient because of its size or of its dominant position in its industry, nor recommended that it should be broken up so as to increase competition in an industry. The recommendations of the Commission have been designed rather (i) to prevent the abuse of monopoly power, e.g., by imposing official supervision over prices and costs, or by prohibiting discrimination in the treatment of customers; (ii) to prevent the extension or entrenchment of the monopoly position, e.g., by preventing or weakening exclusive dealing arrangements, by controlling new acquisitions, and prohibiting the use of "fighting" companies; and (iii) to prevent the use of practices, such as in some instances resale price maintenance, which restrict competition among the monopolist's customers.

Four mergers have been the subject of references to the Commission since in 1965 the scope of its duties was extended to mergers; other mergers have been allowed to proceed without such a reference. Two reports have been made by the Commission—one favorable to a merger which was allowed to proceed, the other unfavorable to a merger where the plan was suspended by the Board of Trade's intervention. The Board also suspended the plan of a third proposed merger pending receipt of the Commission's report but has not done so in the fourth.

The Commission consists at present of eighteen members and its membership has included lawyers, businessmen, trade-union leaders, chartered accountants, university economists and former civil servants. It thus has a wide background of experience. Moreover, its reports are published and the reasons for its views are, therefore, available to all concerned. If any of its members dissent from a majority finding their minority report is included in the published material. The Board of Trade is entirely free to adopt or reject recommendations made by the Commission and to decide on the executive action, if any, which should be taken. These features of the situation together with the width of interests contained in the Commission's membership appear to afford useful safeguards for securing that its conclusions shall be characterized by a sense of responsibility and that the public shall be informed adequately about the facts elicited in its investigations and the reasons for its findings.

This is all that I can say in the time available about public controls in the United Kingdom over large businesses and mergers. I hope that my description of these controls will not have left upon you the impression that the businesses are under constant inquisition by government authorities. If you have derived such an impression from my remarks let me assure you that it is erroneous. British government policy aims at the promotion of business growth through mergers which are thought to be in the public interest and the prevention of mergers only where they are deemed to be contrary to it. There is no initial bias against take-over bids, mergers and the like merely because they create large units or enlarge units which are already of great size. The approach to the matter is empirical; it is an endeavor, where circumstances arise in which prejudice to the public interest seems likely either to be present or likely to develop, to form a judgment on the available evidence as to whether present or prospective activities or the enlargement of a business unit will be good or bad for the economic health of the nation.

There is no absolute or statutory standard for making such a judgment. The decision is made by the Board of Trade in the light of the circumstances of the particular case, and it has the Monopolies Commission at its disposal to investigate, report and make recommendations to assist it. The Board is not obliged to seek the advice of the Commission nor to take any action, nor has it invariably done so. It would, presumably, always do so when the Board has reason to think that there is a need for investigation in order to ascertain the facts in a particular instance or that a situation is or may be developing which is contrary to the public interest.

The United Kingdom accounts for and its economy in large measure depends upon nearly 7 per cent of the non-communist world's productive capacity. Its exports and imports together account for about 9 per cent of total world trade. The attainment and maintenance of industrial efficiency are, therefore, of vital importance to both its present and its future. Those concerned in government circles and in industry are fully conscious of the benefits which are obtainable in this connection from healthy expansion in the size of the business unit and of its potential contribution to national economic growth. They are alive to the need for the presence of efficient and energetic management to lead and direct such expansion, of the need of facilities for training those who will provide that management in the future, and of the urgent necessity in the interests of all our people to ensure that every resource of the country both human and material shall be employed in the most efficient and effective manner for the common good.

We seek, as you do, those three objectives of high economic growth, full employment and price stability to which I referred at the outset; their full attainment will require a unique combination of imagination, wisdom, enterprise and adaptability to ideas as well as unceasing readiness on the part of all in your country, my own and other countries to work and work hard towards that end. Let us go forward together and bring them nearer, so far as in us lies, to attainment in our generation.

IX CAPITALISM, CULTURE, AND THE ARTS

CHAIRMAN: H. Bruce Palmer

· *Introduction by Mr. Palmer*

· *Capitalism, Culture, and the Arts,*

  David Rockefeller

· *Comments, Mr. Palmer*

W<small>E</small> <small>TURN</small> <small>NOW</small> to a significant aspect of capitalism that we have not heretofore considered in this great convocation. It is capitalism's past, its present, its prospective sponsorship and financial support of culture and the arts.

David Rockefeller needs all the time that he has at his disposal, even if he is just to touch lightly on capitalism's contributions to culture and the arts.

I don't think I shall be poaching on his area, however, if I mention briefly something that I read recently. The Chinese have been very marvelous workers, as all of us know, in the silk industry for many hundreds of years. Chin Lung tapestries are fine examples of the world's taste in artistic skills.

Under Communism, that art of silk work in Red China has come down to this: tens of millions of portraits of their leaders. They're beautifully done, but these fellows that they depict in silk were not very pretty to start with, and they haven't improved with age. They ought to do better than that. Even the way-out art that we have today is original, and whatever anybody might think of it, it doesn't show obvious signs of arm-twisting by political commissars. Perhaps David will mention the problems of artists and the teachers of the cultures and the arts under Communism in this commentary.

After graduation from Harvard, David took several advance courses there in economics, and spent a year at the renowned London School of Economics. He proceeded to the University of Chicago for his doctorate.

His war record also warrants mention. He enlisted as a private in 1942, was in North Africa and France, and was discharged with the rank of captain in 1945. He was awarded the Legion of Merit, the Army's Commendation Ribbon, and the French Legion of Honor.

Aside from his banking career, he has devoted much time and energy to the various Rockefeller philanthropies. He has been especially involved in civic problems, as we who live in New York all know.

He helped to create Morningside Heights, Inc., a nonprofit organization of fourteen groups, including Columbia University, that are concerned with the improvement and the redevelopment of that area as a residential and educational and a cultural community. He was the first president, and then became chairman, and is now a member of its board of directors. In recognition of this and many other outstanding civic contributions, he has been the recipient of many honors, numerous honorary degrees, medals and citations.

His deep interest in international affairs (and our paths have crossed here, and it has been my delight to be with him) has led to his command of French, Spanish and German. He is a director and vice-president of the Council on Foreign Relations.

Mr. Rockefeller is a stout champion of the liberal arts. He has said, "The conduct of modern enterprise is so complex, that a person who knows and understands something about philosophy, literature, the arts and history is a type of person who is most likely to succeed in business." I can think of no one more qualified to discuss the relationship of capitalism, culture and the arts.

—H. Bruce Palmer
PRESIDENT
NATIONAL INDUSTRIAL CONFERENCE BOARD

Capitalism, Culture, and the Arts

DAVID ROCKEFELLER

President, The Chase Manhattan Bank, N.A.

BY INVITING a banker to talk about culture, The Conference Board has raised several intriguing questions in my mind, and I suspect, in yours as well.

Did the board do so with tongue-in-cheek, perhaps, as an appropriate way of celebrating a Golden Anniversary?

Or was it simply an acknowledgment of the banks' expertise in the one aspect of culture that seems to enjoy universal appeal among businessmen—namely, its tax deductibility?

Or was it a recognition of the fact that many cultural organizations wind up their fiscal year in such shape that they badly need "a friend at Chase Manhattan?"

Without presuming to answer these questions, I think it only fair to warn you at the outset that I have had a long-standing attachment to the arts. This is something I came by quite innocently, having been born in a house on Manhattan's 54th Street, on the present site of the Museum of Modern Art!

However, I make no apologies for my interest in the arts, nor should The Conference Board assume a defensive posture for devoting time at this memorable convocation to the subject. Bankers and businessmen from the Medici to the Mellons have often been enthusiastic patrons of the arts. Cosimo de' Medici established Europe's first public libraries as far back as the fifteenth century, and supported such men as Donatello, Brunelleschi, Ghiberti and Fra Angelico. At one time, his private contributions to cultural and related activities were said to have amounted to twice the income of the entire Florentine state. His descendants carried on the family tradition of artistic patronage in still more lavish fashion, encouraging among their protégés such Renaissance figures as Michelangelo and Cellini.

Today, we hear exuberant talk of a "new Renaissance," a "cultural explosion," and the statistical evidence, at least, is impressive. Americans spent some $4 billion on cultural activities last year— twice as much as a decade ago. By 1970 this figure is expected to top $7 billion. The 750 groups now presenting opera in the U.S. are almost double the number so engaged a decade ago. Theatrical enterprises now number about 40,000, again a substantial increase over the past ten years. More people saw "Hamlet" on television in a single night than had seen it in live performances in all the years since it was written. Some 300 million people visit art museums each year, about 150 per cent more than a decade ago, and 14 million American homes contain an original work of art.

These statistics point up with startling clarity the fact that we live in a period of increasing cultural interest that is not mere lip service but is genuine and active. Impressive as the figures are, though, they don't tell the whole story. Interest is only one side of the coin; quality can be quite another. Most of the expansion in the creative arts has been among amateurs. Professional artists and art organizations have barely held their own. Of the 800 American cities with populations of 25,000 or more, only one in five has been visited by a professional theatre group or heard a professional orchestra in the past three years. Millions of our fellow citizens have never seen a professional performance of any kind.

This is a situation that should concern us all, both as businessmen and as citizens. For the arts are a vital part of human experience, and surely our success as a civilized society will be judged largely by the creative activities of our citizens in art, architecture, music and literature. Improving the condition of the performing and visual arts in this country calls, in my judgment, for a massive cooperative effort in which business corporations must assume a much larger role than they have in the past. The corporate community as a whole has a long way to go in accepting the arts as an appropriate area for the exercise of its social responsibility.

I'd like to share with you my own reflections on why I feel business should consider substantially greater involvement in the arts, and how it might go about this.

Almost imperceptibly over the past several years, the modern corporation has evolved into a social as well as an economic institution. Without losing sight of the need to make a profit, it has developed ideals and responsibilities going far beyond the profit motive. It has become, in effect, a full-fledged citizen, not only of the community in which it is headquartered, but of the country and indeed the world.

The public has come to expect organizations such as yours and mine to live up to certain standards of good citizenship. One of these is to help shape our environment in a constructive way. When I speak about environment, I mean the vast complex of economic, technological, social and political forces that influence our cities and the people who live in them. In shaping this environment, the corporation must initiate its share of socially responsible actions, rather than merely responding passively to outside forces.

Mainly through the impetus provided by our business corporations, we have achieved in the United States a material abundance and a growing leisure unprecedented in history. It is sadly evident, though, that our cultural attainments have not kept pace with improvements in other fields. As people's incomes have risen, a proportionate share has not been devoted to artistic and intellectual pursuits. As leisure has increased, so has the amount of time given to unproductive and often aimless activities.

Corporations genuinely concerned about their environment cannot evade responsibility for seeing that this leisure is channeled into rewarding activities such as those the arts afford. We must face up to the task of bringing our cultural achievements into balance with our material well-being through more intimate corporate involvement in the arts.

From an economic standpoint, such involvement can mean direct and tangible benefits. It can provide a company with extensive publicity and advertising, a brighter public reputation, and an improved corporate image. It can build better customer relations, a readier acceptance of company products, and a superior appraisal of their quality. Promotion of the arts can improve the morale of employees, and help attract qualified personnel.

At Chase Manhattan, we have seen firsthand evidence of these benefits from our own efforts in art and architecture. When we decided to build our new head office in lower Manhattan, we wanted to use modern concepts of architecture to express a contemporary image of banking instead of the traditional stodginess of the past. We were eager to have a building that, in addition to being highly efficient, would enhance the Wall Street area, give pleasure to the thousands who pass by every day, provide a stimulating atmosphere for our employees, and, hopefully, exert some influence toward civic improvement.

Because there are stretches of pavement in the congested financial district which get less than 24 hours of sunshine in a full year, we felt that an open plaza would be a welcome addition to the scene. So we designed our building to occupy only about one-third of the 2½-acre site. The rest was devoted to the plaza which includes sycamore trees, circular granite benches, and a sculptural water garden.

When it came to decorating the interior of the building, we felt that fine art would be the best complement to the contemporary architecture we had chosen. So we set up a special art committee, which included some of the country's leading museum officials, and gave them a budget of $500,000. The works they selected for the reception areas and private offices ranged from primitive Americana to recently painted abstracts. Altogether, the bank has now accumulated about 450 paintings and pieces of sculpture, some of which are lent out from time to time; and a few have been donated to museums.

So far as results are concerned, we believe the building has helped humanize the image of what was once considered a cold and impersonal business. We believe it has enlivened the downtown community and given pleasure, reassurance and delight to employees, customers and visitors. In fact, customers have told us repeatedly how much they enjoy doing business in these surroundings. And many employees have remarked on the added benefits of working in such an environment.

At lunch hour during the spring, summer and fall months, the plaza is a popular strolling place. Band concerts and other forms of entertainment, which are staged regularly, draw capacity crowds and extensive coverage in the newspapers and on television. We have been told frequently—and we like to think it is true—that public spirited gestures of this kind have reinforced our slogan about the "friend at Chase Manhattan."

I am confident that if you were to talk with Tom Watson, Jr., of I.B.M., or Herbert Johnson of S.C. Johnson & Son, or Joyce Hall of Hallmark Cards, or Leigh Block of Inland Steel, you would hear similarly enthusiastic stories about the business-related advantages of using the arts in one form or another to promote corporate goodwill.

Let's turn now from the question why business should involve itself to the equally important consideration of how it can do so most effectively. The truth is that there are almost as many approaches as there are companies, ranging from the modest to the monumental.

For sheer expansiveness of concept, it would be hard to match the program of S.C. Johnson & Son. This company decided it wasn't enough simply to encourage American art; it wanted to encourage artists. So it bought more than 100 canvases of consistently high quality, embracing all the important styles and trends in contemporary American painting. As a gesture of goodwill toward people everywhere, this notably fine and varied collection was sent on a world tour to be seen by millions in London, Paris, Rome, Vienna, Athens and Tokyo. Recently it was donated to the permanent collection of the Smithsonian Institution, where Americans will have the pleasure of viewing it in the months and years to come.

Symphonic music was the particular area selected by the Schlitz Brewing Company. The firm underwrote a series of free summer concerts by the New York Philharmonic. The first concert in Central Park attracted 75,000 people, the largest audience ever to hear a symphony concert anywhere.

The roster of corporate sponsors of symphonies, operas and ballets is expanding rapidly. For years Americans regarded these more or less as the entertainment of the sophisticated few—or, as my Harvard undergraduate friend, Cleveland Amory, put it, "Like a husband with a foreign title: expensive to support, hard to understand and therefore a supreme social challenge."

But, lately, twenty-six companies in the Detroit area contributed to underwrite a reorganization of the Detroit Symphony. The Pantene Company won wide recognition for its sponsorship of a ballet production, the American Export and Isbrandtsen Lines for an opera, and Dell Publishing for Shakespeare-in-the-Park. Some 360 companies gave almost $10 million for the construction of Lincoln Center for the Performing Arts.

Obviously, not every business can pick up the bill for an international art show, a concert series, or a Shakespearean festival. But surely each one can re-examine its own activities in the light of the opportunities which are within its grasp.

For instance, every company has an opportunity to project a corporate identity that is clear, forceful, and unmistakably individual. When the identity scheme is artistic and is a planned one, so that each visual element is blended within the others, the result can be quite striking. This can find expression in many forms—in fresh concepts for buildings, offices, showroom displays, furniture, advertising, brochures, letterheads, and of course in products themselves.

Without question the arts provide a fertile field for building the corporation's image. It has been estimated that the business community in the United States and Canada spends some $625 million a year on public relations. If only a small percentage—say 5 per cent—of this expenditure were directed into the field of the arts, the arts would receive over $31 million annually from this source alone. Added to the total support now received through corporate gifts, it would more than double the business community's present contribution to culture.

Businesses can see to it that their products are tastefully and well designed and that the appeal made through advertisements and other media caters to something more than the lowest common denominator. The level of general merchandise today is certainly higher, in esthetic terms, than it was twenty-five years ago. This represents a conscious effort on the part of business. It means that businessmen have come to accept the fact that adopting high standards of artistic excellence in seemingly unimportant items of everyday life not only contributes to raising standards of public taste, but can also pay off in terms of the profit and loss statement. For example, much of our advertising and commercial art has been improved by first-rate typography and photography, as well as by the influx of ideas from other fields such as painting and sculpture.

The architecture of a company's buildings can contribute enormously to its environment—or, if poor in quality, can equally well detract from it. Good design can transform a whole area, and provide relief and refreshment for both the eye and the spirit. Those who have discovered this fact and have acted accordingly will be blessed for it by generations to come. But alas, we have only to look around us here in New York to realize that far too many have still to learn the lesson.

In the area of financial contributions, each company can well afford to take a fresh look at the ground rules it has established for corporate giving. It is a curious but demonstrable fact that while health, education and welfare organizations are now widely regarded as "safe" beneficiaries, cultural groups have not quite achieved the same measure of respectability.

A variety of reasons are offered for this phenomenon. One of the most popular is summed up in the plaintive query: "What would the stockholders say?"

Actually, companies that are major supporters of culture and the arts have encountered very little objection from this source. The fact is that many stockholders, as individuals, are heavily engaged in cultural activities and understand the urgent need for corporate backing.

Only once can I recall a stockholder's raising an objection, at an annual meeting, about the art program at Chase Manhattan. She had stopped off at our ground floor banking office to cash a check and her eye had been caught by a somber abstraction on one of the walls.

"Please, Mr. Rockefeller," she said, "let's have no sad paintings down on the banking floor among the living. Let's move it up to the trust department where they specialize in the estates of the dead!"

Another reason cited by some companies for not contributing is that culture and the arts are controversial. Take a firm stand, they say, and you are sure to alienate some groups who can hurt your business.

In our own case, this has not been so. Most customers coming into our head office or our branches have either expressed themselves in favor of our art work or have accepted it with stoic silence. We have no evidence to date of anyone's closing a checking or savings account because he disagreed with the art committee's selections.

Recently some of our more sensitive individuals in the bank had qualms in this regard when the committee selected a piece of sculpture by Jason Seley for our ground floor concourse. They were worried over the fact that the sculpture's readily identifiable raw materials were automobile bumpers. Curious about the reaction, I watched customers milling around the piece the day it was put up. One of the few critical comments I overheard was from a taxi driver. "They must have picked up those bumpers in Jersey," he said, "because after New York accidents there isn't that much of the car left."

Still another reason given for not contributing is that now that the federal government has moved into the field with its National Endowment for the Arts, there is no longer any need for corporate support. Personally, I am heartened to see the government taking an active hand in encouraging artists. This has worked out satisfactorily in several major countries around the globe, and I think it is a salutary development here at home where we are dedicated to maintaining a healthy balance between public and private endeavor. But the funds appropriated thus far by Congress for the National Endowment are very modest indeed. The Endowment is expected to run a nationwide program on a budget that is less than that of the Metropolitan Opera. By contrast, Austria's government spends more on the Vienna State Opera than on its entire foreign service. So I don't believe the U.S. Government's present role as a cultural "angel" will appreciably lessen the need for corporate support.

The fact is that the sources from which the arts have traditionally drawn their support—primarily wealthy individuals and foundations—are no longer able to cope with the growing needs, and not enough companies have moved in to take up the slack. The recent Panel Report, sponsored by the Rockefeller Brothers

Fund, on the Problems and Prospects of the Performing Arts brought forth some disturbing and challenging facts. Reflecting the examination by concerned and expert citizens of the state of the theatre, the dance and music in America, it noted that only about half of the nation's businesses contribute anything to the performing arts. Altogether, only a tiny fraction of corporate giving goes to meet cultural needs—less than $25 million in total. And a survey by the National Industrial Conference Board has pointed out that contributions to the arts in 1965 amounted to less than three cents of each corporate philanthropic dollar. The result is that progress has been too slow to sustain the necessary breakthrough to a dynamic growth in the arts.

Corporate financial contributions to the arts are in roughly the same situation now that contributions to higher education were a dozen or so years ago. At that time, the foundations became concerned about the problem and resolved to do something about it. They helped set up a Council for Financial Aid to Education to encourage greater voluntary support of colleges and universities, with special emphasis on corporate participation. It is no mere coincidence, I am sure, that over the past decade, corporate contributions to higher education have increased by more than 150 per cent.

Here, in the presence of so many distinguished leaders of business and industry, I should like to propose that we seriously consider the establishment of a comparable organization for the arts—a Council on Business and the Arts.

Such a council, drawn from the ranks of businessmen knowledgeable in the arts, cultural leaders and representative artists, could provide strong impetus and clearly defined direction for what is often rather haphazard progress.

As I see it, this organization would devote itself to broadening the base of corporate support through four main avenues.

First, it would conduct research on a national basis to provide statistical analyses of the voluntary support being generated on behalf of the arts. These reports would furnish an authoritative yardstick for the appraisal of the progress being made in this area.

Second, it would provide expert counseling for business firms seeking to initiate new programs or expand existing ones. Such counseling could range from comprehensive program analyses and recommendations to special detailed treatment of varied kinds of aid.

Third, it would carry on a nationwide program of public information to keep corporations informed of opportunities that exist in the arts, and to apprise the artistic community of what corporations are doing in their particular fields.

Fourth, it would work to increase the effectiveness of cultural organizations in obtaining voluntary support from business and industry, and to encourage the involvement of more businessmen as trustees of cultural groups.

Quite frankly, it has been my observation that some cultural organizations don't always make the most intelligent and forceful case for themselves when they seek corporate support. Their reasoning is often fuzzy, their documentation fragile. Even the most public spirited corporation has, I think, a right to expect the organization seeking its help to prove that it has competent management, a realistic budget and workable plans to attain immediate objectives as well as long-range goals.

I feel it would be enormously helpful for representatives of business and the arts to exchange views face to face, to seek new ideas from each other, to clarify misunderstandings and explore new possibilities. It would help bridge the gap between the sometimes rigid mentality of the businessman and the creative spirit of the artist. Both sides could benefit far more from constructive critical interest than from biased attack or hostile neglect.

Of necessity, the concept of a Council on Business and the Arts must be outlined here in its broadest terms. Yet I would hope that the basic idea has sufficient validity to justify exploration of its possibilities.

What a resounding acknowledgment this would be that the enhancement and development of the arts are worthy objectives for the exercise of corporate social responsibility. Too often the tendency is to regard the arts as something pleasant but peripheral. I feel the time has come when we must accord them a primary position as essential to the nation's well-being.

In our increasingly mechanized and computerized world, the arts afford a measure of consolation and reassurance to our individuality, a measure of beauty and human emotion that can reach and move most men. They are indispensable to the achievement of our great underlying concern for the individual, for the fullest development of the potential hidden in every human being.

Among our own people and those I talk with from other nations, there is insistent questioning about the significance of our material advances. What does it matter, they ask, that America has the largest Gross National Product or the biggest atom smasher or the fanciest automobiles? What does it matter that, in the words of Archibald MacLeish, "We have more things in our garages and kitchens and cellars than Louis XIV had in the whole of Versailles?"

Are these the only hallmarks of a truly Great Society?

Clearly, they are not.

The ultimate dedication to our way of life will be won, I am convinced, not on the basis of economic achievements alone but on the basis of those precious yet intangible elements which enable the individual to live a fuller, wiser, more satisfying existence.

I know of no other area in which we can spend our time and talents and energies more rewardingly.

Comments by Mr. Palmer

OBVIOUSLY we again picked the right man for the subject that we wish to pursue in our deliberations in our convocation.

I'm happy to tell you, David, that while we cannot do the total job that you challenge us with, in recent months we at the Conference Board have deliberated at some length on further research into the contributions of business to culture and the arts. We have done this in other fields, particularly in the field of education, working with the Council for Financial Aid to Education. We have found that apparently the publication of our research reports on what some companies are already doing has been a real stimulus to other companies to do likewise. And I'm hopeful that while we cannot involve ourselves in a full action program, we can make at least some contribution to the challenge which you have presented.

X CAPITALISM, ETHICS, AND MORALITY

CHAIRMAN: J. Irwin Miller

· *Introduction by Mr. Miller*

· *Capitalism, Ethics, and Morality,*

  Dr. John C. Bennett

Two most distinguished gentlemen, both leaders of religion, are here to play an important part in a most important meeting of world business leaders.

These two men stand before you as representatives of organized religion as it exists in most capitalist countries. Fifty years ago these men would have come to this conference, if at all, only to say grace at meals. Fifty years ago the established churches of capitalist countries generally supported the representatives of capitalism within their societies. They received an impressive portion of their money through contributions from capitalists, and they viewed with concern and indignation threats and attacks on laissez-faire capitalism—whether coming from the rising forces of labor, from popular revolutionary movements, from encroaching acts of government, or from lone voices within the churches themselves.

Fifty years ago the relation between the capitalists and the churches bore the appearance of a partnership—capitalists supplying the money, churches supplying respectability.

If such were still the case, there would be no purpose to be served by this panel. But such is no longer the case. To the capitalists it now appears that organized religion has turned on capitalists and capitalism, siding with labor, taking political, even revolutionary positions, criticizing the making of profits. In response the capitalist says to the churches, "Why don't you keep your nose out of business and stick to religion?"

Implicit in such a question is a definition of "religion" which the Western churches reject—the notion that religion ought to be confined to the conduct of religious worship, to the salvation of the individual, and should not soil its hands with the sordid affairs of everyday life.

The Western churches, however, remind us that religion under the Judeo-Christian inheritance is concerned with the whole of a man's life—with his responsible behavior toward his fellow man in every area, and especially toward those men who are in one way or another disadvantaged.

They tell us that the church has a parental responsibility to speak out to individual men, to groups or associations of men, to nations themselves, if these are in any way behaving with lesser responsibility toward others than the situation or time demands. These churches would also call to the attention of their lay critics (whether capitalist or otherwise) the example of one recent church which *did* "stick to religion and keep its nose out of everyday affairs"—the church in Czarist Russia. That church conducted its beautiful services without comment on the growing corruption, decay, cruelty, and immorality of the society outside its doors. For lack of responsible, constructive, audible criticism, that society collapsed, and in its collapse brought down the unconcerned church, too. The churches of the West thus defend their growing criticism of capitalism, as well as of other segments of society.

As capitalists, however, we have something more to say in return than "keep your nose out of our affairs." We have a right to require of the churches that, if they are to discharge truly the full responsibility which they have assumed, they must be a great deal more competent, better informed, and farsighted than they have shown themselves to be up to now.

The businessman finds ethics and morality, the problems of "fair shares," to run through everything he does—labor negotiations, pricing, promotions, relations with competitors, raising of capital. Each decision is a choice, and the choice is seldom between right and wrong, but almost always between two wrongs. Whichever alternative the manager chooses, someone is hurt or deprived or treated unfairly. Were he to approach pastor, theologian or priest with his complex alternatives prior to choosing, these men of religion would most likely flee in terror, pleading incompetence, or piously tell him to "do right, and not wrong," neither of which is of help to him. If they then return, after he has made his choice, and point out the obvious evils in the alternative he finally elected, our capitalist is not to be too severely blamed for an emotional rather than a logical response.

In concluding these remarks of introduction let me now say a word to each of the parties—to the capitalists, and to the churches. To the capitalists: No one should know better than you how swift and violent are the changes that are upon us; nor how hopeless the prospect of slowing the changes, let alone "going back" to anything. History tells us that governments, war lords, merchants, enterprisers—in whatever system they organized themselves—have flourished when they served reasonably well the true needs of their times, and not alone their personal advantage; and that they have perished when they have resisted or refused to recognize change and the new demands of the society in which they were planted. Capitalism will survive and flourish only as it continually and intelligently changes, renews itself, and serves the whole society well. For change and renewal to take place, a constant voice of clear, responsible criticism is a necessity, and of all voices, that of organized religion has the best right to claim that it speaks in the equal interest of every individual and in hatred of no one. The healthiest voice in our society today may well be the uncomfortable voice of the church, which speaks to save society, not destroy it.

Churches are institutions that also exist in a world of violent change, but their history is one of greater resistance to change and renewal than that of the relatively flexible and accommodating merchants and enterprisers of history. I would say to the churches: Unless you identify the shape of the future more accurately than do the capitalists, unless you continually and truly renew yourselves more thoroughly and swiftly than do the capitalists, no one will mark your example, hear your voice, or accept your leadership.

Our speakers are men to whom these hard words of mine do not apply, for they are men of competence, proven courage and vision.

The Reverend John Bennett is a man of great perception and compassion.

On the record, he is an establishment man, educated at Exeter, Williams, Oxford and his own Union Theological Seminary. He is further cursed with honorary degrees from Yale, Harvard and Princeton. And, on his board of trustees he has a number of persons who make their living at the southern tip of Manhattan Island. But the establishment has no grip on John Bennett, nor has his religion ever been confined within the handsome walls of his seminary. If a kindly but prophetic voice of warning or criticism seems due our government or business or education or the church itself, one of the most effective of such voices in our society today is that of John Bennett, president of Union Theological Seminary.

—J. Irwin Miller
CHAIRMAN OF THE BOARD
CUMMINS ENGINE COMPANY, INC.

Capitalism, Ethics, and Morality

THE REVEREND

JOHN C. BENNETT

President, Union Theological Seminary

THE PHRASE, "the Protestant ethic," is familiar in the discussion of the motives that underlie capitalism as a way of life. The use of the phrase in this context was stimulated chiefly by Max Weber's speculation concerning the influence of seventeenth-century Calvinism, especially in its Puritan form, on the development of what he called the spirit of capitalism. There is an enormous literature about Weber's thesis, much of it critical of his claims for it, but there is little doubt that aspects of Calvinistic spirituality help to explain the fact that among middle class Protestants there did develop the tendency to emphasize economically productive work as itself a religiously sanctioned vocation, unlimited production and unlimited profit, and a disciplined life that made it natural to save and invest rather than to spend.

Protestants were not the first people who have sought financial gain, but dedicated participation in this rationalized system of profitable work and saving seems to have been favored by a major type of Protestantism. There was an economic dynamism here that was not characteristic of Catholicism and that cannot be taken for granted in any culture. The early religious sources of this dynamism are now generally forgotten but today among

157

middle class Protestants something of this ethos persists. One illustration is the tendency of Protestants with this Puritan background to feel guilty, or at least uneasy, when they are not working. Deep within the Catholic tradition there is the assumption of the superiority of the contemplative life. Is it not possible that the secularization of the contemplative life may be leisure without a sense of guilt or of uneasiness?

Discussions of the Protestant ethic as a support for capitalism often refer to Richard Baxter whose book on moral theology, entitled *A Christian Directory,* had great influence on seventeenth-century Puritans. He writes: "It is a sin to desire riches as worldings and sensualists do, for the provision and maintenance of fleshly lusts and pride; but it is no sin, but a duty, to labour not only for labour's sake, firmly resting in the act done, but for that honest increase and provision, which is the end of our labour; and therefore to choose a gainful calling rather than another, that we may be able to do good, and relieve the poor." (P. 854.)

The fact that responsible Protestant teachers could write in this way about the *duty* to seek "an honest increase and provision" and to choose a more "gainful calling" is a mark of what we may call the stereotype of "the Protestant ethic." This was not the ethic of the great reformers; it was not the ethic of all forms of Protestantism; but it was an ethic that has been strong among some forms of Protestantism that have flourished in several northern countries, especially our own.

Great changes have come in capitalism with free enterprise finding its place, though still as the dominant factor, in a mixed economy in this country. And also great changes have come in the teaching of economic ethics within Protestantism. It is to the relationship between these two developments that I shall now turn.

Within the past century there have been at least three periods in the corporate ethical thinking of Protestant churches in regard to capitalism. During the first period that extended until about the beginning of the twentieth century, the Protestant attitude toward capitalism was one of uncritical acceptance. This was along the lines of what I have called the stereotype of the "Protestant Ethic." The second period involved an increasingly critical attitude toward capitalism and in the 1930s and 1940s there was a tendency to reject capitalism. A third period in which we are living today is characterized by a more open attitude toward some of the aspects of capitalism combined with hope for the development of present-day capitalism under the pressure for social justice in our society. During this third period I think that Protestant thinking and Roman Catholic thinking tend to converge. Though there are some differences of methodology, I am aware of no distinctive Protestant position now that can be contrasted with the economic ethics reflected in the social encyclicals of Pope Pius XI and Pope John XXIII and in the Schema on The Church in the Modern World of the Second Vatican Council.

The first stage of Protestant teaching within the past century was almost a celebration of capitalism, especially unreformed laissez-faire capitalism. Theologians were uncritical of the productive processes. They opposed all tampering with so-called economic laws which were believed to be God's laws. They had no sympathy with the efforts of labor to organize because this would interfere with the operations of these laws. They often regarded poverty as a sign of sin and wealth a mark of divine favor. Responsible Christian thinkers who in other areas are still much admired were often uncritical defenders of a form of capitalism that is now outmoded.

A great change began to come toward the end of the nineteenth century. There was an increasing tendency to criticize capitalism. During the period between the two world wars, Protestant ethical thinkers became strongly anti-capitalistic. Often they were Christian Socialists. If we take as an example the year 1930 we would find that most of the great names in Protestant theology were opposed to capitalism. This was true of Karl Barth, Emil Brunner, Paul Tillich, Reinhold Niebuhr, and Archbishop William Temple and a host of lesser figures. Of the men whom I have named the most conservative was Emil Brunner, a Swiss reformed theologian who has had great influence in the United States. He wrote about 1930 in his *The Divine Imperative*: The capitalist system "is that system in which all that we can see to be the meaning of the economic order from the point of view of faith is being denied: in which, therefore, it is made almost impossible for the individual to realize, in any way through his economic activity, the service of God and his neighbor. This system is contrary to the spirit of service; it is debased and irresponsible; indeed we may go further and say: it is irresponsibility developed into a system." (P. 423.)

One of the most significant statements that reflect the strong criticisms of capitalism, though it does represent the beginning of the tendency to acknowledge the hopeful side of reformed capitalism, came out of the first Assembly of the World Council of Churches at Amsterdam in 1948. This statement was a part of the report of one of four sections of the assembly. At the time it received a great deal of publicity and was interpreted as more dogmatically anti-capitalist than was the case. It said that the church should make clear that there are conflicts between Christianity and capitalism, as well as conflicts between Christianity and communism. It recognized, however, that capitalism varied from country to country and that "often the exploitation of the workers that was characteristic of early capitalism has been corrected in considerable measure by the influence of trade unions, social legislation and responsible management." The statement then emphasized four criticisms of capitalism. "(1) It tends to subordinate what should be the primary task of any economy—the meeting of human needs—to the economic advantages of those who have most power over its institutions. (2) It tends to produce serious inequalities. (3) It has developed a practical form of materialism in western nations in spite of their Christian background, for it has placed the greatest emphasis upon success in making money. (4) It has kept the people of capitalist countries subject to a kind of fate which has taken the form of such social catastrophies as mass unemployment."

Would you not regard that list of criticisms of capitalism as a good check list of the points at which capitalism is morally vulnerable and which do call for continuous watching and correction in every period? These criticisms are different from the overall Marxist criticism that there is an inevitable historical judgment on capitalism exposing its inner contradictions and causing it to be displaced everywhere as a system through revolution.

A more open attitude toward important aspects of capitalism does characterize the present period—what I have called the third period. There are at least three such aspects. The first is the pluralism of capitalism that is made possible by the existence of many centers of initiative and power in contrast to a collectivism that unites and centralizes political and economic power. This pluralism is favorable to many forms of freedom, not only the more obvious forms of economic freedom such as freedom of enterprise, freedom to choose one's vocation and to some extent one's residence and one's job, freedom of consumer's choice, but also freedom of cultural initiative by providing sources of support for educational institutions and agencies of expression and communication that are independent of the state, and political freedom that comes from the existence of social forces that are not controlled by the state, including the power of private business and organized labor.

The second aspect of capitalism that has always been much praised by its long-time defenders but which now is often acknowledged by those who are inclined to be its critics is its creative dynamism. Critics of capitalism have often contended that the profit *system* as a guide to production and distribution is irrational because, instead of moving directly to meet human needs, it meets these needs as a byproduct of the profit-seeking of individuals. The tendency to overexercise the profit *motive* has often been regarded as immoral because it may make men more acquisitive than they might be under another system.

There is truth in these criticisms and I shall suggest some ways of taking account of this truth later. Yet I think that this self-serving and often family-serving motive is a given factor which needs both to be tamed and to be used. I think that our ethical response to it should be both a *yes* and a *no* and that under some conditions the *yes* should come before the *no*. The energies that capitalism has stimulated because of its use of the profit incentive have led to the great benefits as well as to the many ills of modern industrial society. On balance this process has surely been constructive. This applies to much more than the profit incentive in the restricted sense that relates it only to the return on equity capital; it applies to the seeking of economic advantage down the line to include all forms of income that stimulate effort and efficiency.

There is much foolishness in what is said in this whole area. Collectivists often deny the creative role of these economic incentives. Defenders of capitalism often speak as though these were the only incentives in the business world, thus insulting themselves. They overlook the other incentives which both supplement or correct the profit motive: the fascination of a game and the building of an empire, the enjoyment of status which when it involves social approval can correct raw acquisitiveness and empire building, the love of creating, loyalty to an organization, loyalty to the common good. There is a blend of all of these motives in professionalized management. Today the stress on social responsibility is conspicuous.

Let me state more sharply the moral dilemma. The profit motive as a subjective phenomenon, unless it is very much limited and tamed, is morally objectionable. It tends to corrupt the individual and it becomes the source of temptation, even in far-reaching decisions, to put a very limited interest before the common good. The profit system, in so far as it is a stimulus to initiative and in so far as it provides moments of truth with the prospect of profit or loss by which institutions are shaken out of ruts, is on balance a constructive force. Yet the profit system can easily over-stimulate the profit motive as personal acquisitiveness and thus it becomes morally problematic. This is a moral dilemma that is built into capitalism; it requires both internal disciplines within the system and external checks.

Even in non-profit institutions there is a subordinate place for economic incentives. This is true of differentials in salary that accompany recognized contributions and enlarged responsibilities. It is also true that non-profit institutions, even churches, gain by having to win at least partial financial support from contemporaries instead of coasting indefinitely on endowments. There are problems here when threats to withhold support tempt institutions to betray their essential purposes but the best institutions need to face some equivalent of the moment of truth which the prospect of either profit or loss creates for private business.

The third aspect of capitalism which deserves acceptance within limits is the role of the market in guiding economic activity as an index of what is needed though in the first instance what is wanted by those who are able to pay for it. The market provides considerable freedom for the consumer. Again what is good is on the edge of much evil and corruption. Insignificant wants encouraged by or even created by advertising may have priority over real needs. We should not absolutize a want system and assume that it is always good to produce what is wanted. And yet, as a rough guide to the direction of economic activities the market is preferable to detailed central planning that seeks to impose what the planners believe to be good on a nation of consumers. There are self-correcting elements in an open market which in the long run have their effect in reducing the effects of overeager and sometimes unscrupulous salesmanship. Corrections are needed also by government regulation as well as by improvement of taste in the society and by a juster distribution of purchasing power. No economic system can be free from the defects of the society within which it operates or can be expected to solve all its problems.

I have said many positive things about the embodiment of ethical values in the institutions of capitalism. I can do this in large measure because capitalism has changed so profoundly within the past half century. The rise of the labor movement to check the arbitrary power of employers—it often was extremely arbitrary in this country before 1935—has helped to make capitalism morally tolerable. The social legislation that has gone far to create a welfare society has corrected many of the injustices of traditional capitalism and has done much to save capitalism from itself. Many of you will share my memory that in this country the social changes that have made capitalism morally tolerable have come in the teeth of the opposition of those who dominated our capitalistic institutions. Their successors in many cases—I hope in most cases—have come to accept these changes and would not return to the more ruthless capitalism of an earlier period. Those who today have the power within the institutions of capitalism—both corporations and labor unions—have to satisfy a pervasive sense of justice in the society as a whole. The recent history of countries in which capitalism is dominant indicates clearly that capitalism is not a self-sufficient system, that it exists to a considerable extent on sufferance, that it has been changed and will continue to be changed by political decisions.

In what follows I shall deal with two aspects of this larger ethical frame to which capitalism is subject, first in the United States where we can indicate very precisely some of the limitations of capitalism and, second, in the international sphere where we see capitalism competing with other systems and facing new problems.

In the United States our actions make it clear that capitalism, as the free enterprise system, is not self-sufficient. So much that needs to be done is not economically profitable for any private person or institution. There are large areas of public need on which the institutions of capitalism seem unable to focus. Professor Galbraith has helped to illumine the situation by giving currency to the contrast between private wealth and public poverty. This helps us to see what economic targets are missed when the emphasis is only on maximizing the wealth of individuals even though there may be reasonable success in the case of most individuals. The community may still be very poor in schools, in housing, in opportunities for recreation, in many health services, in the failure to combat the pollution of water and air, in the ugliness of so much of the environment that is allowed to deteriorate, and not least in the public transportation of which so many citizens are daily victims while their excellent private vehicles remain parked near home. This kind of public poverty, which involves real deprivation in fact for citizens in their private capacity, can only be overcome by strong public initiatives which in various degrees may cooperate with or coordinate private initiatives and supplement them.

Those who stress in theory the moral priority of free enterprise may accept in fact most of the institutional changes which now enable society through government to supplement and coordinate and regulate the activities of private agents but there is a lag in basic thinking when it is assumed that private initiative is, except in the case of national defense and a few other matters, inherently better than public initiative. Why should it not be just as sound for the community as a whole to act for its own welfare as it is for any individuals or private organizations to take initiative for profit?

There is one subject that is on the minds and consciences of all of us: the poverty of our cities, in this case often both public and private poverty, poverty that is dramatized for us by the ghettoes in which so many millions of our fellow citizens are imprisoned. These are both a racial and an economic problem. The existence of this poverty side by side with our enormous productivity and prosperity should cause us all to make explicit the fact that capitalism is not self-sufficient. In the 1930s the overwhelming interference with human freedom caused by mass unemployment did a great deal to broaden American thinking about the conditions of freedom. Those who did not learn the lesson then are in many cases learning it now as they see before them the destruction of freedom in our cities today for which free enterprise alone cannot provide the remedy. The whole society working through government has to take bold initiatives to create the conditions that favor more freedom of choice, greater justice and more well-being for the victims of our institutions. One of the things that always has to be learned over again is that comfortable people do not do enough until they are pushed. If the Negro minority did not have votes to threaten our national political parties and if they had not taken to the streets in direct action, middle class Americans would not be as ready as they are now to face the radical action required by the plight of our cities. When shattering events create anxiety concerning the structure of society, consciences are also stirred and changes fortunately are accepted from a mixture of motives.

I said earlier that Protestant and Catholic economic ethics have converged in recent decades. This is especially true in regard to the relationship between public and private initiatives in economic life. Neither Protestants nor Catholics believe in an all-encompassing state. However both emphasize the legitimacy, indeed the necessity, of the increasing role of the state in economic life. Both seek to preserve the social and economic pluralism which is favored by the many units of economic decision and initiative which we associate with capitalism. Both give ethical sanction to private property as a source of and protection for personal freedom, though the arguments for private property must be understood as arguments for the widest possible distribution of such property. The Schema of the Vatican Council to which I have referred has a fine balance in relating private and public poverty.

Pope John's encyclical, *Mater et Magistra*, and reports that have come from the assemblies of the World Council of Churches, are very similar on this issue. Pope John speaks of the "tendency to be found in the ever-widening activity which the common good requires that public authorities undertake." This statement is immediately corrected by these words: "the state and agencies of public law should not extend their ownership except where evident and real needs of the common good dictate it" (p. 177). One of the reports that came from the Evanston Assembly of the World Council of Churches in 1954 preserved the same balance by first saying that "while the state is sometimes the enemy of freedom, under many circumstances the state is the only instrument which can make freedom possible for large sectors of the population" and then by warning "against the danger that the union of political and economic power may result in an all-controlling state" (Section III).

The necessity of supplementation and correction of the effect of capitalism is vividly illustrated by the recommendations of the President's Commission on Technology, Automation and Economic Progress chaired by Dr. Howard Bowen. This commission's diagnosis of trends was certainly free from extreme or alarmist predictions but some of its recommendations broke the pattern of individualistic social thinking very radically, especially its recommendation that "economic security be guaranteed by a floor under family income" and that "this floor should include both improvements in wage-related benefits and a broader system of income maintenance for those families unable to provide for themselves" (*Technology and the American Economy*, p. 110). This recommendation is close to one adopted in February 1966 by the General Board of the National Council of Churches that "our burgeoning productivity makes possible, and our Judeo-Christian ethic of justice makes mandatory, the development of economic policies and structures under which all people, regardless of employment status, are assured an adequate livelihood" (statement on "Christian Concern and Responsibility for Economic Life in a Rapidly Changing Technological Society"). I am sure that both statements presuppose the idea that such income maintenance must be recognized as a basic right such as the right of all children to educational opportunity. This can be defended both in the public interest and as a condition for personal freedom and welfare in the case of millions of persons. This seems very remote from the stereotype of the Protestant ethic to which I referred at the beginning of this address. Someone may be tempted to quote St. Paul's words: "If any one will not work, let him not eat" (II Thessalonians 3:10). But we should not turn Paul's condemnation of an especially obnoxious group of parasites in the first century into a universal law applicable in all centuries to all economies, at all levels of productivity. Moreover there are other verses in the New Testament including the words in the story of the Last Judgment: "for I was hungry and you gave me no food" (Matt. 25:42).

As we look abroad to other countries we can see clearly that capitalism with all of its astonishing creativity is not self-sufficient. The older industrialized countries in which capitalism was dominant have retained many of the elements of capitalism but these have been transformed to meet the needs of welfare societies. Their political parties have abandoned both a dogmatic individualism and a dogmatic socialism. American rightists see in this development a victory for communism as they do in the case of similar trends in this country, but they could not make a greater mistake for these developments have rendered nations immune to communism. Communism as a revolutionary movement and a conspiracy thrives on neglected social problems. Rightists see freedom being lost, for their model of freedom is the uncontrolled economic behavior of strong men in a frontier society rather than the maximizing of opportunities for real freedom of choice on the part of all classes in an interdependent industrialized society.

It is remarkably ironic that while Karl Marx expected a ripe capitalism in western Europe to prepare the way for communist revolution, communism has in fact developed in nations that were in large measure pre-industrial and pre-capitalist and has proved to be a quick and ruthless way of modernizing and industrializing. The developments in communist countries have shown that communism is no monolithic or unchanging system, that it is more open-ended than we in the Western countries imagined to be possible. The irony becomes complete as advanced and mellower communist nations begin to develop some of the characteristics of an open society including a very limited measure of economic decentralization and of reliance on economic incentives. In any case there have been enough changes in European communism to blur the conflict between social systems and to soften the hostilities of the cold war. It is a favorable sign that important business leadership in this country seeks increased East-West trade and is becoming open to trade with Communist China.

Denys Munby, an English economist who has given great attention to the relation between economics and ethics, has recently written that "although the industrialized world is divided between the western and eastern blocs, the old issues of socialism and capitalism are dead." He goes on to say that there are more similarities between Western and Eastern Europe than either side would admit, and as the "East" begins to learn how to apply traditional economic theory and modern mathematics to its directed planning, the "West moves in the same direction from laissez-faire to indicative planning and thence to target planning" (*Economic Growth in World Perspective*, Denys Munby, editor, Association Press, 1966). I can believe that many of you will regard that as a considerable overstatement but it is significant that it appears in the foreword to a symposium representing the thought of scholars in many countries and written in preparation for a world conference of churchmen that met in Geneva in July 1966. At that conference which represented seventy countries there was a continuous expression and even dramatization of the assumption that today the issues between what Lord Franks some years ago taught us to call "the North" and "the South" are becoming far more significant than those that have divided "the East" and "the West."

In relation to the third world, or the southern hemisphere or the so-called developing nations, we need to recognize that American institutions cannot be exported universally, that economies in many developing nations will have a much greater socialistic ingredient than may be desirable in the United States, that foreign aid should not be used to prevent such socialistic developments where strong public initiative is required to do in a few decades what has been done in this country in the course of several generations. Also American corporations and labor unions should not support sterile and oppressive oligarchies in nations to the south of us because they preserve an order which, however unjust, provides some security for business dealings. One major test of American capitalism will be the capacity of its leaders to be open to the possibility that some nations, whose oligarchies have drifted for generations without doing anything important about the massive poverty of their people, may need to be changed by leftist revolutions which often have considerable Catholic support. And we may hope that such revolutions will not be followed by more revolutions but by real nation-building and economic development. Fear of communism should not be used to justify the United States in being a counter revolutionary force in all such explosive situations, especially in view of the fact that we know now that communism is not monolithic and that some communist nations already show signs of being able to develop into more humane and open societies. (Also we see that one communist nation can be a check on another.) We should do what can be done to help any nation that needs radical change to find a constructive alternative to communism, but this may not always be possible. Indeed there are many situations in which our problem is to discern what is the lesser or the least evil.

Capitalism and ethics. Capitalism as we know it today has elements which are ethically desirable even though they may not always be possible. We should be thankful where they now are part of the pattern of dynamic societies which are quite open and which are moving rapidly toward greater social justice. They should also be part of any objectives that we regard as adequate for other societies. Those who stress them should also recognize that capitalism is not a self-sufficient system and that there must be the most varied combinations of private enterprise and public planning and initiative.

There are universal moral norms by which all systems should be judged. All should serve justice, not a static justice but a continually transforming justice, humaneness and diversity in society. They should serve the freedom of persons, of persons under all conditions and not only those who have economic advantages. There is needed a conception of the depth and dignity and transcendence of the person that involves a far more inclusive form of freedom than that associated with the stereotyped and dated "Protestant ethic" that is often associated with traditional capitalism. Professor Brzesinski, who is one of the chief authorities on the conflict between East and West and who has proved his toughness in regard to immediate political problems, says that the issues of the cold war "are no longer the basic issues facing mankind." He says that "in the second half of the twentieth century the developed nations, given new scientific and social developments, will face a real threat to the continued existence of man as a spontaneous, instinctive, rather autonomous and even somewhat mysterious being; the less developed countries, because of overpopulation, economic backwardness and potential political disorder, will be challenged by a fundamental crisis of survival of organized society" (*Foreign Affairs,* July 1966). The phrase "somewhat mysterious being" makes room for the idea that the person is made in God's image, on which Protestants and Catholics stand together.

This position leads me to say that while we should hold fast to universal moral criteria and objectives, not least those that recognize and protect the person as more than an economic being, as a "somewhat mysterious being," we need to be skeptical concerning the absolute claims of institutions and systems. Openness to unimagined institutional developments in the economic sphere and moral discernment concerning what is good for persons are both necessary to prepare us for the future.

XI RELIGIOUS POSTULATES OF THE ECONOMIC-SOCIAL ORDER IN FREEDOM

CHAIRMAN: J. Irwin Miller

· *Introduction by Mr. Miller*

· *Religious Postulates of the Economic-Social*

Order in Freedom, His Eminence

Paolo Cardinal Marella

No MORE remarkable events have occurred during these past few years than those which have taken place within that ancient institution, the Roman Catholic Church. These events have occurred in recognition of the extraordinary changes that are occurring in world society, of the vital role which organized religion is called upon to play at a time when the forces of depersonalization, of inhumanity, and of fear are all over the world.

His Eminence, Paolo Cardinal Marella stands in the very center of this new and significant activity of the Catholic Church. He was born in Rome, he was educated in Rome and almost immediately entered into the important service of the Vatican itself. He has seen long service throughout the world, in Washington, in Japan, in Australia, in France.

In 1959 he was created Cardinal by Pope John XXIII and in 1965 he was made president of that remarkable new activity of the church, the Secretariat for Non-Christians.

We are extraordinarily honored to have His Eminence Paolo Cardinal Marella, who has come to us directly from the Vatican to share with us his own thinking and that of his Church on the subject of the future of capitalism.

—J. Irwin Miller

Religious Postulates of the Economic-Social Order in Freedom

HIS EMINENCE

PAOLO CARDINAL MARELLA

President, Vatican Secretariat for

Relations with Non-Christians

I HAVE ACCEPTED with pleasure—and, I may say, with admiration—your invitation to speak at this solemn fiftieth anniversary meeting of one of the world's greatest research organizations, dedicated to the study and presentation of truth concerning the economic and social activities in the United States and the international community.

My intimate joy and profound consideration for the National Industrial Conference Board has been caused also by the fact that you have wished to have men of God in your midst, and in particular, a Cardinal of Rome.

Before I left Rome, the Holy Father, in an audience dedicated to these meetings, manifested great personal interest in my mission. He desires that I bring to this important organization and to this eminent audience his warmest greetings and a brief expression of his thought. He asked me to convey to all of you his heartfelt wishes for each of the participants, for their families, and for those who will benefit from your work. He prays that a great good in society will come from this constructive discussion, and from the follow-up action, not only in the United States, but also in other continents and especially in Latin America, and this not only for what concerns the field of production and commerce, of economic, technological and scientific progress, but also for the promotion of human, moral and spiritual progress.

I want to state first that, in Rome, we are constantly studying the leading nation of the free world in all of its aspects. We are conscious of the results of the latest opinion polls which indicate that the percentage of citizens in the United States who declare themselves believers in God is as high as 97 per cent—while church attendance for all religious groups reaches 67 per cent.

I have been impressed with the important papers presented by eminent economic-social leaders and by great statesmen of different continents at this important gathering.

I see that out of the initiative of the National Industrial Conference Board international agreement can grow on the basis of great common principles which guarantee the future of a developing and irresistible economic-social order inspired by human freedom. I will do my best to follow in this line. I will strive for the union of minds and hearts by reducing some of the postulates of individual and social life to a simple synthesis of ten basic principles which are, in a certain sense, ten basic commandments for better living. Five of these principles are general and five are specific, applied to the natural requisites of economic-social order.

But before I do this I want to define the terms. As you know, this is a Roman specialty, based on the lasting philosophy most concisely expressed by Aristotle and Thomas Aquinas. Correct definition of terms is the first basic condition for any kind of agreement. The lack of it is often a cause of heated conflict. Consequently I am sure you will want to join me in this exercise in logic which makes for better dialectics. I think that there is a spontaneous agreement on the need for correct definition of terms between businessmen and churchmen. We can perhaps inspire some political leaders, who have forgotten this exercise in logic, to concentrate on definitions before going in for denunciations, agitations or other forms of unwarranted accusations.

The title of my address is "Religious Postulates of the Eco-

nomic-Social Order in Freedom." The first word is an adjective—
"religious"—which is derived from the noun—religion. Now the
word religion comes from the Latin—*religare*—which means "to
link." It is evident that man is linked to a reality, greater, higher
and more perfect than himself. Most men know about this link.
All religions stress its primacy as the ultimate concern of man.
It is in this sense that I am here as president of the Vatican Secretariat for Relations with Non-Christian Religions.

In his first encyclical, "Ecclesiam Suam," on "The Ways of the
Church," the present Pope, Paul VI, has enlarged the circle of
interest to include in constructive dialogue not only all Christians
but "all believers in the one God" and, ultimately, "the whole
of mankind."

In a special message on Easter 1964, Pope Paul declared that:
"Every religion has rays of light which should not be despised
nor extinguished." Thus he recognized the genuine values and
spiritual elevation in all peoples, so necessary nowadays to con-
vince the world of the degrading effect of materialism on the
human race. The Secretariat for Relations with Non-Christians,
over which I have the honor to preside, was established by Pope
Paul VI in this spirit, manifested by a special declaration of the
Ecumenical Council Vatican II. This was indeed timely in a
world becoming smaller every day, where human thoughts and
endeavors are tending towards common expression, in a world
where all peoples are struggling to coordinate their aspirations
in a common effort. All this will promote the much desired har-
mony and peace for all mankind.

We are thus realistic when we say that the "religious" quality
is, indeed, becoming one of the most widely recognized values
of civilization. But its immense potentialities have not yet been
tapped.

The second word in my title, the noun "postulate," is not
yet clear or popular. And yet the world's greatest nation, of
which I am a guest today, was born out of a set of postulates which
were presented by Thomas Jefferson as "self-evident truths." In
short, there are some basic assumptions upon which we can all
agree, before we start disagreeing over incidentals. The American
Webster's Dictionary says that postulates are "assumed without
proof, as basis for argument, stated as facts taken for granted."

This is the first and most critical thing we must do together—define our postulates of individual and social life. Without this, a disagreement becomes destructive and, in this nuclear era, potentially suicidal. With a solid basis of unshakable postulates we can start thinking, feeling, acting to create that rich diversity which is necessary for human unity.

You will understand now, I trust, why I had to choose as my subject the religious postulates for the economic and social order. There is one central sentence in the Charter for Democracy Under God, launched by Pope Pius XII in his Christmas message of 1944, which may have been forgotten: "Democracy is seen as a postulate of reason." This means that if we are to be religious, we must be reasonable and accept the postulate that the political, economic-social, cultural order for society must be established through democratic freedom.

But this means also that, if we are democratic, we must be at least implicitly religious. If we accept the totalitarian principle that the state is the source of our rights, then we must accept the fact that the state can take these rights away, as some states have done in practice. It is not just a paradox of history that the greatest, most solid and most permanent democracy was born out of a declaration of national independence which started with a declaration of dependence on God.

Before explaining what we mean by religious postulates of the social order, I cannot do better than ask here if anyone disagrees with the following principles: "that all men are created equal, that they are endowed by their Creator with certain inalienable rights, that among these are life, liberty and the pursuit of happiness." I hear no dissenting voices. I know there is consent. These self-evident truths were launched in the preamble of the American Declaration of Independence. They were presented by the Continental Congress "as a standard to which all wise and honest men can repair." Now this proclamation is beginning to move all nations throughout the world.

I have chosen the words, "economic-social order in freedom," rather than the word capitalism. In the first place, capitalism is too narrow; it does not include the nonmaterial parts of the common good, such as education, culture, ethical customs. In the second place, the word capitalism, like many other words used in politics, has become a living thing which is deeply hated by a great part of mankind and is not entirely loved by the other part. In contrast, the word democracy creates sympathy in all languages, so much so that not only anticapitalistic, but even totalitarian regimes pay lip service to it. We recognize that the time has come to enrich the political forms of democracy with the necessary economic and social applications of democracy. By stressing the future growth of the truly social order effect of economic democracy, we can succeed more quickly and more completely in acquiring the necessary majority consent.

I have added the words, "in freedom," to avoid any possible confusion. Totalitarianism can try to give the name democracy to total economic-social state control. But it cannot support the idea that any such totalitarian order, and specifically the economic-social order, can be the fruit of freedom.

Now that we have carefully defined our terms, we can progress to some self-evident truths or postulates of the economic-social order in freedom. While economics and social studies, and freedom itself, are immensely complicated, the sources from which they spring are basically simple. We arrived at the formulation of these postulates by asking "why" after every important achievement in economics and politics, in culture and social life. When we reached certain simple truths which were so self-evident that their "raison d'être," or their know-why, was part of them, we then had our system of civic consensus, our postulates for order in freedom. As you can understand, I can only give you a summary of the results of this work. The complete work of synthesis has taken decades of study in many nations and five years (1960-65) of writing and rewriting for the pastoral constitution on "The Church and the Modern World." This constitution was passed by a 96% majority of more than two thousand bishops at the end of Vatican Council II, December 8, 1965. The document was addressed to all men of good will of all continents. As the basic postulates express common conclusions of sound reason and respected traditions, there has been an unprecedented consensus of world opinion favorable to this appeal to the conscience of mankind. In fact, the church, in the introduction to this largest and newest social document, has recognized that "she gladly holds in high esteem the things which other Christian churches or ecclesiastical communities have done or are doing cooperatively by way of achieving the same goal. At the same time, she is firmly convinced that she can be abundantly and variously helped by the world. This help she gains from the talents and industry of individuals and from human society as a whole. The council now sets forth certain general principles for the proper fostering of this mutual exchange and assistance in concerns which are in some way common to the church and to the world."[1]

The five general religious postulates for economic-social order can be presented as follows:

First postulate: human brotherhood. This is the premise of the very first sentence of the council's constitution: "The joys and the hopes, the griefs and the anxieties of the men of this age, especially those who are poor or in any way afflicted, these too are the joys and the hopes, the griefs and the anxieties of the followers of Christ."[2] It is said more concretely further that "everyone must consider his every neighbor without exception as another self . . . so as not to imitate the rich man who had no concern for the poor man Lazarus.

"In order to do this a special obligation binds us to make ourselves the neighbor of absolutely every person and to actively help him when he comes across our path."[3]

The council states also that, *"before all, the obligations of justice should be fulfilled, so as to avoid offering as a gift of charity what is already due by right of justice."*

Second postulate: updating of religion in the age of technological and scientific revolution. The council invites all to: "recognize and understand the world in which we live, its expectations, its longings and its often dramatic characteristics . . . a true social and cultural transformation, one which has repercussions on man's religious life as well."[4]

This presupposes a need for "a more critical ability to distinguish religion from a magical view of the world and from the

1. Guild—America—Association Press—edition on the *Documents of Vatican II,* p. 239.
2. *Ibid.,* p. 199.
3. *Ibid.,* p. 226.
4. *Ibid.,* p. 202.

superstitions which still circulate. This purifies religion and exacts day by day a more personal and implicit adherence to faith."[5]

Applying this to the economic order, we must consider this order as being subordinate to the religious and moral order. Thus, economics and its development must respect and be of service to the promotion of individual and social dignity of the entire person.

At this point the Vatican Council II sets itself in the wake of the previous papal teachings, according to which neither selfish economic individualism nor absolute collectivism can be in accordance with the religious and moral order.

Third postulate: increased social responsibility. The council states: "Throughout the course of the centuries, men have labored to better the circumstances of their lives through a monumental amount of individual and collective effort. To believers, this point is settled: considered in itself, such human activity accords with God's will. For man, created in God's image, received a mandate to subject to himself the earth and all that it contains, and to govern the world with justice and holiness."[6]

Then the council strengthened this position by stating that: "This mandate concerns even the most ordinary activities. For while providing the substance of life for themselves and their families, men and women are performing their activities in a way which appropriately benefits society."[7]

The root problems of socio-economic life of the modern world have been faced by the council. Their answer is summed up in the principle that those who have economic power should not consider this power only as a means for their own well-being, but also, and in the first place, as a means to promote the common good.

Fourth postulate: autonomy of the laymen in earthly affairs. The council makes it clear: "If by the autonomy of earthly affairs we mean that created things and societies themselves enjoy their own laws and values which must be gradually deciphered, put to use, and regulated by men, then it is entirely right to demand that autonomy. Such is not merely required by modern man, but

5. *Ibid.*, p. 205.
6. *Ibid.*, p. 232.
7. *Ibid.*

harmonizes also with the will of the Creator.[8] This autonomy must be promoted, therefore, by methodical investigation within every branch of learning, carried out in a genuinely scientific manner and in accord with moral norms, which never truly conflicts with faith. For earthly matters and the concerns of faith derive from the same God."[9]

Fifth postulate: religious depth of freedom of conscience. As developed in a special declaration on religious liberty, the council stresses that: "Only in freedom can man direct himself toward goodness. Our contemporaries make much of this freedom and pursue it eagerly; and rightly so, to be sure."[10]

The reason for this is given: "All believers of whatever religion have always heard His revealing voice in the discourse of creatures. But when God is forgotten, the creature itself grows unintelligible."[11]

The specific postulates of a socio-economic order in freedom are logical implementations of the five first postulates. These postulates can be presented as follows:

Sixth postulate: The human person as the beneficiary of economics. This premise is expressed in the following first two sentences of the chapter on socio-economic life. "In the socio-economic realm, too, the dignity and total vocation of the human person must be honored and advanced along with the welfare of society as a whole. For man is the source, the center and the purpose of all socio-economic life."[12] In another text the council stresses that: The *equal dignity* of the human person requires the achievement of a more human and fair condition of life. In fact, the *too great economic and social inequalities* between members and between peoples of the one human family arouse scandal and are contrary to social justice, to *equity*, to the dignity of the human person, as well as to social and international peace. But this, *for the same reason*, also means that equity, mentioned in the text just quoted, should determine a universal distribution of goods, to be implemented not really according to a guiding

8. *Ibid.*, p. 233.
9. *Ibid.*, p. 234.
10. *Ibid.*, p. 214.
11. *Ibid.*, p. 234.
12. *Ibid.*, p. 271.

criterion of arithmetical measurement—which would certainly be difficult, if not impossible—but according to a criterion of goodness, of brotherhood, of personal understanding.

Seventh postulate: The pluralistic responsibility in economic-social planning for the common good. The council has been exceptionally clear and precise in negating any ethical justification for total government planning. The following declarations are a challenge to all: "Economic development must be kept under the control of mankind. It must not be left to the sole judgment of a few men or groups possessing excessive economic power, or of the political community alone, or of certain especially powerful nations. . . . Growth must not be allowed merely to follow a kind of automatic course resulting from the economic activity of individuals. Nor must it be entrusted solely to the authority of government."[13] This postulate is implemented not only in the sections concerning management and labor, but also in the chapters concerning political life and international welfare and peace.

Eighth postulate: The creative economic primacy of private enterprise. In the same pastoral constitution on the Church in the Modern World the Ecumenical Council includes the following decree: "Ownership and other forms of private control over material goods contribute to the expression of personality. Moreover, they furnish men with an occasion for exercising their role in society and in the economy. Hence it is very important to facilitate the access of both individuals and communities to some control over material goods.

"Private ownership or some other kind of dominion over material goods provides everyone with a wholly necessary independence, and should be regarded as an extension of human freedom. Finally, since it adds incentives for carrying on one's function and duty, it constitutes a kind of prerequisite for civil liberties."

I am not an expert in economic affairs and do not have to be to draw from this solemn commitment of common sense and conscience a positive statement concerning the necessity of at least a minimum of economic incentive for those who invest their savings in modern enterprise. It is understood that the worker

13. *Ibid.,* p. 273.

has a right to a just reward for his labor. The investor is a worker too, but, rather than consuming all of his earnings, he puts a part of them back in private enterprise, thus providing work for others. The facts concerning the division of income between workers and investors reinforce our moral judgment. Mr. George Moore has given these facts so precisely at this NICB anniversary meeting. The Conference Board has explained clearly the significance of these facts in the foreword of the special chart study for their 50th Anniversary Convocation. As educated men, we have naturally read the "surplus value" theories of Marx and have also read the famous statement of the American Marxist, Deleon, who misinterpreted American government figures and influenced Lenin to repeat the accusation that private capitalists in America steal from the workers 80% of the wealth they produce. We now have the facts, and they completely refute the Marxist calumnies. For we must use the exact term for one of the greatest sins: to calumniate is to rob an innocent person of one of his highest human achievements, his good reputation, by means which consist of falsifying the truth. It is in the spirit of this principle that we solemnly encourage all businessmen to publicize, always faithfully, the facts concerning the division of their income between workers and shareholders.

Dissemination of the facts concerning distribution of income is of great importance to all religious and moral forces of the world in their work of religious social education.

Ninth postulate: The political necessity of subsidiarity of the state to private initiative of individuals and groups. This postulate has long been the central principle of Christian social doctrine. To make it more impressive, it is presented in the section of the Vatican Council document which describes the building up of the international community and stresses that individuals and groups must undertake, as part of their responsibility toward the common good, multiple activities to overcome hunger, illness, and ignorance. It is repeated again as follows:

> The principle of subsidiarity formulated by Pope Pius XI in the encyclical letter "Quadragesimo Anno" reads: "This supremely important principle of social philosophy, one which cannot be set aside or altered, remains firm and unshaken: Just as it is wrong to withdraw from the individual and com-

mit to the community at large what private enterprise and endeavor can accomplish, so it is likewise unjust and a gravely harmful disturbance of right order to turn over to a greater society of higher rank, functions and services which can be performed by lesser bodies on a lower plane. For a social undertaking of any sort, by its very nature, ought to aid the members of the body social, but never to destroy and absorb them." (AAS 23 [1931], p. 203; quoted by Pope John XXIII in encyclical letter 'Mater et Magistra,' AAS 53 [1961], p. 414.)[14]

Tenth postulate: The ultimate option in social life: for God or against God. This tenth and final postulate is best expressed in the central motto of the encyclical published by Pope Pius XI on May 6, 1932, at the trough of the great economic crisis of the thirties. It was the first encyclical addressed not only to church members but to "all men of good will." When social unrest was becoming tragic also in Europe, Pope Pius XI did not limit himself to asking unity in prayers and in churches, but he clearly challenged humanity to make the decisive choice in daily social life. His appeal has become exceptionally timely in our present crisis: " 'PRO DEO AUT CONTRA DEUM'—'For God or Against God.' This is once more the choice upon which hangs the fate of the world. For in every department of life, in customs, arts and sciences, in politics and economics, in the state and in the civic and domestic societies, in the East and in the West, everywhere there is this choice, whose consequences are of vital importance."[15]

It was this text that inspired the vast program of "Pro Deo," International Movement for Democracy Under God.

A charter "For the memory of future generations," contained in an apostolic brief concerning Pro Deo, was officially presented on April 29, 1965, by His Eminence Cardinal Cicognani, who states: "That His Holiness Paul VI has willed to sign the apostolic brief with His own hand is very significant." For this reason, it is necessary that I translate very carefully the central part of the Latin text of this apostolic brief, which is in fact the most precise expression of this final postulate. I can address this as an appeal for implementation to all the responsible leaders here present, for

14. *Ibid.*, p. 300.
15. Encyclical "Caritate Christi compulsi"; AAS XXIV, 1932, p. 184.

they should all pursue, as the Pope asks, "the aim that men of study and men of action from different nations and those of different social and religious backgrounds, who recognize in God the supreme source of authority in public and private life, should join in a common work to establish unity among all those who inhabit the earth . . . and to scatter fertile seeds in the culture of the spirit, in the political, economic and social thinking of peoples who desire to be brought together by the links of brotherhood."

The same apostolic brief establishes that the policy-making body of the International Movement for Democracy Under God shall be interreligious, composed of a majority of laymen of different continents, cultures and religious beliefs, with a minority participation of prelates and religious order members specializing in social studies. The charter ends by stressing that the activities must be practical: "to gather conclusions useful for solving the spiritual problems of our time and correlated problems which concern civic matters."

I am conscious that these ten postulates for the economic-social order in freedom will need further reflection before they can become a guiding influence. But I am already informed through the Pro Deo staff, which follows so carefully the American way of life, that each of these postulates has been fully developed in hundreds of books and addresses of leading Americans. I know particularly that each speaker, called to this meeting to express his deepest convictions, has for years based his actions upon these principles.

I wish to conclude my address with a special appeal for coordinated action to save our Latin-American brethren from totalitarianism. As you all know, the Catholic Church is a great "grass-roots" organization that unites this continent in its deepest, lasting traditions and in its spiritual dynamism. To overcome totalitarianism, the church is convinced of the necessity for an emergency program of economic-social education and persuasion in the light of the postulates I have extracted from Vatican Council documents and Papal Encyclicals.

But now that action has started through our own efforts reaching all priests, sisters and Catholic Action leaders in Latin America, it is my duty to stress again that the socio-economic development of Latin America can now be achieved in time, only if there is also a very special coordinated effort of the American economic-social leaders so well represented here.

We will have, I hope, reached at the end of this meeting a broad and strong consensus of great creative forces. But consensus in society is thought which precedes action. So I conclude my presentation of the postulates, with the challenge so often repeated by Pope Paul VI: "The actions must follow the ideas, the facts must follow the words." You are all men of action; you will all desire to apply common principles to practice. This is, I hope, the decision which will be made at the end of this great gathering. If this decision is clear and productive, then the Convocation Board will go down in history as a turning point in the age-old struggle between slavery and freedom.

XII CAPITALISM— AN AGENDA FOR THE NEXT HALF-CENTURY

CHAIRMAN: W. O. Twaits

· *Introduction by Mr. Twaits*

· *Capitalism, an Agenda for the Next Half-Century,*

The Honorable Paul Martin

THIS CONVOCATION has already presented a comprehensive and penetrating examination of modern capitalism: its social, economic, political, cultural, ethical—in fact, all the aspects.

Now, we come to that challenging and elusive question of the future. "Capitalism—An Agenda for the Next Half-Century" is an intriguing topic, deceptively simple, a peek at the menu for tomorrow. It contains an essential dichotomy, I think; on the one hand it involves the perils of prophecy, and on the other hand the freedom of the crystal ball gazer.

I think there are only two things certain about this. There will be many many changes, probably at a greater pace than those of us who are depression oriented have seen in the evolution of modern capitalism in the last thirty years.

The second thing I'm relatively certain of is that none of us will be available to audit the results fifty years hence, except perhaps possibly by remote control. I don't treat this latter possibility lightly. We should remind ourselves that colonization of outer space is almost a certainty in the forecast period. We can anticipate that the term "departing" this mortal earth may acquire a more physical than spiritual interpretation.

When I couple this prospect with new time-space capsules, the Einsteinian, if I may say so, slowdown of the aging process when you exceed the speed of light, then I am virtually certain that some of our present critics or advocates of contemporary capitalism will not remain silent beyond so-called temporal limits. It's rather a frightening thought, isn't it?

Now no country has benefited more dramatically from twentieth-century capitalism than Canada and I include not just capital dollars, but technical and managerial know-how. Whatever our definition of capitalism, we must never forget that money without know-how is ineffective and self-defeating. No country, I think, has more to gain in the future from a free, intelligent, self-motivating capitalist movement than Canada.

As a country of 20 million people, 85 per cent living within 150 miles of the United States border, we are more exposed to the pressures and to the advantages of the world's largest common market and its most aggressive society, than any other nation in the world.

The exigencies and the severe demands of public life are such that political leaders are subject to the equivalent of a shareholders' meeting every day. It is these circumstances, entirely unpredictable, that prevented The Right Honourable Lester B. Pearson, Prime Minister of Canada, from being with us.

188

I need hardly introduce to you a speaker so well-known internationally as The Honourable Paul Martin, but rather remind you of the many attributes which commend him to an audience of businessmen. He is and was a brilliant scholar, studying on scholarships at the Universities of Toronto, Harvard, Cambridge (that's Cambridge, England) and the Geneva School of International Studies. His background as a Canadian of French descent, completely bilingual, his development of a successful law practice in the city of Windsor (which I note parenthetically is the only Canadian city which has the United States as a northern neighbor) give him a broad understanding of human beings and this has been the real foundation of his career.

It led him to the House of Commons where he has represented his constitutents continually since 1935, no mean feat. In government, his international aptitudes were soon recognized and as early as 1938 he was Canadian representative with the League of Nations. He is, I believe, the only person who has represented his country at the League of Nations, the United Nations General Assembly and the NATO Council.

A Cabinet Minister in 1945, he subsequently spent eleven years in the post of Minister of National Health and Welfare, and since April of 1963 has had the important post of Secretary of State for External Affairs.

Quite obviously he has been a successful statesman. Obviously, too, he has been a highly successful grass-roots politician with an unbroken record of electoral success for over thirty-one years. I might remind you that under the Canadian system, cabinet members must also be elected members of the House of Commons. If I had to compress this introduction (which I haven't), I would say that you're going to hear from a man who successfully negotiates such important and technically difficult treaties as those governing the Columbia River power, and the Automotive Trades Agreements between Canada and the United States. He is also the same man who still finds time to answer personally a dozen or so letters a day from his constituents.

—W. O. Twaits

PRESIDENT
IMPERIAL OIL LIMITED

189

Capitalism—An Agenda for the Next Half-Century

THE HONORABLE

PAUL MARTIN

Minister for External Affairs, Canada

I HAVE BEEN ASKED to speak on, "Capitalism, an Agenda for the Next Half-Century." As a member of a government, one is necessarily preoccupied with the actual decisions of today, but these must be taken in the light of one's conception of the opportunities and problems of tomorrow. I do not want to suggest that my remarks will be predictive—I do not have much confidence that a prophet's chance of honour is greatly improved outside his own country. Nevertheless, in finding the right path through some of the more tangled thickets of our own time, it is good to pause for reflection on the direction in which the broad currents of history are carrying us.

The vastness and complexity of the convocation theme is suggested by the variety of subjects on its agenda and would be confirmed by the contents of any good library. After all, capitalism, in its most general sense, embraces the economic and social system under which we of the Western World have lived and worked to achieve unprecedented material progress over the past century and a half.

It would be impossible for me to cover the whole subject in the short time available. Indeed, you will expect me to speak from the vantage point of one responsible for Canada's foreign policy and active in public life. Even so, my remarks can only be illustrative and will be directed toward three problem areas in the hope of suggesting the kind of challenges our system must meet in the decades ahead. I will consider the roles of government and private enterprise in the future evolution of capitalism, the problem of economic development in the developing countries and the relations between ourselves and the state-trading nations.

In reflecting on these subjects I have been much impressed by the way in which they defy easy analysis in terms of a clear-cut division of responsibilities between government and private enterprise. The lesson of history is beyond dispute: society is in a state of continuous evolution. Whatever the original definition of capitalism, it is now a commonplace that the success of our system depends upon a partnership between all elements in our society.

If there was ever a time when partnership, mutual confidence and a willingness together to examine long-range problems was needed, it is now. It is in the sphere of international relations that this necessity is most urgent.

The reason, of course, is that we find ourselves in an era of technological and social change, and of change in the relations between nations, which can best be described as revolutionary. Capitalism has successfully adapted in the past; without pretending to scientific precision, we might say that the nineteenth century saw the adaptation to new production techniques, while, in this century, we have achieved a better understanding of the role and responsibilities of government in assuring stable economic progress and social justice.

I would suggest that the adaptation we must make in the coming decades, if we are to strengthen the system and get the best from it, is one which takes the international factor particularly into account. You are only too well aware of the economic and technological forces which impel private enterprises to transcend national borders and conduct their activities on an international scale. Paradoxically, the emergence of many new independent nations in Asia, Africa and other parts of the world has produced new tendencies towards political and economic nationalism. The problem of underdevelopment, with its terrible waste of human resources and portentous implications for peace and stability, weighs heavily on the world.

This is also an era in which the experience of governments, both political and economic, has led them to consult and concert to an unprecedented degree, both bilaterally and multilaterally. There are now more points of contact between governments, and between government and business across national borders. We are all faced with a diversity of interests, plans and policies to which we must adjust our own actions.

In this changing environment an intelligent appreciation of the community of interest and responsibility which we share is vital.

In turning more precisely to the problems with which government and private enterprise are likely to be faced in the coming decades, I draw on Canadian experience. You will already have inferred that I attribute progress which has been achieved in our countries largely to the harmonious way in which these two elements in our society have developed their respective and interdependent roles. In our changing world the adaptation of these roles will be an important factor for future consideration.

Let me illustrate. A healthy and vigorous economy is the foundation of a nation's strength and prosperity. It determines the part the nation can play on the international scene, the welfare of its people and the assistance that can be provided to others. The maintenance of a strong economy is thus a major objective of governments and private industry. In the recent past, our goals—one might now speak of them as traditional— have been balanced economic growth, full employment and price stability. We see already the need to redefine and perhaps extend these goals.

The increasing competitiveness of world trade, the demand for yet higher standards of living and welfare, the approach to full employment, the accelerated pace of technological change have all led to a new emphasis on productivity. For example, industry and labor are concerned with different aspects of automation; governments with the problems of upgrading and adapting the skills of the working population.

To cite only one other example of the new situations and challenges with which we shall be faced—what is the proper role of economic planning in a free society? There are already many experiments in planning to draw on—"indicative plans, target plans, prices and income plans." No one would deny the need for planning. It is an essential ingredient of economic activity. But a real consensus has not yet emerged as to the proper and desirable place of the plan in our system, nor of the relationship to it of government and of the business community.

To turn to our experience in Canada, I might mention that it is the stated objective of the government to achieve a balance in our foreign payments within a reasonable period of time. As you know, we have for many years imported substantially more than we export, the difference being offset by foreign investment in our economy. This foreign capital has been welcome since it has made an essential contribution to the more rapid development of Canada than would otherwise have been possible. We look forward to the continuation of this capital flow under appropriate conditions for some time to come but it would be imprudent and improvident to plan on living indefinitely beyond our earning capacity.

Hence the ultimate goal we have set ourselves. We are already engaged in a series of policies designed to promote domestic industrial development and increase productivity, to upgrade the skills of Canadians and to elicit a still greater volume of domestic savings. More will undoubtedly be necessary but the essential point I wish to make is that these measures by the government must be viewed as complementary to the adaptations which the private sector is called upon to make. Industrial development is achieved through the myriad activities of private business under our system; the individuals concerned and the economy as a whole must know how to profit by programs of manpower retraining if they are to be of value. I believe that in the future, even more than in the past, we will need a conscious and coordinated effort by all segments of society if our goals, however they may be defined, are to be achieved.

There are implications in what I have said for the future of Canada-United States relations. You all know of the multiplicity and scope of the trade and financial links between our two countries. You may not be consciously aware of the fact that our trade is now at a level of more than $12 billion a year or that we have averaged a current account deficit with you of more than a billion dollars a year for more than a decade. Nor is it generally appreciated that this deficit more than outweighs our favorable trade balance with the rest of the world.

An approach towards our ultimate objective will in all probability have to involve a reduction in this bilateral deficit. This in turn will entail adjustments in thinking and action on both sides of the border which, I would contend, it is very much in our mutual interest to make as harmoniously as possible. Let me cite but two simple examples: first, we will need to find progressively larger markets for our goods in the United States if we are to earn the wherewithal to continue importing your goods at the present (or higher) levels; at the same time, the Canadian subsidiaries of United States corporations must be encouraged to play their full part in the achievement of Canada's objectives, particularly by developing their export potential though they may have been established in the first place to serve the Canadian market. While it is designed to meet a situation which is in some ways unique, I regard the Canada-United States Automotive Agreement as the kind of imaginative measure we can take for the mutual benefit of both our countries.

This brings me to another important development in the structure and operation of business on which some attention has recently focussed in my own country. In a process which dates back at least to the inter-war period, but has greatly accelerated in recent years, corporations have extended their operations beyond their national boundaries by establishing branches, subsidiaries or other associated companies in foreign countries. The advantages of this process are obvious in an era when large accumulations of financial and technical resources are required to exploit the potentialities of mass production and rapid technological advance. In fact these corporations may be regarded as typical of modern business organization; they are to be found in every corner of the globe where free enterprise is welcome and they are, needless to say, established in relatively large numbers in Canada.

Like many significant developments, this one has created some difficulties in addition to the evident benefits it confers. There must for example be a parent corporation, subject to the laws, policies and public opinion of the country in which it is incorporated. There are likely to be substantial numbers of the citizens of that country in the management of subsidiary companies abroad. There is always the suspicion that the latter are run essentially for the benefit of the parent organization rather than to maximize their own returns.

I do not mean to suggest that the internationaal corporation, as it is known, would deliberately direct its subsidiaries to operate in ways which are contrary to their own interest or that of the host country. It is nevertheless clear that foreign control leaves subsidiaries open to external influences which may not always be consistent with their own best interests or with those of the community in which they operate.

In extreme cases what may be involved is an apparent or genuine conflict of national policy or law. Let me illustrate this by reference to Canada-United States relations which, perhaps because of the advanced state of industrial development on this continent, so often seem to anticipate developments of more general application.

As part of the 1966 program to improve the United States balance of payments, a number of large United States corporations, including many with branches and subsidiaries in Canada, were requested to increase further their contribution to the United States balance of payments by expanding exports, repatriating income and short-term capital to the United States and by seeking to finance their further expansion through funds obtained abroad.

Insofar as the Canadian subsidiaries were concerned, this raised a very real possibility of disruption in the regular patterns of trade, procurement and capital movements which, if they had materialized, would have had an adverse impact on our own balance of payments without, in our opinion, significantly improving the United States situation. More seriously, this development raised fundamental questions concerning the extent to which the operations of these Canadian companies should be subject to policies formulated in foreign countries and, in this instance, by a foreign government.

After careful discussion between our two governments, the

problem was resolved to our mutual satisfaction, the basis of the solution being perhaps most aptly summarized in the communique issued after the meeting last March of the Canada-United States Ministerial Committee on Trade and Economic Affairs which stated that the "United States members reemphasized the view that United States subsidiaries abroad should behave as good citizens of the country where they are located."

Conflicts of national law can, of course, give rise to even more fundamental difficulties. I refer to the case, for example, of a subsidiary company that is inhibited (or perhaps prevented) from undertaking sales, which are permissible under Canadian law, due to the fact that such sales are forbidden to the parent corporation and to United States citizens by United States law. You will know of instances of the extraterritorial effect of laws relating to foreign assets control, antitrust and the sale and distribution of securities, to mention only a few that come to mind. I have made it clear that the extraterritorial application of the law of another country in Canada is unacceptable as a violation of national sovereignty and as inconsistent with national integrity.

Happily incidents of the kind I have cited have usually been quickly resolved on a sensible and pragmatic basis by our two governments. However, there remains the fact that differences of national law and policy can exercise a subtle but effective inhibiting influence on the activities of the subsidiaries of international corporations, and I wonder whether the time is not approaching when we must seek to minimize or eliminate this irritant in relations involving nations and also business.

Certainly, if the present trend towards the development and expansion of the international corporation continues, private business will necessarily become increasingly involved in the reconciliation of interests of the kind I have described. I would add, without comment, that business also seems destined increasingly to have to take account of the views and activities not of one government only (as has been traditional) but of many; and not just of sovereign governments, but of international organizations. Conversely, the activities of an international corporation may be of interest, not merely to one or two governments, but to many.

One of the subjects which must be high on the agenda of any developed country is that of economic assistance for the developing nations. This is a question to which a great deal of study, energy and resources have been devoted since it first commanded our full attention about fifteen years ago. It is one whose essential issues are only too often confused by a surfeit of statistics and a preoccupation with technique. Yet the lessons of our experience in the short period of a decade and a half are surely clear.

The problems of underdevelopment are intractable and will yield only to a sustained and prolonged effort on the part of both the developed and developing nations. Yet their solution is vital if we are to realize the hope for progress toward a world society in which peace and political stability will reign. In this situation we face urgent tasks of expanding the flow of resources to the developing nations and of helping them to meet a greater proportion of their needs through trade.

However, the problems of economic development are too difficult and the impediments to growth too varied to justify the hope that we can find some formula, some combination of assistance and self-help, which will provide an easy and early path to economic maturity for most of the developing nations. Education, population growth, food shortages, lack of trained personnel, social and political problems and the overriding shortage of foreign exchange earnings all enter into this complex situation. It poses a severe test for the optimism, unique to our century, that science and technology, entrepreneurial energy and economic foresight can transform the world.

We do well to consider these matters in the context of a conference in which the trends of a half-century are being reviewed. We do well also to consider the partnership of government and business in the endeavor that faces us.

For our part, it has been against the background of the sense of urgency created by these basic facts that the Canadian Government has expanded its aid program rapidly in the past three years and will continue to move as quickly as circumstances permit towards the levels of aid now internationally recognized as desirable. Our aid program is not, of course, as big as that of the largest developed countries. We do, however, extend aid through a variety of channels to sixty-five of the developing countries in all the major areas where assistance is required. We are engaged both in English- and in French-speaking regions. Our programs include all the major types of aid, from capital projects to pre-investment studies and educational assistance, with which you will be familiar through the activities of your own country.

This extensive experience has made us acutely aware of the difficulties involved in the effective mobilization and use of aid in developing public understanding and support and in bringing to bear on the problems of development all the resources of skill and experience available in our society. I can say, as a member of the government, how important we consider it to encourage the interest of business and other private agencies, not only as sources for private aid funds but as participants in the attack on underdevelopment. As in the United States, we have endeavoured through certain aspects of our aid program to provide an opportunity and stimulus for the business community in this regard.

In my opinion, the opportunity and the responsibility cannot but increase dramatically in the decades ahead. While we cannot afford to be dogmatic about the means to the agreed end, our economic system with its great range of incentive, motivation and technique, has been the fundamental element in our own economic progress. The validity of this experience, and the variety of ways in which our system can be adapted to the needs of the developing nations, can best be conveyed through partnership in which government and private enterprise each makes its appropriate contribution. We can thus bring the developing nations the resources and the knowledge on the basis of which—largely through their own efforts and institutions which correspond to their own traditions—economic growth may be achieved. We can make real their hope and our belief that the most stagnant of economic waters can be made to move and the most barren of regions to flourish.

The tasks ahead may seem superficially to call for an effort by the private sector beyond the traditional response to the profit motive. I would not personally be averse to making this call nor surprised if it were generously heeded. However, trade has always flourished best among the most prosperous nations, and I have no doubt that on any longer calculation the economic progress of the developing nations will yield a handsome return.

Not that this should be a dominant motive in our actions. The issues are immeasurably greater. In addition, economic betterment is now a matter of national pride and policy in most developing countries.

When this is associated with belief in international cooperation of the type set forth in the United Nations charter and trust in the sincerity and efficiency of the developed nations, a positive force is created which has immense implications for the peace and welfare of the world. What, however, may be the reaction to economic stress if hopes of progress under conditions of freedom are long deferred? There are few of us, looking back over the last half century, who can not recall where the collapse of economic and political confidence has led in the past.

If some nations eventually resolve to pursue the goal of economic betterment not by the processes of a liberal internationalism but by rigid authoritarianism, by an embittered regional isolationism or, in the case of smaller countries, through amalgamation brought about by force, then all of us who have hoped for the development of a world community of the new type will have suffered a great defeat.

We are, therefore, on trial. Our ability and willingness to transfer resources in a way likely to stimulate economic growth, our willingness to work out trading relations and adjust our own markets in a way which will permit the developing countries to earn necessary amounts of foreign exchange, and our understanding of national sensitivities will be examined and judged over the coming years. On that judgment much depends.

We can help to create a new climate in international economic relations in which private investment and enterprise will make an increasing contribution (perhaps on new conditions and with new motivations).

Or we can delay, neglecting our own traditions of innovation and adaptation, and so lose opportunities irretrievably.

In this perspective we cannot, in the end, separate precisely what will be the appropriate roles and responsibilities of government and business, nor can we draw too sharp a distinction between foreign aid and the contribution which international trade will be called on to make to economic development.

The United Nations Conference on Trade and Development in 1964 revealed how many far-reaching and difficult questions of fair trade relations had to be faced. We know the developing nations must diversify and expand production and trade; we know this will call for assistance and adjustments on our part—that is on the part of both government and the private sector in our countries.

It is my own belief that the developed nations must be prepared to make adjustments in their economies to facilitate the development of reasonable market opportunities for the goods exported by the developing countries. I do not know what combination of tariff reductions, commodity agreements or compensatory financing might be found most effective, but I am sure that we should accept and encourage some innovations, with their risks, in our changing world. The progress in war and peace in this country and elsewhere in the fifty years during which the National Industrial Conference Board has been in existence has not been achieved by solving easy problems only.

I do not believe that the deeper wells of national character from which the qualities of inventiveness and industry are drawn are running dry.

Turning now to the last of my illustrative topics, trade relations with the communist countries, I might, I suppose, take the simple and straightforward view which was held by many not so long ago that no such trade should occur because our two systems were basically inimical. This has, in fact, never been the view of the Canadian Government and I am encouraged in the policy we have pursued by the significant evolution which is taking place within the communist world. The familiar images which we learned to associate with the communist movement no longer accurately reflect the changing character of international communism. It is, of course, not long since they did so. Under Stalin, the monolithic unity of the bloc was a harsh and inescapable reality and political and economic relations with the West were dominated by the full intensity of the cold war.

What is the nature and significance of the changes which have taken place? With the passing of Stalin and the subsequent emergence in China of a second center of communist power, a pattern of decentralization and diversity has begun to develop in the communist world. Reversing the earlier repudiation of the Yugoslav experiment, the possibility of different roads to communism is now accepted. In eastern Europe, communist regimes have the opportunity, within limits, to pursue policies of national differentiation, particularly in the fields of economic planning and trade. One example is the resumption and increase of trade between the countries of eastern Europe and their former trading partners in the region, marking in some measure the reassertion of natural economic patterns over earlier tendencies to centralized control. There has been an increased, if qualified, recognition of the profit motive. In the case of Yugoslavia we have an astonishing example of the degree to which a state-controlled economy has moved in the direction of the "mixed" economy.

It is too early to say whether these stirrings of change portend anything comparable to the profound changes in traditional capitalism to which I alluded earlier in my remarks. Certainly the process has not yet led to any significant departure from the main lines of communist policy towards the Western world.

Nevertheless, we must ask ourselves how our evolving free societies should take account of these changes, on the assumption that they are not reversed.

The first comment I would make is that the European communist states have made considerable progress in the process of industrialization and economic diversification. It seems to me very much in our interest that this progress should be channeled along constructive lines, and I welcome the opportunities which are presented for developing and expanding trade. This form of contact, profitable in itself, has traditionally provided a means toward greater understanding, particularly when other contacts are limited.

Some communist countries, Yugoslavia and Poland in particular, have in recent years come to play an increasing role in the international trading system. Their interest in greater contact with us must, I believe, be met seriously and constructively for both political and economic reasons. It will, however, pose problems because experience indicates the difficulties of organizing trade between nations with such fundamental differences in economic philosophies.

It would, I think, be premature to try to suggest how, in their own interest and in the interest of the Western world, business and industry might pursue the possibilities which seem to be opening up for greater exchange and contact with the communist states. Let me merely say that insofar as we welcome the growth of pluralism and adaptability in eastern Europe, insofar as new concepts of enterprise may be needed to develop market opportunities and insofar as extensive personal contacts serve our general interest in promoting understanding, businessmen will be in a good position over the next decades to help, through responsible business activity, in reducing the gap between the two types of society.

I have done no more than draw attention to a few general problems which will certainly require a good deal of our attention in the next half century if our system is to respond to the challenges which time and change will bring. I believe that it is not beyond our powers to deal with them effectively. We have certain reserves of economic strength on which to draw. The experience of recent years suggests that we have learnt at least to mitigate the internal economic crises which created severe difficulties in earlier periods. The progress we have achieved testifies to the vitality of our peoples and institutions, private and governmental.

However, we shall not fully develop ourselves, we shall not promote relations between nations on the best and most harmonious basis, without considerable effort and without a willingness on the part of all to take a long view of world prospects. As a smaller nation, Canada is particularly aware of the interdependence of the world economy and of the importance of our economic relations with other countries for our own welfare. This is why we consider it to be particularly important to discuss, to exchange experiences, to foresee and to forestall the effects of changing world conditions.

Some have spoken of the period since the Second World War as a second Industrial Revolution in the economically advanced nations. If we succeed in meeting and solving the problems of which I have given some examples, then historians will, I am sure, speak of another world economic revolution in this and the next century, a revolution of economic progress fundamental to political stability and peace.

This time of change is a time for enterprise. I have always understood this word in its most generous connotations of initiative, effort, confidence and courage. It applies to the contributions made by individuals, to the intelligent application of skill and energy to new commercial undertakings, to the devoted effort of those seeking new levels of welfare and human rights in society and to the search for justice, order and peace by the elected authorities of a nation. I believe that it is found in its richest form under conditions of political freedom and that this, in essence, constitutes our agenda for the next half century.

XIII CAPITALISM AND WORLD MONETARY PROBLEMS

CHAIRMAN: The Honorable Henry H. Fowler

· *Introduction by Secretary Fowler*

· *Capitalism and World Monetary Problems,*

Dr. Karl Blessing

IT IS A PLEASURE for me to escape from the Ways and Means Committee this afternoon to be here in a somewhat dual capacity, having undertaken initially the privilege and honor of introducing the main speaker for this occasion, but now, as a result of intervening developments of the last ten days to two weeks, being pressed into service as an additional speaker on the program.

I shall not be talking about the future, but very much the present. I shall not stray over into the more interesting and romantic territory of international affairs, which is the province of the guest speaker, Dr. Blessing, but will keep more on the domestic level.

I am very pleased to be with you on this very auspicious occasion —the fiftieth anniversary of this distinguished organization. In my position as Secretary of the Treasury I am often reminded of the many and profound contributions the National Industrial Conference Board has made to our understanding, and how important that is, of how a free economy works and how it should work. Much that is embodied in public policy today is the result of your fifty years of patient research and illuminating reports and exchanges. If I were asked to summarize this work in a line, I would say, from my own experience and observation, and I think perhaps you wouldn't disagree with me, that the board has been engaged in exploring the potentials of a partnership for economic well-being between the government and the business community of a free nation that wants to remain free.

I believe the idea that free people can collaborate with their government to get the most out of their economy is one of the most important—and, nowadays, one of the fastest spreading—political economic concepts in the world.

Our public-private partnership has been of unparalleled benefit to our own country and its people, as demonstrated by the studies made for this particular occasion. I hope that before this fiftieth anniversary meeting closes, there will be a resolve to carry forward this work at least another fifty years, for I can see no time in the future when the contributions to knowledge such as have been made will not be needed at least as greatly as they have in the past.

I am glad to note that this meeting is dedicated to the future. I hope that my remarks, which deal with the newly announced program by the President on September 8, will throw a contemporary sidelight of some value on the theme, "The Future of Capitalism."

It is my view—and your work indicates that it is also your view— that the future of capitalism is a future of responsible economic behavior by government, by the public, by labor, by farmers, and, as the very existence of the NICB suggests, by the business community, great and small.

The President's anti-inflation program is nothing more and nothing less than a call to a new level of responsible economic behavior by all segments of the American economy. It is a program for maintaining and continuing the unprecedented economic gains we have made during the long climb over the past six years out of something that borders on economic stagnation.

It is a program for maintaining and extending these gains by preserving the balance between our various demands for goods and services and our capacity to satisfy rising demands, a balance that has been the unique, and the uniquely beneficial, aspect of our economic growth over the past six years.

The economy has now come under special strains that threaten that balance. These strains arise largely, although not exclusively, from two sources: exuberant capital expansion by business and demands arising from our defense of freedom in Vietnam. I do not think that any of you here today, faced with this problem, would choose to curtail the defense of freedom in order to let business plant and equipment expansion go unchecked, nor did the President. He asked the Congress to suspend temporarily special tax incentives to business investment during the next sixteen months.

Nor did the President stop there. He committed himself and the administration to a strong program to reduce lower priority federal programs, including an estimated cut of 10%—or approximately $3 billion, depending upon Congressional action on remaining appropriation bills—in that limited portion of the budget which is under and subject to direct Presidential control.

The President's program also pointed the way toward balance in another aspect of the economic policy—the application of fiscal and monetary measures in balance, whether in seeking stimulus or in seeking restraint. In this connection, he called upon the Federal Reserve Board in executing its policy of monetary restraint, and our large commerical banks, to cooperate with the President and the Congress to lower interest rates and to ease the inequitable burden of tight money. He called upon the whole economy, and all those responsible for it, for measures of restraint.

Now, this program which I want to just summarize briefly today is designed to do four things, at least:

1. To contribute to a restraint of inflationary developments that are proving disruptive of the financial markets and placing excessive strain upon one key segment of our economy, the capital goods industries.

2. To promote a more sustainable rate of balanced economic growth in the next sixteen months and thereafter.

3. To suspend special fiscal stimulants to investment, and thereby support and complement a policy of monetary restraint without incurring the burdens and without running the risks of excessively tight money and high interest rates.

4. To complement the other measures enacted by the Congress or pending before it and being undertaken through administrative action to reduce upward pressures on interest rates and minimize the discriminatory impact of tight money and high interest rates on the housing sector of the economy.

Now, the strains on the economy show up in three clearly discernible ways—in the money and financial markets, excessive demands for credit and monetary restraint interacting together have created severe tightness and a very sharp rise in interest rates, with highly selective impact on several sectors, particularly single family housing.

The second area is in the market for capital goods. The ever-mounting flow of new orders by business firms, coming on top of an unprecedented rate of outlays for plant and equipment, is generating rising prices, rising wage rates and shortages of some skilled labor, and is augmenting the large demands for capital from banks and the securities market.

The third force is the rising rate of government expenditures, federal, state and local, highlighted by the steadily expanding defense and public works outlays, which are adding steadily to aggregate demand at a high rate.

Now, these three sources of pressure are interrelated and reinforcing. Accelerating business spending breeds demands for credit from banks and for financing in the capital market. Higher government spending also generates credit demands, by the government itself, and by private firms which receive government orders and work on borrowed funds to fill new contracts. And tight money itself causes additional government spending, particularly to help finance areas of important economic activity such as homebuilding, from which the supply of private capital has been diverted.

The program contained in the President's message is designed to deal with these three pressure points. The program is primarily economic and financial in its objective and thrust. It represents the most carefully chosen and prudent means consistent with preserving stable economic growth within the framework of a free economy to ease the strain of the pressures described.

Let me emphasize that the President's proposal to suspend the investment tax credit and accelerated depreciation for buildings for the next sixteen months is not a tax reform proposal. It is temporary in its design and purpose.

Let me emphasize also that it is not primarily a revenue-raising measure in its purpose and in its objective. The revenue aspects are only incidental. This proposal and the entire program announced on September 8 is basically an anti-inflationary action designed to relieve the pressures, clearly observable in the money markets and capital goods sector, which have produced the highest interest rates in forty years, and a perceptible trend towards a general condition of economic instability.

Let me relate the tax aspects to the balance of the President's program. The proposed suspension of special incentives to undertake major programs of business investment should relieve to some extent the credit market by moderating business needs for funds. To what degree is unpredictable. The President directed me to review all federal security sales and present them to the President for approval with the objective of lessening and reducing the magnitude of these sales and the burden of federal finance on the markets. The memorandum to all federal departments and agencies of September 9, calling for careful pruning of federal lending and borrowing activities, should reduce aggregate federal credit demands on the private market.

It has already been decided to cancel the sale of the Federal National Mortgage Association participation certificates tentatively scheduled for September, and to have no FNMA participation sale in the market for the rest of 1966 unless market conditions improve, nor will there be any Export-Import Bank sale of participation certificates in the market in the rest of this calendar year. Market sales of federal agency securities, meanwhile, will be limited in the aggregate to an amount required to replace or roll over maturing issues, while new money, to the extent genuinely needed, will be raised by sales of agency securities to the government investment accounts.

Another important ingredient in the President's program is the legislation passed last week and signed by him this morning and implemented by the regulatory agencies in the course of the late morning, to give the bank regulatory agencies and the Federal Home Loan Bank flexible authority to halt and hopefully reverse the harmful process of excessive interest rate escalation in the field of consumer savings.

The announced program for reducing federal expenditures for fiscal 1967 is yet another and key related measure to minimize the drain of federal financing on the credit market in addition to reducing aggregate demand in the economy. The President has made clear his firm determination to hold down all lower priority expenditures by means of deferrals, stretching out the pace of spending and otherwise reducing contracts, new orders and commitments—a policy and program with which I have been actively and affirmatively concerned from the initial preparation of the January budget.

Of course, any precise description of the amount and nature of the spending cuts must await action by the Congress on the eight major appropriation bills still pending before it. When Congress gives us the bills, we will try to do the job of expenditure control on the remaining segments of the budget.

Let me stress that all along we have been exercising a more vigorous control of federal expenditures than is generally realized.

In the fiscal years 1965 and 1966, and as proposed by the President in 1967, federal budget expenditures—*including in the latter years, large amounts for Vietnam*—were respectively, 14.8%, 15.0% and 14.7% of our Gross National Product. With the exception of 1958 and 1951 fiscal years, these are the lowest percentages since 1942—a period spanning 25 years, five presidents and a large growth in the responsibilities of the federal government.

When President Johnson took office, the budget under which he was operating, that for fiscal year 1964, called for $98.8 billion of expenditures. Three years later, exclusive of the special costs of Vietnam which had arisen, his budget called for expenditures of $102.3 billion —an average increase of slightly over $1 billion per year. And this increase in the total of federal outlays is much smaller than the added costs over this period of federal pay raises and increased interest expense on the public debt alone. And I might say that at an average increase of $1 billion a year it compares quite favorably with an average rate of increase of $3 billion per year in the ten years preceding fiscal 1964.

In each of the fiscal years 1965 and 1966, the federal deficit was lower than the prior year. The deficit in the administrative budget in fiscal 1965 was $4.8 billion lower than the year before, and $8.5 billion below the 1964 estimate prevailing when the President took office. In 1966, the fiscal year just concluded on June 30, despite the added expenses of Vietnam, amounting to $5.8 billion, the deficit was cut another $1.1 billion below that of 1965, bringing it down to a $2.3 billion total. In fact, on a national income and product account budget basis, favored by many economists as the true measure of the stimulus or restraint of federal activities, the 1966 budget was in a surplus of about $1 billion.

The President announced on September 8 that he had directed federal agencies to defer, stretch out, and otherwise reduce contracts, new orders, and commitments by $1.5 billion in this fiscal year. The total amount of the reductions which will ultimately be required must, as I have said, await Congressional action on the remaining authorization and appropriation bills. But, as I indicated earlier, given our best estimates of likely possibilities, we believe a total of at least $3 billion below the final appropriations figures will be called for, and we are prepared to make such reductions.

Since his program was announced, the President has begun the implementation of his promise to seek additional economies in government by issuing to the various departments and agencies a new six-point economy program. For example, he has ordered a 25% cut in federal overtime pay.

Now, I will turn to the part of the President's anti-inflation program that calls for temporary suspension of the 7 per cent investment tax credit for machinery and equipment and a suspension of the option to elect accelerated depreciation on buildings, for the period September 1, 1966 through December 31, 1967.

As everyone here is probably well aware, I have been a very strong exponent of the investment credit, having worked strenuously to secure its original enactment in the Revenue Act of 1962, together with the administrative liberalization of depreciation which took place in the summer of that year.

Our experience to date has justified the faith I had in 1962 in the efficacy of the investment credit, and my belief that it should be a permanent part of our tax structure. Since then industrial production has increased three times as fast as in the previous decade, real business fixed investment has increased nearly four times as fast, and our economic growth generally has far surpassed its previous rate. This remarkable achievement is not due solely to the investment credit, but I firmly believe the investment credit has contributed substantially to it. Moreover, looking to the long-term future, I am convinced that the encouragement provided to business by the credit to modernize and expand its use of capital equipment is essential to maintaining full employment with stable prices, and to keep our industry competitive with foreign goods. The President and his administration fully share these views.

It is therefore, as I am sure you understand, only with very considerable reluctance and after very careful study that we reached the conclusion that suspension of the investment credit was an appropriate measure at this time. I stress suspension—and not repeal—since the credit should be regarded, as the President's message indicated, as an essential and enduring part of our tax structure.

Not only do I regard the investment credit as a permanent structural component of our tax system, but also one that should be suspended only in times of active hostilities at least on a scale such as characterizes the present situation. Even in such circumstances I would, as I have in the past made clear, be chary of suspending the investment credit unless the combination of a rapidly expanding civilian economy and increasing and special defense demands made this course compelling. I am opposed to treating the investment credit as a counter-cyclical device, to be suspended and restored with the normal ups and downs of the economy.

The present situation is unique and was quite unforeseeable when the credit was adopted and stress was put—and properly so—on its permanent character. We then contemplated a peacetime economy and thoughts of a country engaged in hostilities on the present scale were far from our minds. But hostilities can cut ruthlessly across many plans and procedures designed to meet problems of a country at peace, as of course our experiences during the time of Korea, and prior to that, have made us so keenly aware. We are deeply committed to an extensive military operation in Southeast Asia which shows no signs of early termination. Its effects on our economy are clearly evident. We are also confronted with a monetary situation of almost unparalleled tightness, which is producing distortions in our economy and the highest levels of interest rates in more than 40 years.

Early in the year when the question of suspending investment credit was raised in the Senate, in connection with the Tax Adjustment Act just passed in March, we hoped this change in the law could be avoided. In March, the President invited to the White House more than 100 chief executives of companies which, together, are responsible for making a large portion of business plant and equipment outlays. At that dinner, the President made a strong personal appeal to those present to carefully review their investment plans with the objective of screening out and setting aside for deferral whatever projects and expenditures they possibly could. Many of the executives did just that and wrote letters to the President confirming their plans to moderate their investment outlays.

Nevertheless, the level of investment in both plant and equipment has remained too high under present circumstances and it is taking place despite sharp increases in interest rates paid by corporate borrowers which some thought would restrict capital expenditures. Undoubtedly, the increase would have been larger without the influence of the President's appeal for restraint and the cooperation of those that did respond. This made clear the need for temporary suspension of special investment incentives, accelerated depreciation as well as the investment credit.

It would be dangerous to let the economy proceed on its present course without a release from these pressures that the suspension will help accomplish, along with and as a part of the remainder of the program set forth.

The unforeseeable escalation of Vietnam in mid-1965 gave a strong upward thrust to the demand on our resources. In response, the policy of the Administration has been to take fiscal steps designed to meet conditions as they unfolded. This was exemplified in the Tax Adjustment Act of 1966 which applied the degree of restraint that conditions and prospects at that time required. Similarly, we are now proposing another appropriate step responsive to prevailing conditions. In view of the uncertainties with which we are still confronted, we cannot offer blueprints for future programs. The only prudent course is to maintain a flexible, step-by-step approach which will maintain the stable growth and prosperity of the last five and one-half years, and in the President's words, "pay for current expenditures out of current revenues, as we are now doing."

* * *

It is my pleasure to turn to the main occasion for this meeting, and to introduce Dr. Karl Blessing, President of the Deutsche Bank of the German Federal Bank.

I cannot recommend too strongly that you follow his remarks with the utmost attention, for he comes remarkably well-equipped by experience and natural endowment to speak to you with wisdom on the very important subject that he has chosen, "Capitalism and World Monetary Problems." I know from my own meetings with Dr. Blessing that he is a worthy negotiator, strong in support of his views, and strongly inclined to a view of the world that is creative, receptive, and at the same time practical.

This attitude, I believe, flows from a background that combines extensive public service with long experience in the world of business.

Dr. Blessing entered the banking profession in 1920 in the Reich Bank in Berlin, and for the next twenty years had many varied and important assignments from the German Central Bank. He subsequently became associated with the great international trading concern Uni-Lever, where he rose to high office in private business as he had previously in official banking.

Dr. Blessing became President of the German Federal Bank in 1958. Since then, he has been influential in the development of German and European thinking and policy in the field of monetary policy and international finance, and has also had a very great effect in the exchanges we've been fortunate to have with him on the course of our own thinking in this area.

He has gained a reputation to be envied as a banker, always to be found in the forefront of new, cooperative ventures aimed at strengthening the international monetary system without ever sacrificing any part of his own renown as a prudent man, a man as firm as he is friendly in councils for sound economic procedure in his own country and among the nations. These are councils that I know well, for Dr. Blessing and I are associated in negotiations among the Group of Ten, the ten principal industrial nations, which negotiations are aimed at finding agreement and charting a path to substantial improvement in international monetary arrangements, including new means for supplying reserves.

I look forward, as I know you do, to his expositions of this enormously difficult, but at the same time, tremendously important subject and hearing his suggestions for dealing with it. I am very proud to call Dr. Blessing my friend. I have never found my confidence in him as a friend disappointed. I am privileged to have the honor of introducing him to you as a man of strength, courage and friendliness, and as an advocate of that old school of sound conservatism, and at the same time the school of the liberal world trader.

—Henry Fowler

U.S. SECRETARY OF THE TREASURY

Capitalism and World Monetary Problems

KARL BLESSING

President, Deutsche Bundesbank

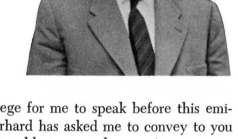

I
T IS A SINGULAR privilege for me to speak before this eminent gathering. Professor Erhard has asked me to convey to you his regret at not having been able to come here owing to pressing matters of state.

Allow me to begin with a personal observation. The Spanish author, Professor de Madariaga, once said, when embarking upon a speech he had to deliver in English: "My relation with the beautiful English language is exactly the same as my relation with my wife. I know her and I love her, but I have no control over her." I am in a similar position, so that I must request your indulgence.

The subject "Capitalism and World Monetary Problems" has a special attraction because it permits the monetary problems of our times to be viewed in a wider perspective.

I should like to define the term "capitalism," which in some European quarters has an unpleasant flavour, as an economic order founded wholly or preponderantly upon free property, free competition and free enterprise—in other words, an economic order in which the forces of the free market are the foremost element, government intervention being duly limited. Such a "free market economy," as we call it, is superior to any other economic order, but it can only be maintained as long as the national and international monetary system functions satisfactorily. Capitalism and sound money are twins. To prove this close connection I should like to quote, not an exponent of free market economy, but a prophet of the communist doctrine, none other than Lenin. He once said that a particularly effective means of destroying capitalism was to destroy its monetary system.

In spite of this communist thesis it is unfortunately not a matter of course in the free world that a liberal economic order and a sound monetary system are conditional upon one another. The protagonists of monetary stability, who naturally include in the first place the central banks, frequently face the reproach that they maintain this view as an end in itself and that they defend an anachronism. We encounter such criticism both on the part of the private groups in search of abundant cheap money for their expansion and on the part of the academic quarters seeking to use monetary policy for the purpose of obtaining maximum growth, even at the price of creeping inflation. In international monetary relations, too, some quarters hold that it is simply reactionary to call for greater monetary discipline in order to eliminate sustained balance of payments disequilibria. Even among governments of the industrial countries there is no complete agreement on the improvement of the international monetary system and on the future supply of additional monetary reserves for the world. By contrast, I should like to make the point that the liberal economic order we have today can be maintained only at the price of keeping discipline in national and international monetary policy.

It is not amiss to recall some historical experiences. During the first half of this century we have witnessed several collapses of the international monetary system. The first one, which occurred during and after the First World War, marked the end of a bygone era of the capitalistic system. This collapse had consequences not only in the economic but also in the political and the social sphere. During the 1920s ineffective attempts were made to restore the previous world economic order and the gold currency system. Thereupon in the early 1930s we experienced the second collapse, which turned out to have even more disastrous consequences than the first one. The "sauve-qui-peut" attitude, which people adopted to mitigate the consequences of the world crisis for themselves, resulted in world-wide disintegration; in a sharp decline in international goods and capital transactions; in rivalry among currency blocs; in flexible exchange rates in the sense of a "beggar-my-neighbor" policy and in restrictive practices of every kind, culminating in wholesale foreign exchange control; in bilateralism and autarchy.

The disastrous social and political consequences of the great crisis—in particular mass unemployment—are unforgotten to this very day. We in Germany had our own particularly grim experiences; had there been no world crisis, there would probably have been no Hitler and no Second World War. The economic and monetary disorder persisted more or less up to the Second World War, which intensified its virulence. Not until the end of that war did one begin to conceive a new order on a liberal and multilateral basis, an order which found expression in the International Monetary Fund and in G.A.T.T. Marshall aid and O.E.E.C. subsequently led to rapid and gratifying success and finally brought about convertibility of the principal currencies. The Federal Republic of Germany was among the first after the war to subscribe to the principles of a free market economy and a hard currency and to direct its policies systematically towards this target.

Whether capitalism would be capable of once again surviving a collapse of the international monetary order is doubtful. Presumably another collapse would submerge us in dirigism or even collectivism. In saying this, I am far from identifying myself with the scaremongers and alarmists who deem such a collapse to be imminent and inevitable. On the contrary, by uttering this warning I wish to make sure that the monetary problems are no longer regarded as isolated phenomena and that the potential dangers are clearly recognized. To recognize the dangers is a prerequisite to overcoming them. The international monetary system has during the past 15 years induced an expansion of world trade and a level of general prosperity never before witnessed. We cannot expect the system without further action on our part to solve in a similarly satisfactory manner the tasks which will face us during the coming fifteen or twenty years.

The dangers threatening our monetary system as it stands today are partly of a national, partly of an international character. I shall begin with the national ones—all the more so since it is a truism that international monetary problems begin at home.

We know of very few cases in which balance of payments deficits and the resultant disturbances of international equilibrium cannot be traced back to excessive domestic demand. In other words, certain countries are living beyond their means, or have done so. I do not propose once again to raise the old issue as to whether the responsibility for a disequilibrium should more often be laid at the door of the deficit countries or of the surplus countries. Postwar experiences with persistent creeping inflation, however, permit the assumption that the propensity to live beyond one's means is rather more common than the opposite. This can take the form of consuming beyond one's means and also of investing beyond one's means—in fact, one can even invest abroad beyond one's means. Overspending can take place in the private sector as easily as in the public sector. Unless the authorities succeed in bringing the situation rapidly under control, costs and prices will rise and competitiveness in world trade will decline, whereupon the balance of payments will become more and more adverse and can only with great difficulty be returned to normal.

In this respect almost all countries have suffered bitter experiences. Let me briefly characterize a few aspects responsible for excessive demand.

1. The fact that today a far greater portion of national income than formerly passes through government hands means that everything which is done or left undone in the public sector exercises an immediate influence on the business cycle and on monetary stability. In the era of mass democracy and of organized group interests, of the progressively expanding welfare state and of economic growth worshipped as a fetish, the risk that the fiscal authorities misuse their power is extremely great. Certainly it would be illusory to believe that the process which brought about the expansion of the public financial sector could be reversed in any appreciable measure. But to direct this process in future into a more orderly course is definitely a thing which is both possible and imperative. It is therefore an urgent postulate that politicians and parliaments should learn better than hitherto to adjust financial policies to the requirements of the business cycle. I know very well how difficult it is to turn fiscal policy into a modern instrument for

monetary stabilization, all the more so in a federatively organized country such as mine in which a multitude of competences emphasize the handicap of every fiscal policy, namely its lack of flexibility. But to capitulate in the face of these difficulties might be fatal. In Germany we are at the moment in the midst of legislative efforts to set up at least the basic elements for a stability-oriented budget policy. A particularly dangerous factor is what we in Germany call "Gefälligkeits-demokratie" which might be translated as "democracy to please everybody." Election favors accorded to certain groups have a demoralizing effect. Such favors frequently set in motion an inflationary spiral which it may be very hard or impossible to reverse, and, besides, it means underestimating the intelligence of the voter, who will certainly realise what is going on.

2. The power to make inflation is however by no means limited to public authorities only. It is unfortunately also exercised in the private sphere and is particularly apparent in the abuse of autonomy in collective wage agreements by trade unions and employers' associations. The solution of this problem may confront the free market economy with its possibly hardest test. I do not belong to those who look upon free bargaining about wages and the existence of a free market economy to be incompatible with one another, but I do believe that here again, the responsibility of the parties concerned is not yet recognized with sufficient clarity. The experiments conducted by governments in the field of what is known as incomes policy are still in the very early stages. In any event, endeavors to counteract the danger of a cost inflation by "guide lines" should not be ridiculed or cynically belittled. If it were possible to evolve out of these endeavors a sort of "contrat social" under which all parties concerned would undertake to contain their demands on the social product within the limits drawn by internal and external equilibrium, this would, in the interest of economic growth, be preferable to drastic monetary or fiscal measures, such as would otherwise undoubtedly be necessary for the enforcement of equilibrium. So far, however, we have not reached this point; all endeavors in the direction of incomes policy—and this is proved by the latest experiences in

Germany, Great Britain and the United States—are bound to
fail unless it is possible to strike at the root of excessive demand.

3. The central banks by themselves are not in a position to make
up for mistakes and omissions in the field of fiscal and incomes policy. Those who base their confidence in the future
of the market economy solely on monetary policy merely skirt
the issue. No matter how great their sense of responsibility, the
central banks cannot play their part properly without a sound
"policy mix," that is to say, jointly with fiscal and incomes policies aiming at stability. Of course central banks can regulate
demand by keeping the money supply short and by exercising
a drastic influence on bank liquidity and short- and long-term
interest rates, provided no disturbing influences emanate from
foreign countries. If, however, monetary policy is overburdened, disruptions and losses in growth may ensue. The more
assistance therefore the central banks receive from other quarters, the less severely will they have to act on their own to
allow economic development to take the course of sound expansion without excessive fluctuations.

But even if all countries pursue a policy of stability to the best
of their ability, there will in practice always be certain disturbances of international equilibrium, induced by seasonal, cyclical
or structural factors. There is nothing to be said against this as
long as no major, and especially no persistent, deficits or surpluses occur. If these deficits or surpluses, however, are large and
sustained, they are apt to endanger the international monetary
system. This is why they must be counteracted by appropriate
adjustment processes. To my mind, however, it would not make
sense, and would even be detrimental to the free market economy, if in this adjustment process the way of least resistance were
followed, i.e., if the countries that do not indulge in inflation were
forced to conform by continuous price and cost increases to those
who take monetary discipline rather less seriously.

After all, this kind of adjustment process would mean marching in step into inflation, and this could easily turn into marching
in step into the abyss, as Lenin predicted it. During the past few
years attempts have been made to solve the problem by interna-

tional coordination and confrontation of the economic and monetary policies of the major countries, and by multilateral surveillance. The progress made, in this field especially with regard to deficit and surplus financing, is encouraging. These efforts should be continued and intensified with the aim of reducing payments disequilibria; in particular the proposed establishment of an "early warning system" seems to me to merit all the support it can get. The improvement of the adjustment process, and a national economic and monetary policy that nips in the bud major payments disequilibria or prevents existing deficits from continuing, are exactly what is required. To this end, however, it will be necessary not only for the national experts but also for national politicians to become aware of the meaning of multilateral surveillance; in fact, it is generally necessary that squaring of the balance of payments behavior. Let us be quite clear in our minds economic objectives. Freedom from the shackles of the old gold standard must not be considered as a license to indulge in lax balance of payments behaviour. Let us be quite clear in our minds that in the long run one of two things must become more elastic: either the adjustment process or the exchange rate. All those who, like myself, are opposed to flexible exchange rates should therefore emphatically support the efforts now being made in Working Group 3 of O.E.C.D. to improve the adjustment process.

As a result of the large and persistent payments disequilibria and of the insufficient adjustment process, conditions have emerged in the international monetary system that give rise to concern. The monetary system existing today is the gold exchange standard, under which the official monetary reserves are held partly in gold and partly in dollars. The long-standing payments deficit of the United States in particular, which has persisted, with a single interruption in 1957, from 1950, has produced a situation calling for reform. The short-term liabilities of the United States at the end of May 1966 amounted to $24.5 billion, of which $13.9 billion are held by foreign monetary authorities. American gold holdings have fallen from their peak of $24.6 billion at the end of 1949 to $13.5 billion at the end of June 1966. Neither can the United States go on increasing its short-term liabilities to foreign countries substantially, and permit its gold stock to decrease heavily, nor are the other countries prepared to continue building up their dollar balances in the same measure as hitherto. The figures for the past year show that the United States was obliged to cover its deficit in 1965 of $1.3 billion fully by gold.

The postwar trend which at first led to a desirable replenishment of the monetary reserves of the world, subsequently however gradually bringing on an overabundance of dollars, cannot be repeated in the period to come; nor can it be denied that there is a risk of some portion of the existing dollar balances getting into the hands of central banks making it a practice to convert them into gold. The other reserve currency, sterling, is in an even more difficult position than the dollar.

The Group of Ten was quite right when in its latest study it subscribed to the view that the most important means of maintaining confidence in the reserve currencies and strengthening the monetary system is the restoration of equilibrium in the balances of payments of the reserve countries. There is indeed no alternative to this if we want to avoid grave consequences for the international monetary order and the capitalistic system. If no additional fresh dollars or pounds sterling were to be generated and fed into the international system, the danger of a sudden drastic shrinkage of existing exchange holdings with its possible deflationary consequences would doubtless be considerably less, although even then this danger would not be altogether eliminated. That is why I regret that the Group of Ten has not seen its way to endorse the German and Italian proposals of step-by-step harmonization of the ratio between gold and foreign exchange in the monetary reserves of the major countries. Fortunately, international cooperation and consultation have nowadays, compared with the anarchy during the period between the two wars, been greatly developed. Thus they can be expected to forestall dangerous disturbances that might result from a sudden conversion of exchange reserves into other reserve media, particularly into gold. Nevertheless we shall do well to bear in mind the susceptibility of the present monetary system and to keep the fire brigade which we possess today in the form of the International Monetary Fund and international cooperation ready for action. As long as the present situation continues, speculative money movements and gold hoarding tendencies may however occasionally emerge.

What also needs to be reformed is the present system of reserve creation, especially once the American payments deficit will have been eliminated. More than two thirds of the increase in monetary reserves during the past six years were contributed by the U.S. balance of payments deficit. This kind of reserve creation is both arbitrary and uneconomical; neither do the U.S. payments deficits coincide with the actual reserve needs of the world, nor can the system, for reasons that I mentioned before, be maintained for very long. The U.S. Dollar cannot in future remain the sole source supplying the world with monetary reserves; the burden must be shared by other strong currencies. Gold alone is not sufficient to supply the world with reserves. During the past few years gold contributed no more than about 600 million dollars to the monetary reserves, which is less than 1 per cent annually. An increase in the gold price, which has many advocates, cannot be envisaged as a solution to this problem, because initially it would swamp the world with inflationary liquidity, while later on it might prove to be insufficient and have to be repeated. Consequently, there is hardly anything left but to evolve some other reserve medium to supplement gold. How such a reserve medium should be conceived is a question that is now being pondered by the International Monetary Fund and the Group of Ten.

All the countries of the Group of Ten are agreed that the present world supply of international liquidity is sufficient, and that no new reserves need be created as long as high American balance of payments deficits serve as a source of reserves for the rest of the world. Except for France, however, they are of the opinion that it would be useful already now to enter upon some contingency planning. This means that a distinction must be made between preparing a contingency plan and actually creating additional reserves. There are people who feel that the mere existence of machinery for the creation of additional liquidity will always entail the temptation to put it into operation, without regard to risks of inflation. In order to allay such fears, safety measures against premature or improper use must be taken.

An important question in this connection is who is to make

decisions on a new reserve medium and in what way. An important clarification on this point has already been achieved in the Group of Ten. When making future decisions, the following two points are to be observed: first, the interest of all countries in a smooth functioning of the international monetary system, and, second, the responsibility of a limited group of major countries who in practice would have to provide a substantial part of the financial backing for any new reserve asset. I think it is fitting to point out that the new reserve media, whatever shape they may take, must not dislodge the dollar from its present position; the dollar holdings in the official monetary reserves should be maintained at approximately their present volume.

The intention clearly expressed by the Group of Ten to the effect that this problem, should it call for action, must not be solved by means of an increase of the gold price but by creating new reserve assets, is designed to dishearten those who believe that hoarding gold might become a profitable venture.

I have tried to outline the national and international problems that appear to me to play a major role for the maintenance of a sound monetary system. In conclusion, let me repeat: No monetary system, however ingenious its technical design, can function satisfactorily unless monetary discipline obtains in the leading countries. If we do not succeed in reaching a greater measure of equilibrium in the balances of payments and improving the adjustment process, all reformatory efforts will be of little use. The essential thing is willingness to accept the restraint a sound monetary system calls for, and not so much the emphasis on monetary techniques. Let us be quite clear about one thing: a liberal economic system cannot exist, either nationally or internationally, unless it is based on a sound monetary order. Sound monetary conditions, however, must be fought for day after day. To quote Goethe: "He only merits liberty and life who daily has to strive for them anew."

XIV THE OUTLOOK FOR FREEDOM

CHAIRMAN: Roger M. Blough

· *Introduction by Mr. Blough*

· *The Outlook for Freedom, The Honorable*

Dean Rusk

· *Recapitulation by Mr. Blough*

Our DISTINGUISHED SPEAKER has served the United States as Secretary of State longer, I believe, than the incumbent foreign secretaries of state of any other principal free nation he deals with.

He has dealt with an imposing and changing array of the representatives of foreign governments amounting to hundreds. He has lived through over fifty coups d'état. In these trying days, this itself is a notable accomplishment. I would say that he could be described as possessing an almost elemental patriotism, for the nature of his work demands an immeasurable dedication to duty.

It is only rarely that one can detect a thrust in a direction in a man's career which seems to indicate his education and training were aimed specifically for preparing him for his present responsibilities, but that is the case tonight.

Born on a tenant farm in Georgia, the son of a Presbyterian minister, Dean Rusk supported himself at Davidson College by working at a bank and waiting on tables, yet he somehow found the time and energy to play center on the basketball team, win a Phi Beta Kappa key, and a scholarship. He was graduated magna cum laude with a major in political science.

At Oxford, Secretary Rusk studied philosophy, politics and economics, earning both a bachelor's and a master's degree, and an essay he wrote on international relations won the Cecil Peace Prize. After teaching at Mills College in Oakland, California, he was named dean of the faculty there in 1938. At the same time, he studied law at the University of California. During World War II, he served as an infantry officer in the China-Burma-India theater of operations.

In 1943 he was appointed Deputy Chief of Staff for the Burma theater. He was even then becoming an old China hand. Except for eight years as president of the Rockefeller Foundation, Mr. Rusk has devoted his time fully since World War II to our government's international problems.

In 1946 he joined the Department of State as Assistant Chief of the Division of International Security Affairs. Then for nearly a year he served in the War Department as Special Assistant to the Secretary of War. In 1947 he was named director of the Office of Special Political Affairs for the Department of State where he was preoccupied with problems related to the establishment of the State of Israel. Later he was appointed Assistant Secretary of State for Far Eastern Affairs. He served in the State Department during the Communist takeover of Mainland China and during the Korean War.

He also served as an advisor to John Foster Dulles on the Japanese Peace Treaty, so it is fair to say Secretary Rusk knows a little about the Orient. He has been an outstanding Secretary of State since 1961. President Johnson properly said of him, "He is one of the most able and most competent and most dedicated men I have ever known."

A young college student recently said she had great confidence in Dean Rusk because, in her language, he never loses his cool. Having completed a major reorganization in his department, as announced by President Johnson, he brings to this audience an informed, perceptive and persuasive mind and personality.

—Roger M. Blough

The Outlook for Freedom

THE HONORABLE DEAN RUSK

U.S. Secretary of State

I T IS A VERY great privilege, indeed, for me to spend this dinner with those who Mr. Khrushchev would have called the ruling circles of the United States.

I think I should say of those fifty coups d'état that you mentioned, Mr. Blough, that I'm sorry that I had nothing to do with any of them.

It is also a privilege for me to be able to bring to you, on this closing meeting of your great convocation on the "Future of Capitalism," the personal congratulations and the best wishes and greetings of President Johnson.

You have spent three days in an exercise of high statesmanship. You are concerned with the preservation and the continual improvement of the most productive economic systems the world has ever known. Its health and success are primary concerns of the government of the United States.

We are in a turbulent world situation, a world of change. It is important for us to try to think simply about what it is we're after and the main directions of our course. I continually recall General Omar Bradley's remark many years ago in commenting upon this turbulence, "The time has come for us to shape our course by the light of a distant star and not by the lights of each passing ship."

The central purpose of our foreign policy is what it was when

228

we wrote the Preamble to our Constitution—to "secure the blessings of liberty to ourselves and our posterity."

We can no longer find national security through policies and defenses limited to the North American continent or the Western Hemisphere or the North Atlantic basin, for in this age of instant communication and intercontinental missiles with thermonuclear warheads, distance does not spell safety and no part of this small planet is remote.

Our security depends upon a generally peaceful world, an organized peace, and that cannot be achieved merely by wishing for it or talking about it, or even carrying placards. It has to be organized and maintained by hard work, determination, and, at times alas, by sacrifice on the part of those who want a peace that is safe for free institutions.

The kind of world we seek is sketched out in the Preamble and Articles One and Two of the United Nations Charter. We are deeply committed to the principles of free choice, to self-determination, to the right of every nation to choose and change its own institutions. Unlike the communists, we do not try to impose our system on others. We don't even ask other nations to copy either our political or our economic institutions; but we have, nevertheless, some basic convictions about these matters—convictions which are rooted not only in experience, but in a discourse about ethics and morality which has been going on for more than 2,000 years.

There are those who accuse me of being trite when I remind you that the American people really do believe in government with the consent of the governed, to use Jefferson's phrase. The United Nations ambassadors coming to Washington to represent their countries from all parts of the world have an easy instrument of prediction as to the reactions of the American people to the greatest variety of circumstance that might arise in some distant place, because the American people instinctively ask: what do the people concerned think about it?

We believe that democracy, with its capacity and its great variety of forms and institutions, is the type of government most consistent with the dignity of the individual and the rights of man.

We believe in economic institutions based on private enterprise. We regard private initiative as the engine of economic progress. It may be that in earlier days, and you can have some interesting discussion about this, the engine was not very well harnessed to our society as a whole and, periodically, it broke down. But immense progress has been achieved in improving the capitalist system to make it serve better and more steadily the needs of man. To this end, both government and enlightened leaders of business have made enormous contributions.

The modern capitalism which you have been discussing here has knocked the bottom out of Marxist-Leninist economic doctrine, which continues to talk about a capitalist world that never was, compared with a utopia that they have not been able to bring into existence.

We must, and undoubtedly will, continue to improve our economic and social system, but already it provides, on the average, the highest level of living for our people as a whole that the human race has ever known.

We, in our department, are deeply and constantly aware of the vital stake our foreign policy has in the success of the American economy. Our economic strength is the backbone of our international position. Without a strong economy, we cannot sustain the effort which is necessary to preserve the security and to build the strength of the Free World—our necessary military establishment, our relatively modest foreign aid programs, our overseas information program, our diplomacy.

Beyond that, the ability of the American system to provide an ever better living for all our people is a very important asset in the contest between freedom and regimentation.

Promotion of the economic growth of the United States is one of the oldest objectives of our foreign policy. It was the central preoccupation of our first ministers to Europe after we won independence, such men as John Adams and Thomas Jefferson. In fact, they set in motion our first national export promotion drive.

We are seeking access to goods from abroad which our economy needs, and enlargement of foreign markets for American products. In line with those objectives and with the paramount purpose of preserving our national security and way of life, the United States in recent decades has pursued several closely related policies: lowering of trade barriers; strengthening of the international financial system; aid to the economically advanced countries of the Free World in recovering from the destruction and disruptive effects of war; and aid to the developing nations in modernizing their economic, social and political institutions. These have been bipartisan policies, or, as the late Arthur Vandenberg put it, "unpartisan" policies of our nation.

We in the State Department recognize that we ourselves have special responsibilities for furthering the successful international operations of American business. You are all aware of the keen commercial competition we face from other industrialized nations. Even with an overall increase in our exports, there has been a gradual reduction in our share of foreign markets. Our trade surplus diminished somewhat this year because of increased imports. We must, of course, do all that we can to expand our exports.

For several years I have emphasized to all our ambassadors overseas the importance of maintaining friendly and helpful relations with the American business community abroad, and I've urged on all of them the importance of working with American business to expand our exports. We expect our ambassadors to be salesmen, just as Benjamin Franklin was when he first went abroad for the colonies with an instruction from the colonies to promote trade overseas.

We have welcomed the increasing number of businessmen who have been coming into the department and our embassies abroad in order that we might find a better way of helping them accomplish this great expansion of activity.

As you know, we have a Deputy Assistant Secretary for Commercial Affairs and Business Activities who is giving leadership to this program. We have enlarged, and I hope revitalized, the Department's Advisory Committee on International Business Problems. And I'm encouraged by what has happened at two very useful meetings in the last several months which that committee has held.

We have also enlarged our consultation program through the Business Council for International Understanding, under which our ambassadors and other senior officers meet with senior repre-

sentatives of American business firms with overseas interests before they, the officials, go out to their posts. More than a hundred
such consultations have taken place in the past year.

Cooperative efforts have been undertaken with the Department of Commerce to upgrade the economic and commercial
function abroad and to see that the total resources of our missions
are used to forward the commercial and economic interests of
the United States.

These are simply illustrative of our interest and our concern.
They are in keeping with the paramount objectives of our foreign
economic policy: to cultivate an international environment that
encourages and expands the interchange of goods and capital,
technology and ideas. And they have accomplished considerable
results.

Trade among Free World countries has doubled in a decade.
Last year, Free World exports totalled $165 billion. Capital is
moving across international boundaries in increasing volume,
thereby contributing to a more effective use of the world's resources and special skills and to higher world income. The countries of Free Europe and Japan, long since recovered from the
war, have advanced to new levels of productivity and well-being.

We have an immense and vital interest in the North Atlantic
Community, with its combined gross national product of more
than a trillion dollars, as well as a vital interest in the new and
democratic Japan.

In the Western Hemisphere, that great cooperative enterprise in social reform and economic development, the Alliance
For Progress, is meeting over-all goals. However, some countries are lagging, the performance is somewhat uneven, and the
over-all goals may need to be lifted. Politically, the main trend
has been toward moderation and democracy in this process.

In the Dominican Republic we joined with other members of
the Organization of American States to assure the Dominican
people a free election, relying upon their judgment, thus avert-
ing a take-over by either the extreme right or extreme left,
both of which had earlier been condemned by the O.A.S.

In Free Asia, the Middle East and Africa economic progress
has been uneven, but some countries have made solid and relatively rapid advances. As a rule—and this is very interesting to

be able to say in the middle of the 1960s—as a rule, those countries that have made the most impressive advances have been those that have provided a favorable environment for private enterprise. In the developing areas, there is a growing trend away from doctrinaire leadership.

But not all of the indices are favorable. Overall, the gap between the developing countries and the advanced countries is widening. The world stands at the threshold of a food-population crisis, which cannot be overcome by exports from the countries which produce more food than they need, but requires immense efforts on the part of the developing nations themselves.

At President Johnson's direction, our AID programs are putting increased emphasis upon agriculture, as well as on health and education, as the basic building blocks of development.

We have a great stake in the success of the populous democracies of the Asian subcontinent—more than 600 million people— and we hope that India and Pakistan will move toward settlement of the disputes which have so long divided them, so that the energies and resources of both countries can concentrate more on internal development and make the best use of the assistance they are receiving from other Free World nations.

We have a vast stake in the security and progress of the Free Nations of East Asia and the Western Pacific. The protective shield we are helping to provide for those countries is already yielding important results. I think those of you who have visited that part of the world in recent months would perhaps agree with me that, from Australia on the South to Korea and Japan on the North, the Free Nations of that area are moving forward with renewed confidence.

Indonesia, potentially a very rich country, seems to have turned away from adventurism and is coming to grips with its economic and social problems. One can be much encouraged by new regional initiatives and institutions in that part of the world—the Asian Development Bank, which will open its doors next month; the Southeast Asian Development Conference under the leadership of Japan; ASPAC, the group of Asian and Pacific nations brought together on the initiative of the Republic of Korea; the renewed activities of the Association of Southeast Asia: Thailand, Malaysia and the Philippines.

Those who sit back here and speak for the Asians, rather than listening to what the Asians say, make a mistake when they say that what we are doing in South Viet Nam lacks understanding and support in the western Pacific and East Asia. Those who predicted that it would cost us the friendship of other Asian nations were wrong. The new sense of confidence in that part of the world is mainly due to the conviction that the United States has the means and the will to meet its commitments and that aggression in the face of a commitment of ours will not be permitted to succeed.

Side by side with our endeavors to deter or repel aggression and to increase the strength and well-being of the Free World, we also pursue another policy, and that is to search persistently for areas of common interest and agreement with our adversaries, and to remove that term adversary from any necessary vocabulary. In President Johnson's phrase, we are trying to "build bridges" of human contact and trade and understanding with the nations of Eastern Europe.

We earnestly seek agreements or understandings with the Soviet Union to blunt disputes and to reduce the danger of a great war. We hope for international agreements on the peaceful uses of space and on non-proliferation of atomic weapons. We hope the time will come when, by permitting effective inspection, the Soviets will make possible more rapid progress in reducing armaments. We certainly shall try to do what we can to increase our contacts with the peoples of Eastern Europe.

We believe that our national interest and the cause of peace would be served by increased trade with Eastern Europe and the Soviet Union. In February of last year, President Johnson appointed a special committee on that subject, composed of American business, labor and academic leaders under the chairmanship of Mr. J. Irwin Miller, who, you know, is Chairman of the Board of Cummins Engine Company.

The recommendations of that committee led to the proposed East-West Trade Relations Act, submitted to Congress in May of this year. This act would give the President authority to extend most-favored-nation tariff treatment to individual communist countries when this is determined to be in the national interest.

It could be exercised in a commercial agreement with a particular country in return for equivalent benefits to the United States.

It is in our interest to encourage the communist countries to devote primary attention to the well-being of their own people, and to realize that peaceful relations with the nations of the Free World can serve that end. We believe that that policy is sound, even when we are required to resist aggression actively in Viet Nam. We think we should do all that we can to make it clear to communist leaders that they have a constructive alternative to the support of costly and futile attempts to gain advantages through the use of force.

Most of the eastern European nations have been seeking increased trade and other contacts with the West, including the United States. More such trade with these countries could be profitable in itself. As their national economies turn more and more toward consumer desires, they will become more attractive markets for our own exports.

Between 1956 and 1965 for example, our exports to Poland increased from less than $4 million in 1956 to more than $35 million, and our imports from Poland from $27 million to almost $66 million. In the first quarter of 1966 our trade with Poland was running at an annual rate of about $60 million of exports, and about $80 million of imports.

In the case of Rumania, our trade was nominal for many years, but, with recent improvement in our bilateral relations, our exports to Rumania rose to more than $6 million in 1965 and were close to $6 million in the first three months of 1966 alone. Because Rumania is still subject to discriminatory tariff treatment, its exports to us have not shown a comparable increase. They have grown only to about $1.8 million in 1965.

Since Yugoslavia embarked upon an independent course of policy in 1948, we have treated it accordingly. About 65 per cent of Yugoslavia's trade is now with non-Communist countries.

President Johnson has said that "the intimate engagement of peaceful trade, over a period of time, can influence eastern European societies to develop along paths that are favorable to world peace."

We also look forward to the time when it will be possible to have more normal relationships with the Asian lands which are now under communist rule. We have tried to break through some of that self-imposed isolation, in the case of Mainland China, by probing the possibilities of exchanges in a variety of fields, by attempting to talk about some of the larger world problems such as peace in Southeast Asia and the possibilities of disarmament, but the time for that, in their minds, apparently has not yet come.

Despite dangers and crises and setbacks, the Free World continues to grow in strength. The gap in gross national product between the advanced nations of the Free World and the communist states has widened. The combined GNP of the European members of NATO is approximately equal to that of the entire communist world, and our GNP is substantially larger. Internal pressures for better living conditions and more personal freedom are bringing about evolutionary changes in most of these countries of Eastern Europe.

I think it is accurate to say that, overall, progress has been made in building the foundations of peace. When Hanoi and Peking realize, as they must, that aggression will not be permitted to succeed and their militant doctrines will have been discredited, I believe the world will have a good chance of organizing a peace that is safe for free societies, and in which all peoples can make a better life for themselves and their posterity. Such a peace is our constant goal.

You have been talking here about the future of capitalism. That requires you to think hard about the future of peace. This great Conference Board is fifty years old. I suppose that there are a number of us in this room who are themselves fifty years old and perhaps a little older, but on your banner is the year 1916. Can we recall that yesterday when we were young? Those two world wars which came about because the governments of the world were not able to organize a peace, that period when the United States was itself not prepared to take an active part in mobilizing the decent forces of mankind to insure a peace. Those years when, some said, Manchuria was too far away, Ethiopia was not our problem, and perhaps the next bite by Hitler would satisfy him and bring him into some sort of serenity and repose with his neighbors.

Can you remember what it was to be young and to be trapped

into the conflagration of World War II? Can you remember the exhilaration with which an entire generation came out of the grievous wounds of that war, desperately hoping that the United Nations would succeed in eliminating that scourge from the face of the earth—that scourge of war—who looked upon the charter as the lessons of World War II, and who must now realize that in this nuclear world there will be no chance to draw the lessons from World War III?

Can those of us who were young in those days be forgiven for feeling a certain passion about the necessity of organizing a peace? A certain concern about repeating in the 1960s some of those slogans which led us all into disaster in the 1930s? This does not mean a Pax Americana. No one has elected us to that role, we ourselves would not accept it, and it is not necessary.

The overwhelming majority of the disputes and the acts of violence which have occurred since 1945 have been settled without our own direct involvement. The United Nations itself has taken more than thirty of these disputes and, with discussion and debate, has found a way of preventing those disputes from slipping down the slippery slope to World War III. Regional organizations, such as the Organization of African Unity, have managed to bring to the conference table and to resolve some of the disputes which have divided their hemisphere, and the constant processes of diplomacy are busy around the world, trying to find better answers, as sometimes the headlines reveal.

We have undertaken certain commitments with those who are committed to similar purposes, commitments basically in this hemisphere and in the North Atlantic and on the other side of the Pacific: commitments undertaken in order to avoid the mistakes of the past, to make it clear that those with appetites must restrain them, that the time to stop aggression is at the beginning, and that miscalculation should not be allowed to destroy the peace of the world.

In this postwar period, it has been necessary for us and for a number of other countries to demonstrate a concern toward organized peace by being firm in certain situations, by resisting force with force.

Have you ever tried to redraw the map of the world as it would have been had those efforts not been made? Or to speculate about where the prospects for peace would be if those sacrifices had not occurred? At the same time, it has been necessary to act with considerable restraint, not to open up a war because of the Greek guerrillas, or because of the Berlin blockade, not to let Pandora's box of nuclear war open because of Korea, to handle the Cuban missile crisis in such a way as to permit the peaceful extrication of those missiles from Cuba, to wait five years filled with efforts to produce peaceful settlement before bombing North Viet Nam, and to carry the banner of peace and negotiations about Viet Nam into every country of the world over and over again, to say yes to every formal initiative taken to initiate those negotiations or discussions over the past two years while Hanoi was saying no, to exercise restraint because there is too much power in the world for fury; but, nevertheless, to accept some additional casualties because we dare not follow the past into the pit of a general war.

It is tragic that we should call once again upon our young people for this kind of sacrifice and service, but the survival of the human race is no more a figure of speech, it is an operational problem among the governments of the world to control this unbelievable power that is now in the hands of mankind.

Let us think back on your fifty years, our fifty years, not to build upon the prejudices and passions of the past, but to think of our youth of yesterday in order to be able to build a tomorrow in which our children and our children's children can endure. I have no doubt that that is the central commitment of all of us who have subscribed to the Charter of the United Nations. I have no doubt that that is the greatest passion of the President of the United States in trying to manage our relations with other nations in this present world situation. I have no doubt that that is the deepest yearning of the ordinary men and women right around the globe.

It is easy to say "too far away." It is easy to say "none of our business"; so simple to say "well, perhaps, but not this time." But this time we cannot afford to be too late, and we must try; and, when this nation tries, it shall succeed.

Recapitulation

THANK YOU, Mr. Secretary, for a most interesting and impressive statement of our policies, our positions and our reasons. We all wish you the greatest of success in your very strenuous work.

This has been a historic convocation.

Some of you, I have no doubt, will attend the Hundredth Anniversary of The Conference Board. Some of the rest of us may not. This has been a memorable session—we not only had Secretary Rusk but also Secretary Fowler with us, and our Cabinet Minister, Mr. Martin from Canada and many other distinguished guests. I know you would all feel remiss if I did not extend our thanks, too, to Bruce Palmer and the staff of The Conference Board.

Because this is an unusual occasion, I would like to do an unusual thing, with the help of Martin Gainsbrugh, the Board's chief economist, and his gifted ideas. I would like to review in a brief few minutes some of the major themes that have been developed here.

We began with a brilliant keynote address by Lord Franks who took a long look back at the changes that have come about in the character and structure of capitalism in the first fifty years of The Conference Board's existence. We have moved in that time, we were told by Lord Franks, from an essentially laissez faire society at the start of the century to one marked by increased government regulation. Between World War I and World War II this trend in the evolution of modern day capitalism intensified, as was evident in the United States by the introduction of the SEC and related government commissions and agencies. Since World War II we have moved into the third stage of development, this characterized by an increased degree of direct government intervention designed to assure full employment and sustained economic growth. And as we enter the final third of the twentieth century, inflation has now replaced earlier problems of depression and mass unemployment as the great threat to the continuance of capitalism.

The Honorable Giscard d'Estaing in his address dealing with "Free Enterprise and the Individual" further pursued this analysis of the evolutionary stages of capitalism. As government steadily increases its influence in market decisions it inevitably exercises more control over what shall be produced, where and by whom. It thus poses, according to Monsieur d'Estaing, a growing threat to personal liberty and individual freedom. This may well foreshadow the fourth stage in the evolution of modern day capitalism, namely legislative determination of the extent to which the government—particularly the executive or the executive officer —can directly intervene in the planning of investment, in collective bargaining or in the flow of commerce, domestically or internationally.

Dr. Lee DuBridge skillfully demonstrated the extent to which the more rapid pace of economic growth under modern day capitalism has stemmed in good part from the intensification of scientific research and its high yield of technological innovation. Here again, personal freedom and opportunity for individual initiative are highly essential ingredients. But all of us have learned that a most constructive role has and can be played by government, too, in fostering scientific and technological advances.

The less industrialized countries, our honored guest from Colombia, Dr. Alberto Lleras, reported, are impressed with the growth potentials of free enterprise. Even so, they may find it necessary to develop, with perhaps a greater degree of government determination as to the allocation of resources than prevails in the developed nations, their own style of capitalism. Personal freedom would still be inviolate, but the state necessarily plays a more active role in determining how and where the all-too-limited capital these nations possess is to be invested in new plant, equipment and in construction.

Attorney General Katzenbach warned that under contemporary capitalism business enterprises have so grown in size that this brings with it not only benefits but also potential social costs and threats to the desired degree of competition. Regulatory measures are therefore needed, he contended, to maintain the intensive degree of competition essential for national economic growth without necessarily curbing the efficiencies arising from large-scale production and distribution.

As capitalism steadily augments man's ability to produce more and better goods in fewer working hours, the problem of productive use of leisure grows more pressing. Viewed against this background, business would be well advised, in the words of our friend at Chase Manhattan, David Rockefeller, to give thought and support to more active cultivation of the arts, much as it has over the past decade seen the warrant for intensifying its efforts and financial support of education. An initial constructive step in this direction would be the creation of a Council for Business and the Arts designed to stimulate and organize industry support for all forms of cultural activities.

The spiritual roots of capitalism underwent a most intensive and inspired examination in these proceedings that was in many ways unprecedented. Personally I thought that particular session was the most unusual and that the remarks delivered by Cardinal Marella and Dr. Bennett were most memorable. Capitalism's emphasis is not only on personal freedom and the right to benefit from the fruits of one's production but it is also exhibiting a growing degree of social consciousness and responsibility for action in the public good in its pursuit of private profits.

Few will forget Cardinal Marella's stirring appeal, "Pro Deo aut Contra Deum." The word he brought from Rome was that the Church is now actively enlisting itself in the promotion and support of democratic freedom, particularly in Latin America. This is a new and most impressive development of far-reaching significance. We are in turn asked to make our employees there and elsewhere more conscious of the equitable manner in which the fruits of capitalism are distributed to all who contribute to its success, and most especially to labor.

American industry has been contributing to the full in the

battle against inflation through its managerial discipline over prices and costs and by an unprecedented wave of investment in new tools and equipment and technology designed to enlarge and render more efficient this nation's capacity to produce, particularly under forced draft. And yet, under the strains of the war as it escalates in Vietnam, it may be necessary that the special stimuli to investment in the United States which helped so to touch off this investment upsurge be suspended temporarily. This message was all the more noteworthy in that it was voiced, almost reluctantly it seems, by the man, Secretary Fowler, who had done so much to bring these very investment stimuli into being.

In the closing hours, we learned anew from Karl Blessing of Germany that self-discipline in internal affairs is essential if a nation's currency is to command respect internationally as well as domestically. A soft currency at home ultimately undoes its hardness abroad. The future of capitalism, too, he sagely advised, is inextricably interwoven with problems of international monetary accord and reform, for which the need is greater than at any time since World War II.

Finally, the stirring words of our Secretary of State are still ringing in our ears, so that there is no need in this instance for recapitulation.

This brief catalogue of our proceedings is all too replete with problems that confront democratic capitalism as it enters upon the final decades of the twentieth century. But along with these problems, our speakers have also proclaimed and heralded the progress mankind has made under modern day capitalism—greater personal freedom, more material goods, a richer cultural growth, higher education and scientific attainment, and the rebirth of spiritual faith. Are not these proofs indeed that mankind has flourished under this way of life?

This system has demonstrated in the past fifty years in its flexibility and its adaptability to change that free men working together under the market mechanism can better the faith of mankind more than any other economic system ever known to man. Further changes in the face of capitalism will undoubtedly occur. But let us not let the unresolved problems becloud the record of solid accomplishment. Our achievements should, and will, spur all of us on.

As a parting word, I give you hope and confidence and resolution. In your hands, capitalism has a future indeed. Its rightness gives it might.

—Roger M. Blough

Progress / Problems / Potentials

A Chart Guide of Modern-Day Capitalism

The chart study that follows was prepared by Martin R. Gainsbrugh, the National Industrial Conference Board's chief economist, and Gertrude Deutsch, one of the Board's senior economists. They were assisted by Daniel Creamer, Fabian Linden, Gregory Kipnis and John Myers of the Board's staff.

LIFE   *Progress Against Disease*

The physical health of the American people has been improved markedly over the past half century, gains in longevity being particularly impressive. Almost 18½ years have been added to life expectancy in little more than one generation. The American infant born in 1916 could boast a life expectancy of no more than 52 years. Today's child, in contrast, can top the biblical "three-score-years-and-ten."

Female life expectancy is currently 6.8 years higher than for males, as compared with a 4.7-year differential in 1916. While the difference in longevity of men and women has increased over this half century, the difference in the life spans of white and nonwhite Americans has been greatly reduced. Nevertheless, the expectation of life at birth for nonwhites is still considerably below that for the white population—6.6 years among males and 7.9 years among females.

Progress in lengthening the average lifetime reflects primarily a reduction in mortality at childhood and early adult ages. In 1963, the death rate among white males was less than two per 1,000 in the age range from one through 33 years—and less than one per 1,000 at ages 2 to 15 inclusive. In 1910, a death rate as low as two to three per 1,000 was recorded only for those eight to sixteen years old. Among the very young, it ranged from 28 deaths per 1,000 for the one-year-olds to 3.4 for the seven-year-olds. Even for those in their twenties and thirties,

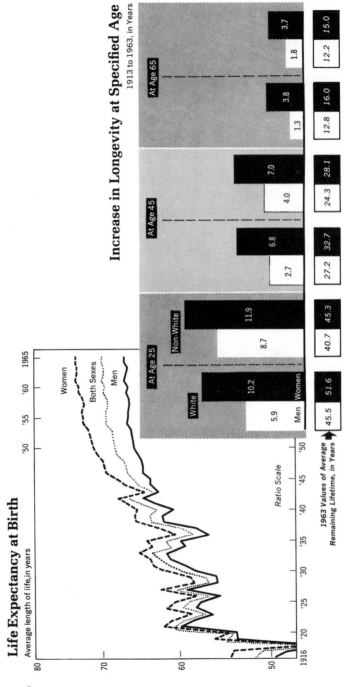

246

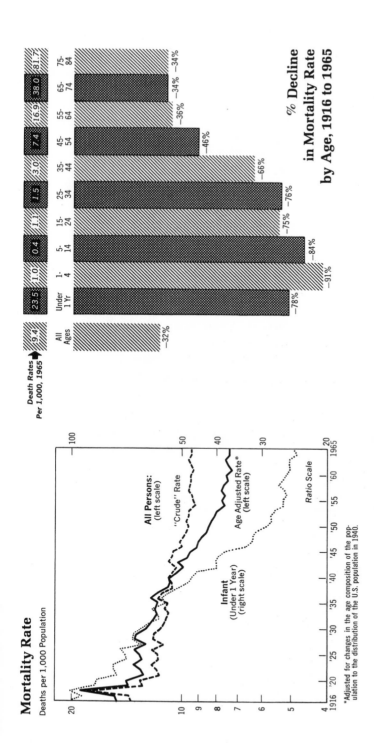

Mortality Rate

Deaths per 1,000 Population

% Decline in Mortality Rate by Age, 1916 to 1965

Death Rates Per 1,000, 1965

All Ages: 9.4 | Under 1 Yr: 23.5 | 1-4: 1.0 | 5-14: 0.4 | 15-24: 1.1 | 25-34: 1.5 | 35-44: 3.0 | 45-54: 7.4 | 55-64: 16.9 | 65-74: 38.0 | 75-84: 81.7

All Ages: −32%
Under 1 Yr: −78%
1-4: −91%
5-14: −84%
15-24: −75%
25-34: −76%
35-44: −66%
45-54: −46%
55-64: −36%
65-74: −34%
75-84: −34%

All Persons:
"Crude" Rate (left scale)
Age Adjusted Rate* (left scale)
Infant (Under 1 Year) (right scale)
Ratio Scale

*Adjusted for changes in the age composition of the population to the distribution of the U.S. population in 1940.

247

mortality then varied between five and seven per 1,000 persons. Only a limited stretching of the life span has been made, as yet, in the older ages.

Improved health and extended life expectancy have sharply boosted the chances of surviving from one age to another. Under the mortality conditions prevailing in 1910, one of every four newborn boys died before reaching his twenty-ninth birthday; currently only about one in 20 will not attain that age. Similarly, half the male children born in 1910 could expect to survive to almost age 60; of the current newborn, half should live on close to their seventy-first year.

Sources: National Center for Health Statistics; The Conference Board

LIFE   *Progress: Toward a Younger Population*

When this century began, this nation's numbers fell just short of 75 million and at the outset of World War I, about 100 million. Today, we number close to 200 million. The pattern of increase, however, has been erratic. In some periods, the population clock ran fast, in others, slow. The birth rate is extremely sensitive not only to economic conditions, but also to social and cultural changes.

The Changing Profile of Age Distribution

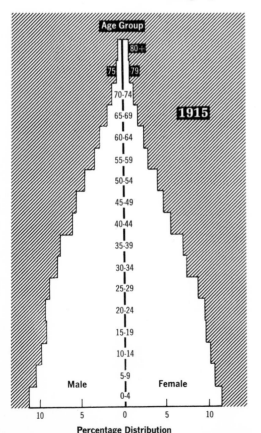

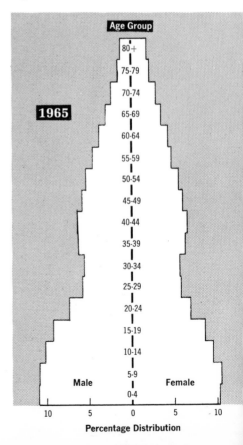

The Ages of Growth

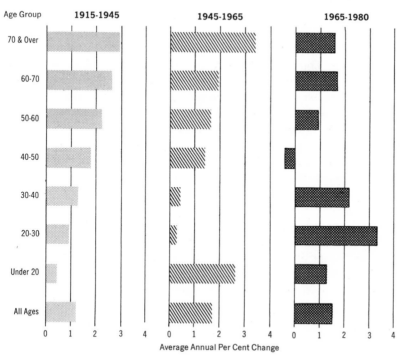

Age Group — 1915-1945 — 1945-1965 — 1965-1980

70 & Over, 60-70, 50-60, 40-50, 30-40, 20-30, Under 20, All Ages

Average Annual Per Cent Change

Population: Past, Present, Projected

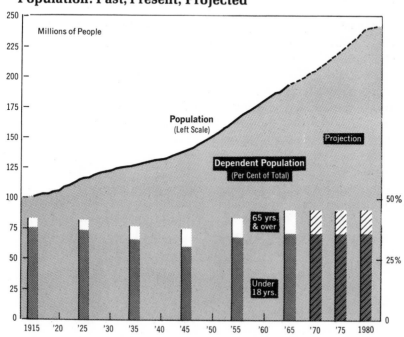

Millions of People

Population (Left Scale)

Projection

Dependent Population (Per Cent of Total)

65 yrs. & over

Under 18 yrs.

Twentieth-century capitalism has undergone the severe test of two major wars and a pronounced economic depression. Currently it is experiencing an unprecedented economic boom. These five decades of turbulent change have left their mark on our demographic profile. Two major shock waves are still working their way through the population age structure. The first was triggered by the decline in births during the depression and war years, the second by the postwar baby boom.

Extensive alterations in the nation's age composition are evident in the accompanying population pyramids. The age profile of 1915 is classical—each upcoming generation was modestly more numerous than the one preceding. The growth progression was orderly and uninterrupted. In contrast, the present age category 25-35 represents a relatively sparse generation, echoing the decline in births during the 1930s and early 1940s. Younger people, those under 20, are appreciably more numerous in recent years. Medical science, too, is affecting the age structure; today, persons over 65 represent a larger fraction of our population than at any other period in the nation's history.

In the years ahead, however, the average American family will grow younger. Between now and 1980, persons between 20 and 40 years will increase in number at a rate twice that anticipated for the total population.

Sources: Bureau of the Census; The Conference Board

LIFE *Problem: Conquering Degenerative Diseases*

Medicine has taken giant steps toward eradicating not only plagues but also the infectious diseases, particularly those of infancy and early childhood. The accompanying reduction in mortality has contributed substantially toward aggregate economic progress. Diphtheria has been practically conquered in the United States and the Western World and whooping cough, measles and scarlet fever have been brought under tight control. These four diseases combined kill less than one per 100,000 as against 39 per 100,000 in 1916.

Science, too, is winning its war on tuberculosis, influenza and pneumonia. Thanks to antibiotics and other miracle drugs, the death rate from tuberculosis has been reduced by 97 per cent and from influenza-pneumonia by over 80 per cent. Even so, the influenza-pneumonia group took the lives of over 60,000 Americans in 1965 and was still the fifth leading cause of death. It caused more deaths than hypertensive heart disease; sickness and disability from these diseases also runs high.

Still unconquered are the major cardiovascular-renal diseases (especially heart disease), cancer, mental-nervous disorders and other "de-

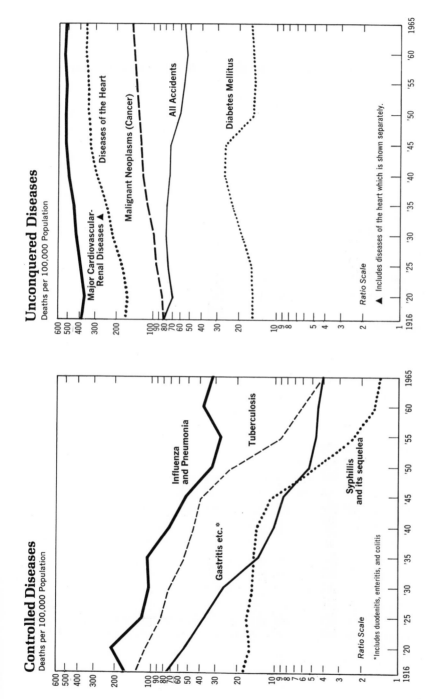

Controlled Diseases
Deaths per 100,000 Population

Influenza and Pneumonia

Tuberculosis

Gastritis etc.*

Syphilis and its sequelea

*Includes duodenitis, enteritis, and colitis

Ratio Scale

Unconquered Diseases
Deaths per 100,000 Population

Major Cardiovascular-
Renal Diseases ▲

Diseases of the Heart

Malignant Neoplasms (Cancer)

All Accidents

Diabetes Mellitus

Ratio Scale

▲ Includes diseases of the heart which is shown separately.

Comparative Mortality from:

Deaths per 100,000 Inhabitants, 1964

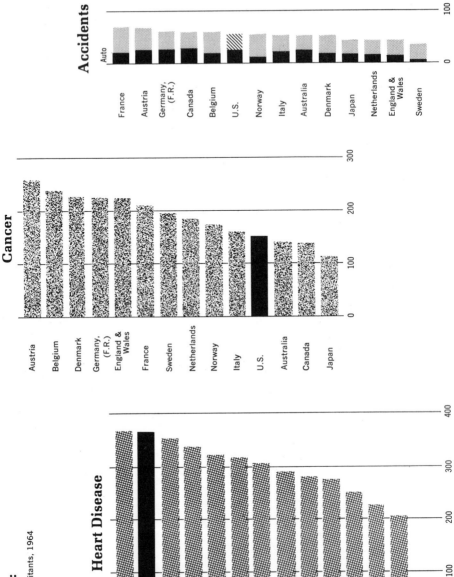

Heart Disease

England &
Wales
U.S.
Sweden
Australia
Norway
Denmark
Austria
Belgium
Italy
Canada
Germany,
(F.R.)
Netherlands
France
Japan

0   100   200   300   400

Cancer

Austria
Belgium
Denmark
Germany,
(F.R.)
England &
Wales
France
Sweden
Netherlands
Norway
Italy
U.S.
Australia
Canada
Japan

0   100   200   300

Accidents

Auto

France
Austria
Germany,
(F.R.)
Canada
Belgium
U.S.
Norway
Italy
Australia
Denmark
Japan
Netherlands
England &
Wales
Sweden

0   100

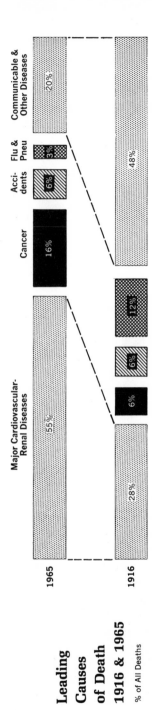

**Leading
Causes
of Death
1916 & 1965**

% of All Deaths

generative" diseases. Close to three-quarters of all deaths are attributed to the various diseases of the heart and blood vessels or to cancer, compared with a fifth of all deaths in 1916. Some of the increased prevalence of heart diseases and cancer reflects the growth in the proportion of older persons in the population as well as refined diagnostic techniques.

"Crude" death rates from heart disease are high in the United States as compared with other industrial countries. In contrast, deaths from cancer rank well below the rates in Western Europe.

Sources: National Center for Health Statistics; World Health Organization; The Conference Board

LIFE *Potential: The Population Explosion— More People, More Markets?*

Twice as many people now inhabit the globe as at the turn of the century. In fact, more people are now alive than had been born previously in all of the world's history. This growth has been most pronounced in the less-developed countries. Their people have nearly doubled in number since World War I, about twice the rate for industrialized areas. So rapid is population growth in some of the less-developed countries that it continues to outstrip economic growth. Statesmen, economists and sociologists as well as demographers and agronomists are concerned about a possible collision course between future population and future food supply. Urgent counsels for population control are widely heard, and in some countries are being heeded.

Long-range population projections are notoriously risky. Recent forecasts prepared by the United Nations, however, suggest strongly that world population will again double by the year 2000—as great a relative gain in just forty years as occurred over the previous sixty years. All regions will participate in the increase, but in the less-developed regions it will rise at a much faster rate, boosting their share of world population from 68 per cent to 77 per cent, under the influence of modern medicine and improvements in sanitation and public health. Of the five less-developed regions shown in the chart, only mainland China is expected to have a smaller share of world population in the year 2000.

Over a billion people now live in Communist countries but the proportion of world population in countries now Communist-dominated is expected to decline from 34 per cent in 1960 to 27 per cent in 2000. This decline results from the expectation that relative growth in mainland China will be lower than in any other less-developed region.

World Potential Population

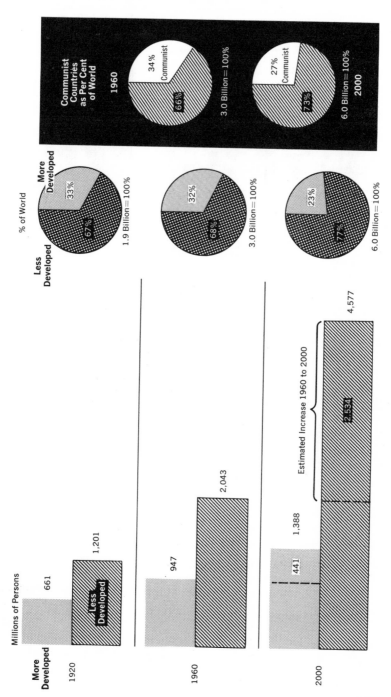

Communist Countries as Per Cent of World

1960
34% Communist
66%
3.0 Billion = 100%

2000
27% Communist
73%
6.0 Billion = 100%

% of World

More Developed
Less Developed

33%
67%
1.9 Billion = 100%

32%
68%
3.0 Billion = 100%

23%
77%
6.0 Billion = 100%

Millions of Persons

More Developed
Less Developed

1920
661
1,201

1960
947
2,043

2000
441
1,388
2,534
4,577
Estimated Increase 1960 to 2000

Regional Changes in Population, 1960-2000

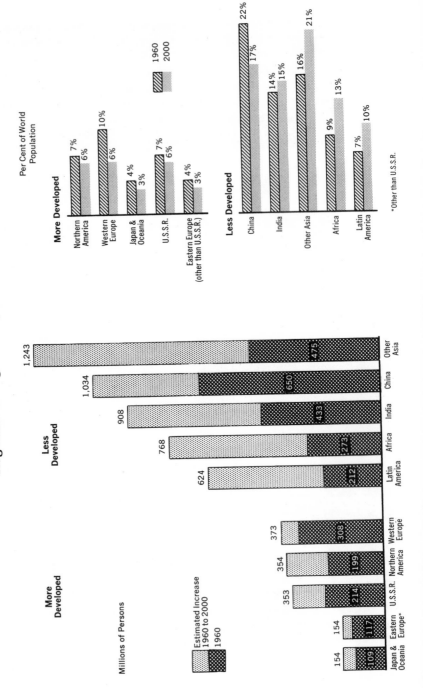

Per Cent of World Population

More Developed

	1960	2000
Northern America	7%	6%
Western Europe	10%	6%
Japan & Oceania	4%	3%
U.S.S.R.	7%	6%
Eastern Europe (other than U.S.S.R.)	4%	3%

Less Developed

	1960	2000
China	22%	17%
India	14%	15%
Other Asia	16%	21%
Africa	9%	13%
Latin America	7%	10%

*Other than U.S.S.R.

Millions of Persons

Less Developed

	1960	Increase
Other Asia	1,243	475
China	1,034	650
India	908	433
Africa	768	273
Latin America	624	212

More Developed

	1960	Increase
Western Europe	373	308
Northern America	354	199
U.S.S.R.	353	214
Eastern Europe*	154	117
Japan & Oceania	154	109

Estimated Increase 1960 to 2000

1960

*Other than U.S.S.R.

Many of the less-industrialized countries remain uncommitted as to the form of economic organization they will eventually espouse. In this battle for men's minds (and stomachs) lies the challenge as well as the potential of modern-day capitalism. Can it perform more effectively than communism in transforming human resources in these areas into increasingly productive economic resources, as has been demonstrated in the United States?

Sources: United Nations; The Conference Board

LIBERTY *Progress: The More Abundant Paycheck*

Labor under modern-day capitalism has steadily gained in economic status. Working conditions, hours of work, vacations and related fringe benefits as well as the real purchasing power commanded by escalating paychecks are indicative of the heightened well-being of all workers, from the charwoman to the chairman of the board.

The minimum wage is twice that of the average hourly rate of a factory worker a brief quarter century ago. The annual earnings of an average full-time worker in manufacturing are now in excess of $6,000 as compared with under $1,400 in 1939. In addition, the presence of many more dual incomes has raised a good proportion of wage-earner families into today's middle-income groups.

Beyond what is in his paycheck, a factory worker today gets medical care, insurance, pensions and many other "extras." Few could make such provision for themselves in 1914. (Gross hourly earnings do not include employer outlays for the bulk of these benefits, and hence are an increasingly inadequate measure of labor costs per hour.)

Increased wage rates have been mainly responsible for the gains in money income since 1914, but other factors have also been at work. Among them are: the shift of a greater proportion of workers to higher-paying durable goods industries; the growing preponderance of skilled and semiskilled workers to meet industry's needs; relatively fewer very young and aged workers; and the growth of labor organization with its economic and political pressure for, as Samuel Gompers put it, "More!"

The more abundant paycheck, even as hours of work were reduced, has been made possible by increased productivity. This ability to make more with less effort has been due to labor-saving inventions, huge investments of capital for modern plant and equipment and advances in scientific management, as well as the worker's better education and training.

Sources: Bureau of Labor Statistics; U.S. Department of Commerce; The Conference Board

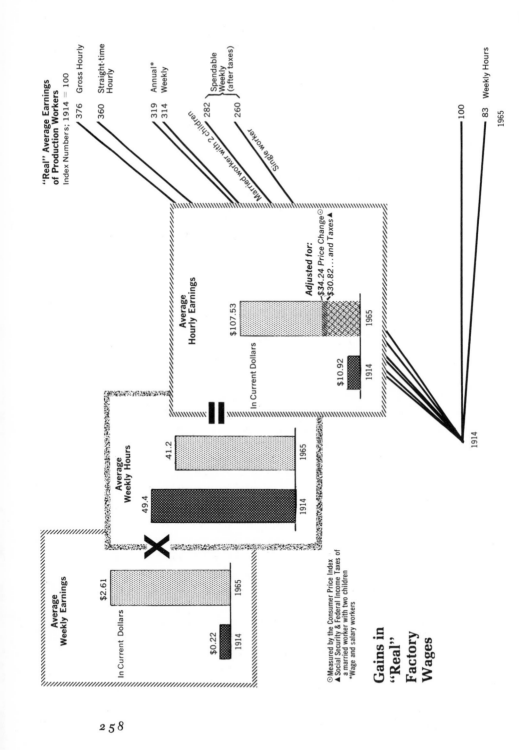

"Real" Average Earnings of Production Workers
Index Numbers; 1914 = 100

- 376 Gross Hourly
- 360 Straight-time Hourly
- 319 Annual*
- 314 Weekly
- 282 Spendable Weekly (after taxes) — Married worker with 2 children
- 260 Spendable Weekly (after taxes) — Single worker
- 100 1914
- 83 Weekly Hours 1965

Average Hourly Earnings

In Current Dollars

$107.53 — 1965
$10.92 — 1914

Adjusted for:
—$34.24 Price Change⊙
—$30.82 . . . and Taxes▲

=

Average Weekly Hours

41.2 — 1965
49.4 — 1914

×

Average Weekly Earnings

In Current Dollars

$2.61 — 1965
$0.22 — 1914

⊙ Measured by the Consumer Price Index
▲ Social Security & Federal Income Taxes of a married worker with two children
*Wage and salary workers

Gains in "Real" Factory Wages

Work Stoppage

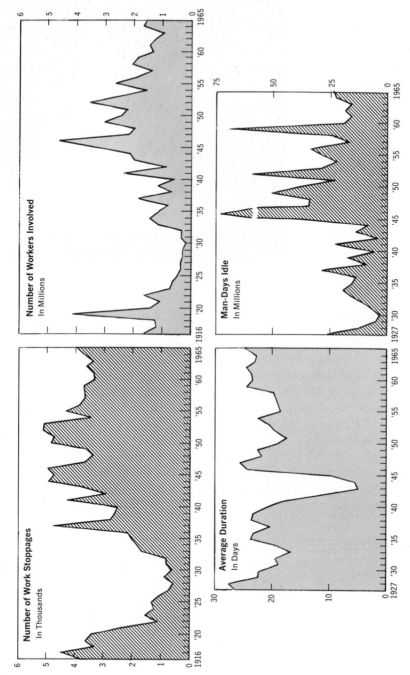

Number of Work Stoppages
In Thousands

Number of Workers Involved
In Millions

Average Duration
In Days

Man-Days Idle
In Millions

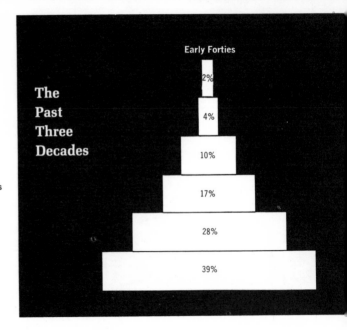

The Changing Profile of Income Distribution

Total Households
Each Period = 100%
All Income Figures in 1965 Dollars

The Past Three Decades

Early Forties

2%
4%
10%
17%
28%
39%

LIBERTY *Progress: Up the Income Ladder*

Few developments have been of greater consequence in the evolution of modern-day capitalism in the United States than the dramatic and unprecedented redistribution of income. At the turn of the century, three out of every five households had an annual income in 1965 dollars of less than $3,000, an amount now widely used in defining the poverty level. Currently less than one in every five households is at the base of the income array.

This "bloodless" income revolution under contemporary capitalism is steadily reshaping, almost inverting, the income pyramid. In the early 1940s, two-thirds of our households had less than $5,000, while now only about a third are in this earning class. As the number at the base

The Long Look

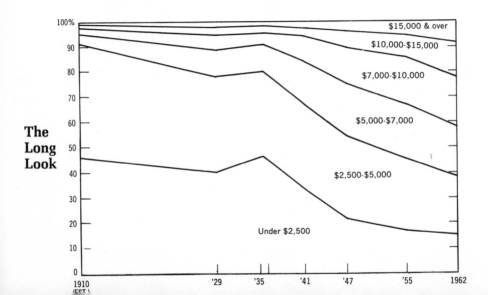

$15,000 & over
$10,000-$15,000
$7,000-$10,000
$5,000-$7,000
$2,500-$5,000
Under $2,500

1910 (EST.)   '29   '35   '41   '47   '55   1962

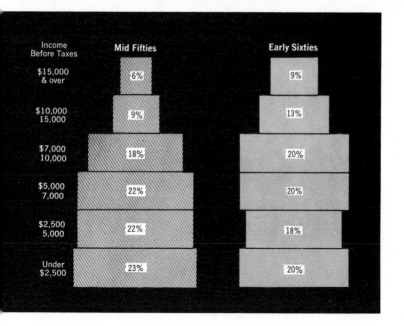

Income Before Taxes	Mid Fifties	Early Sixties
$15,000 & over	6%	9%
$10,000 15,000	9%	13%
$7,000 10,000	18%	20%
$5,000 7,000	22%	20%
$2,500 5,000	22%	18%
Under $2,500	23%	20%

diminished, the population of the higher income brackets exploded. Shortly before World War II, a little better than one home in twenty had the income equivalent of $10,000. The figure is now one in four. The number of households that has climbed up the income ladder and crossed the $10,000-income threshold has grown from 2.5 million to about 14 million.

This great income upheaval is to be explained in part by the rise in wage rates and the allocation of a larger share of the gains in na-

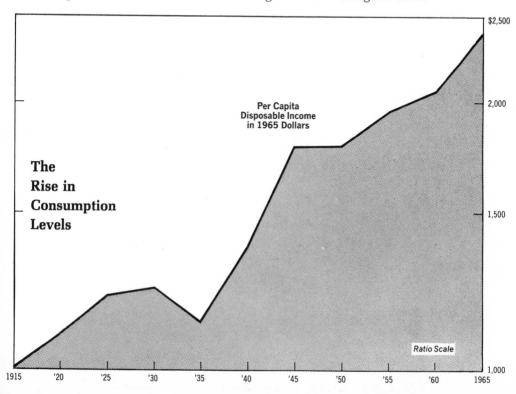

The Rise in Consumption Levels

Per Capita Disposable Income in 1965 Dollars

Ratio Scale

tional productivity to labor. In part it stems from the upgrading in the education and skills of this nation's labor force, as well as from the shift in employment from agriculture and from low value-added industries. The working wife's pay check, too, has played a role in this redistribution of income. Economic, social, cultural and political factors have all contributed toward the realignment of income, bringing with it extensive changes in the quality of American life. The mass market has become increasingly a class market. As higher rungs of the income ladder are achieved, new vistas of goods and services and of cultural and educational outlets become available to a mounting proportion of the population.

Sources: *U.S. Department of Commerce; Bureau of the Census; W. I. King; The Conference Board*

LIBERTY *Progress: Toward Mass Ownership*

Contemporary capitalism has made capitalists of a steadily rising proportion of this nation's population. Today over 60 per cent of all non-farm homes are owner-occupied and only 40 per cent tenant-occupied. As late as 1920 the proportions were exactly the reverse.

Mass ownership of cars sets this country apart from all others. Per 1,000 population the number of privately owned automobiles in the United States now approaches 400 as compared with 23 in 1915. One in every five families already owns two or more cars. As of 1962 the value of all durables held by consumers—cars, homes and appliances—totaled $192 billion and that of privately owned homes and land, $548 billion (at replacement or market value). During 1912-62 the value of the stock of assets held by non-farm households multiplied fifteenfold.

Mass ownership of financial assets—savings and checking accounts, life insurance reserves, pension funds and securities—also highlights the balance sheet of the American economy. Between 1915 and 1965 the number of ordinary life insurance policies in force increased from 90 to 552 per thousand persons. The number owning shares in corporate enterprise now tops 100 per thousand population. In 1929, when stock-ownership was at its pre-World War II peak, the estimated comparable number ranged only between 57 and 74 per one thousand people.

Debt, too, is a more prominent feature in the consumer's current way of life. The total liabilities of all non-farm households had risen from $8.5 billion in 1912 to $250 billion in 1962. Debt was thus equivalent to about 13 per cent of non-farm household assets as compared with 7 per cent a half century earlier. This is primarily a reflection of more widespread resort to the use of credit by a far greater proportion

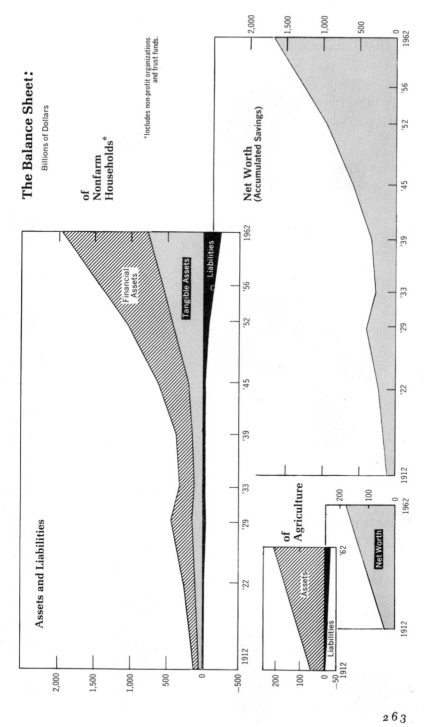

The Balance Sheet:

Billions of Dollars

of
Nonfarm
Households*

*Includes non-profit organizations
and trust funds.

Assets and Liabilities

Financial
Assets

Tangible Assets

Liabilities

Net Worth
(Accumulated Savings)

of
Agriculture

Assets

Liabilities

Net Worth

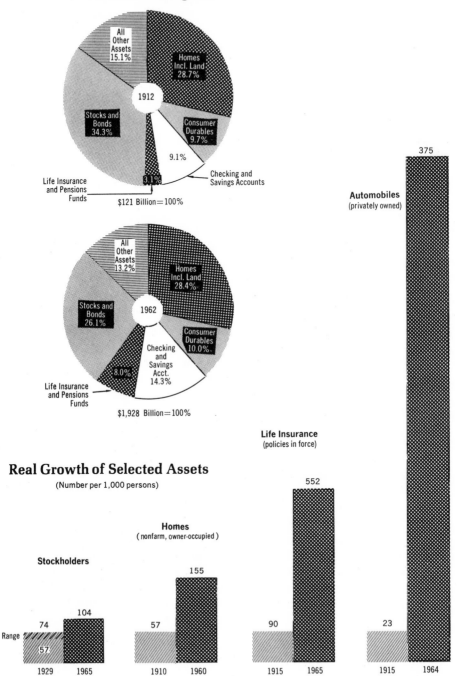

Distribution Among Assets

1912

All Other Assets 15.1%

Homes Incl. Land 28.7%

Stocks and Bonds 34.3%

Consumer Durables 9.7%

9.1%

3.1%

Life Insurance and Pensions Funds

Checking and Savings Accounts

$121 Billion=100%

1962

All Other Assets 13.2%

Homes Incl. Land 28.4%

Stocks and Bonds 26.1%

Consumer Durables 10.0%

Checking and Savings Acct. 14.3%

8.0%

Life Insurance and Pensions Funds

$1,928 Billion=100%

Real Growth of Selected Assets
(Number per 1,000 persons)

Stockholders

Range

74

57

104

1929   1965

Homes
(nonfarm, owner-occupied)

57

155

1910   1960

Life Insurance
(policies in force)

90

552

1915   1965

Automobiles
(privately owned)

23

375

1915   1964

of families than it is of greater reliance upon debt by the average borrower. Even so, the latest survey of consumer finances reveals that half of all families were free of installment debt. Despite the greater popularity of debt presently, net worth—assets less liabilities—of non-farm households had already reached $1.7 trillion in 1962. In 1912, the comparable total was barely $115 billion.

Sources: Raymond Goldsmith; National Bureau of Economic Research; Federal Reserve Board; U.S. Department of Commerce; New York Stock Exchange; Automobile Manufacturers Association; Institute of Life Insurance; The Conference Board

LIBERTY   *Problem: The Welfare State*

Mass unemployment in the Great Depression brought in its wake a social security program that has subsequently been extended to cover additional risks and an ever larger segment of the population.

Expenditures under public programs dealing with social welfare have had a dramatic growth, from about $1 billion in 1913 to about $80 billion at present. Slightly more than half originates in the federal government and the balance in state and local governments. These expenditures have substantially outpaced national economic growth—rising from 2.5 per cent of GNP in 1913 to 12 per cent in 1965. Even so, welfare expenditures are about the same per cent of all government expenditures at the end of the 50-year period as at its beginning.

As with many other expenditures, part of the increase in welfare spending is traceable to the growing population and part to rising prices. But even aside from such increases, they have soared. Welfare expenditures per capita in *constant* prices rose from $31 in 1913 to $395 in 1965, up thirteen times.

Early in this half century expenditures on education dominated welfare programs, accounting for slightly more than half of all such expenditures. With the emergence of social security and related programs, education now represents only about a third of the total.

Modern-day capitalism has brought with it an equally impressive rise in private programs, particularly protection against the risks of illness and old age. In 1940 only 9 per cent of the population was enrolled under private hospitalization insurance programs, 4 per cent under surgical insurance policies and 2 per cent under medical insurance. A quarter century later, the respective percentages for a substantially larger population were 78, 73 and 56. In much the same fashion, coverage under private pension and deferred profit-sharing plans increased from 2.7 million persons in 1930 to 23.8 million in 1963, nearly an eightfold increase.

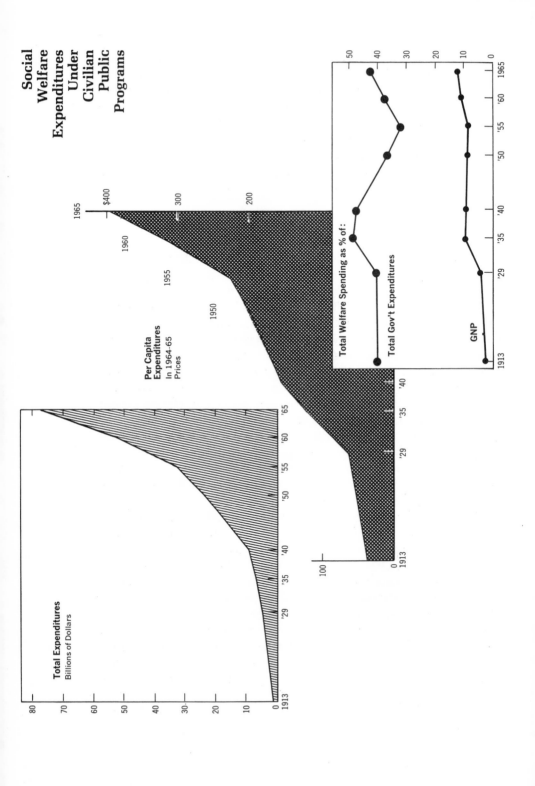

Social Welfare Expenditures Under Civilian Public Programs

Total Expenditures
Billions of Dollars

Per Capita Expenditures
In 1964-65 Prices

Total Welfare Spending as % of:

Total Gov't Expenditures

GNP

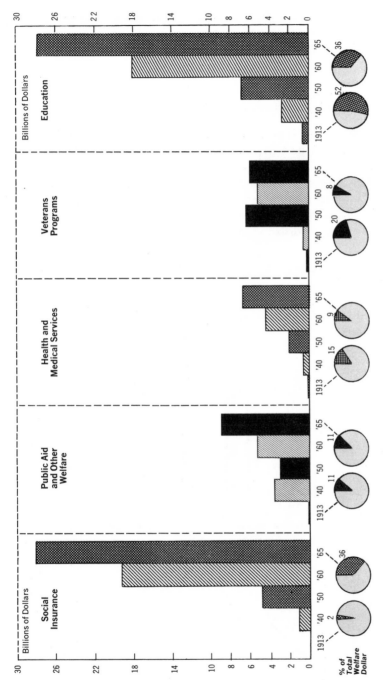

Public Welfare Spending by Program

The challenge that is demanding attention as all these provisions rise toward greater adequacy is the possible impairment under expanded welfare of personal incentives to work.

Sources: Social Security Administration; The Conference Board

LIBERTY   *Potential: Another Doubling in Living Standards?*

Assuming the past is prologue to the future, the growth trend under capitalism over the past five decades may provide some clue to the next half century. For the United States, GNP per capita in 1916 amounted to $1,320 in constant (1958) prices. Fifty years later this had risen to $3,140, a real gain of nearly 140 per cent. This historic outpouring of real goods and services per head of population coupled with broader-based distribution of income among households has

Per Capita GNP

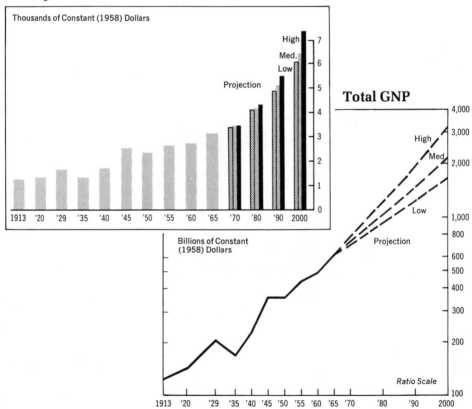

substantially improved contemporary economic welfare. This is not overlooking the fact that there are depressed areas where the rising standards in income, housing and services have not been fully shared.

Are similar gains likely in the decades ahead? Recent projections of population and GNP, using moderately optimistic assumptions, offer the prospect of another real gain per head of population of slightly more than 100 per cent by the year 2000. Should the war against poverty be crowned with success, there would be gains also from further redistribution of income.

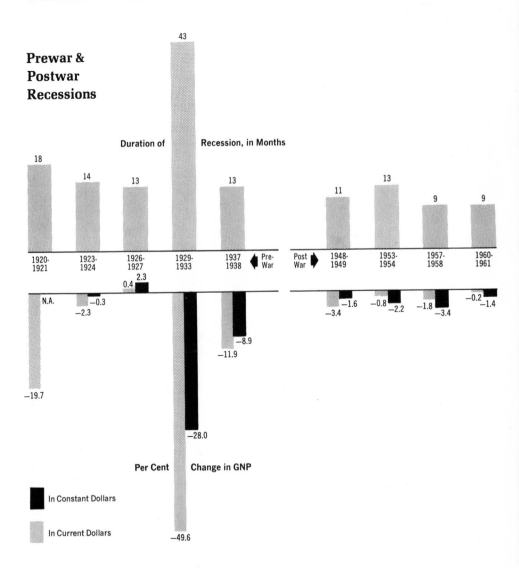

Prewar & Postwar Recessions

Private vs.
Public Share of GNP

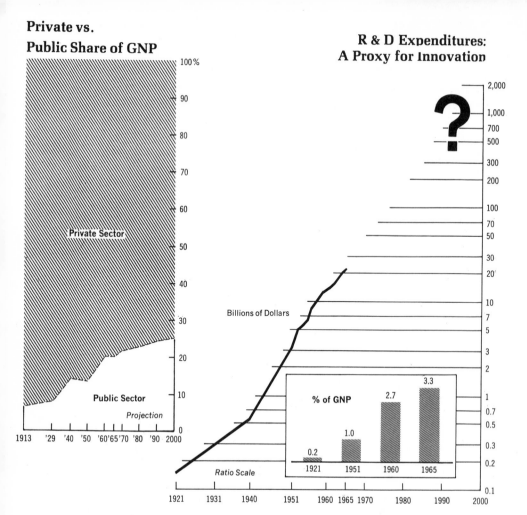

The acceleration in economic growth since World War II is un-doubtedly attributable in good part to the heightened rate of innova-tions accompanying the mounting funds expended for research and development. These have traced a trajectory as steep as an Agena rocket before entering into orbit—from about two-tenths of 1 per cent of GNP in 1921 to 3.3 per cent in 1965. As such outlays level off in decades ahead, will there be a decline in the growth rate in GNP?

Government plays a far greater role in capitalism today than in earlier generations. Some hint of this sweeping change is apparent in the public sector's contribution to GNP—from 6.4 per cent in 1913 to 20 per cent in 1965. Although in the 1960s there has been little change in the relative size of the public sector, those who project the economy look for a gradual increase up to 25 per cent by 2000.

Economic managers in both the public and private sectors are apparently learning how to control, if not master, the business cycle. Recessions have been of shorter duration and of smaller amplitude since World War II, a further reason for optimism about the future of capitalism.

Sources: U.S. Department of Commerce; Resources for the Future; Bureau of the Census; The Conference Board

PURSUIT OF HAPPINESS   *Progress: Toward Optional Consumption*

Americans live twice as well as they did a half century ago, when judged by the goods and services they now consume. Per capita disposable (after tax) income at about $2,400 is slightly more than double what it was in 1915, after adjusting for price changes. But even this arithmetic understates the case, since any time comparison of living standards involves a wide range of intangible values not readily measured by statistics. Today's refrigerator is considerably more efficient in food preservation than yesterday's icebox; television has brought entertainment into the home; and miracle drugs have reduced illness and mortality.

Progress in living standards is perhaps best dramatized by the work-time required to buy consumer items. A pound of bacon currently requires about 17 minutes of work-time of the average factory employee, compared with 65 minutes a generation or so ago. The work-time price of a pound of round steak has decreased to 26 minutes from 56 minutes, a pair of men's shoes to 5 hours and 20 minutes from 10 hours and 20 minutes.

The length of the average workweek has been cut from over 50 hours in 1914 to about 40 today and concurrently the average family has been enabled to reach out for many conveniences and luxuries which in earlier days were available to only a small fraction of the population. As late as World War I, fully three of every four dollars spent by the average family were necessary to meet the basics of consumption: food, clothing and shelter. Today these basics require only one of every two dollars. The food bill, for example, both for eating in and eating out, comes to less than a quarter of the family budget currently compared to two fifths in the earlier era. Fully a third of the present family budget is available for optional consumption—for freer spending for the goods and services that make for the fuller and better life.

Sources: U.S. Department of Commerce; Bureau of Labor Statistics; The Conference Board

The
Family
Budget

Percentage Distribution

Post World War I

Food 40.6
Clothing 17.8
Shelter, Fuel 19.2
Other
A 7.6
B 5.8
C 2.9
D 6.1

Mid-Thirties

Food 34.5
Clothing 11.3
Shelter, Fuel 21.7
Other
A 8.5
B 6.2
C 9.0
D 8.8

Early Sixties

Food 28.2
Clothing 11.1
Shelter, Fuel 17.1
Other
A 10.8
B 9.1
C 15.2
D 8.5

A—Household Oper. & Equipment
B—Medical, Personal Care
C—Transportation
D—Recreation & Other

Worktime Required to Buy
Selected Goods and Services

(Based on Average Hourly Earnings
of Factory Production Workers)

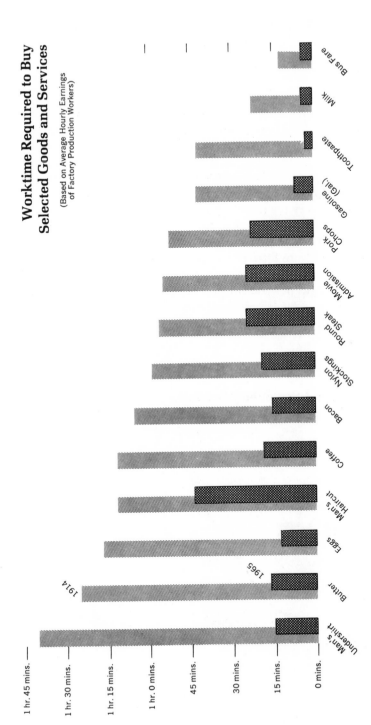

PURSUIT OF HAPPINESS   *Progress: Cultural Explosion*

More leisure under the shorter workweek and more dollars to spend while at leisure leave the great bulk of today's families with both the time and the wherewithal to pursue a richer and fuller life. Leisure and buying power have in turn widened mass participation throughout the broad spectrum of recreational, cultural and religious activities, largely the exclusive privilege of those at the apex of the income pyramid in earlier generations.

Barely one in every ten persons born before the turn of the century had the benefit of higher education. Now one of every four youngsters attends college. Last year this nation's universities conferred over 650,000 degrees, close to fifteen times the number earned at the outset of World War I. Public and private investment in education and learning grows steadily deeper and broader. The academic year of elementary and secondary schools has lengthened by a third in the past half century, and expenditures per pupil are now five times as large, in constant dollars.

Elementary and Secondary Schools: Attendance and Expenditures

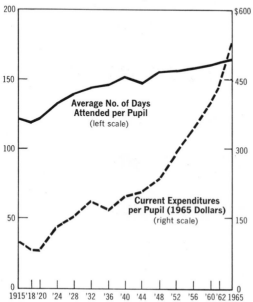

Reading

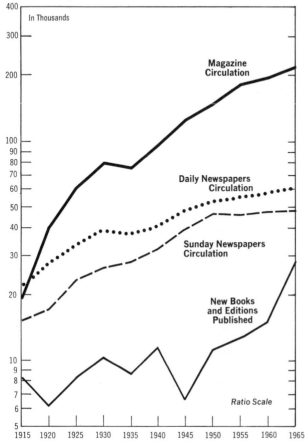

Higher Education: Degrees Conferred

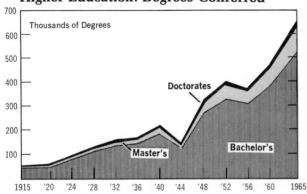

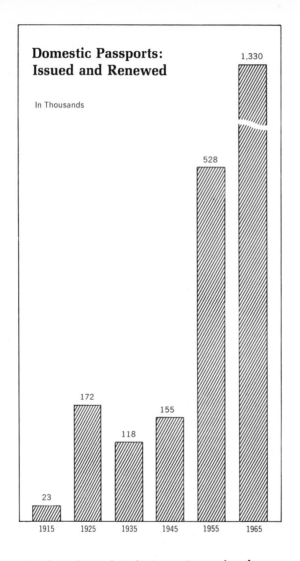

Domestic Passports: Issued and Renewed

In Thousands

Year	Value
1915	23
1925	172
1935	118
1945	155
1955	528
1965	1,330

Membership of Religious Organizations

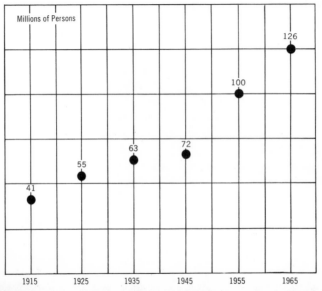

Millions of Persons

Year	Value
1915	41
1925	55
1935	63
1945	72
1955	100
1965	126

Education and culture are more spiritedly pursued in almost all areas of contemporary life. The circulation of newspapers and the publication of books have tripled, while magazine circulation has multiplied more than tenfold. The rising tide of foreign travel by United States citizens is a major contributor to our balance of payments deficit. This year some 1.5 million persons will apply for passports; prior to World War I the number was in the low thousands. This cultural coming of age has been accompanied by a gratifying increase in religious interests. Over the past half century, even as the population of the United States about doubled, membership in religious bodies more than tripled.

Sources: Publishers' Weekly; Magazine Advertising Bureau; National Council of the Churches of Christ in the United States of America; U.S. Department of State; U.S. Office of Education; Bureau of Labor Statistics; The Conference Board

PURSUIT OF HAPPINESS   *Problem: Moral Disintegration?*

Productivity has been so expanded in the twentieth century that levels of living for the bulk of the population of the free world no longer tend toward subsistence but rather toward the more abundant life. Somewhat paradoxically, even as man's age-old struggle to acquire more and better goods with less physical effort is crowned with material progress, concern has deepened and intensified over the moral, social and spiritual problems that growing affluence may have brought in its wake. Social scientists, among other observers, have documented the greater laxity in the moral standards and sexual codes of postwar adolescents than prevailed among their forefathers. Contemporary art, drama and literature are replete with the conflict of the existing order, and with the desire of the individual for identification. They attempt as best they can to depict and understand the tensions and mental strain imposed upon him by the heightened tempo of change. This challenge to the existing order has spread even into religious circles where controversy and debate reign among theologians on questions of population control and use of the "pill" all the way to the thesis that "God is dead."

These are qualitative changes in the world of contemporary capitalism that do not lend themselves to empirical treatment or to graphic analysis. One indication of the quickened change in social behavior is the race between illegitimacy, divorces and marriages. (Other areas of concern are listed in the chart). Holy wedlock is still the traditional prelude to family formation but the proportion of the population that has resorted to divorce is steadily on the rise. For every four marriages today, there is one divorce; in 1915, the ratio was ten to one. The divorce rate has almost doubled over the 50 years. The rate was then

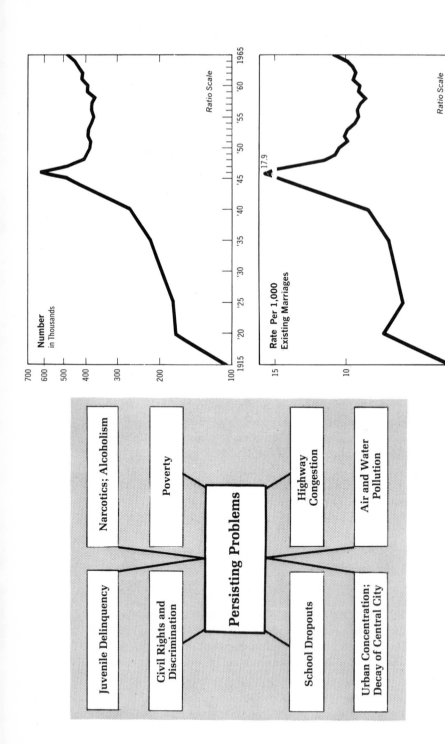

Number
in Thousands

Persisting Problems

Narcotics; Alcoholism

Poverty

Juvenile Delinquency

Civil Rights and Discrimination

Highway Congestion

Air and Water Pollution

School Dropouts

Urban Concentration; Decay of Central City

Ratio Scale

Rate Per 1,000
Existing Marriages

A 17.9

Ratio Scale

Divorces

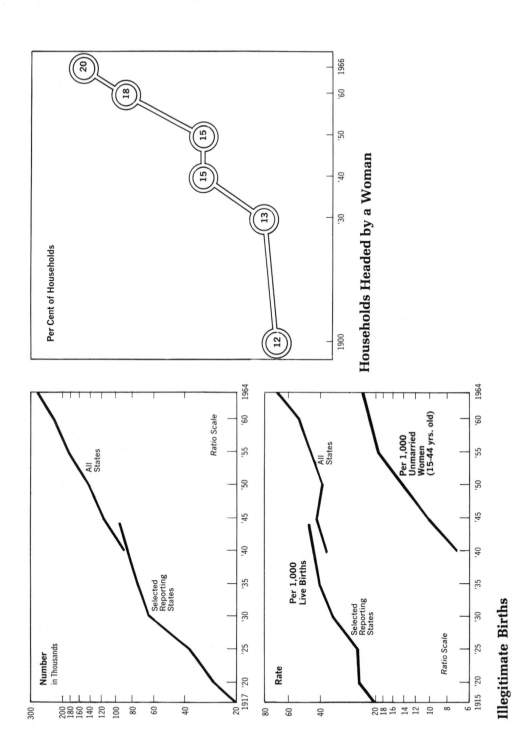

Per Cent of Households

Households Headed by a Woman

Number
in Thousands

All
States

Selected
Reporting
States

Ratio Scale

Rate

Per 1,000
Live Births

All
States

Selected
Reporting
States

Per 1,000
Unmarried
Women
(15-44 yrs. old)

Ratio Scale

Illegitimate Births

less than 6 divorces annually per 1,000 existing marriages. Now it is up to almost 11 per 1,000.

More children, too, are born out of wedlock. Almost 7 per cent of all births in 1964 were illegitimate; only 2 per cent were so 50 years ago. The incidence of illegitimacy is also rising—over 23 illegitimate births per 1,000 unmarried women, as compared with seven per 1,000 in 1940.

Divorce and illegitimacy mean more manless households. These have increased by two thirds over the past fifty years. Many such households are also headed by women who have outlived their husbands. Households in which children are reared with only one parent present are particularly prominent among the minority groups and pose an acute social problem.

Sources: National Center for Health Statistics; Bureau of the Census; The Conference Board

PURSUIT OF HAPPINESS   *Potential: Promise and Fulfillment*

Behind the imposing statistics of America's economic growth is a vital intangible driving force—our aspirations. As a nation, we are disposed to take achievement for granted and be impatient with our imperfections. With each new level of accomplishment we define more ambitious purposes. This is the dynamics of our development. We launch an antipoverty program when the poor are relatively fewer in number than ever before; we are concerned with school dropouts when our general level of educational attainment is beyond even the utopian expectations of half a century ago. But expectations must be tempered by the potential for fulfillment. To reach beyond capacity can make for disruptive stresses and strains. Our current objectives—the elimination of poverty, urban renewal, care for the sick and the aged, civil rights, securing the peace, aiding the developing world and sending a man to the moon—are consistent with our national traditions and our self-image. But, quite evidently, we do not have the wherewithal to accomplish all our aspirations simultaneously. Some system of priority is necessary for orderly development.

The National Planning Association recently attempted to estimate the cost of our major national objectives, using as a point of departure the report of President Eisenhower's Commission on National Goals. Even assuming an optimistic annual growth rate of 4 per cent, the National Planning Association found that its projected 1975 Gross National Product of a trillion dollars would still be some $150 billion short of the resources needed to largely accomplish all of our programs.

There is much to be done if we are to realize even some of our aspirations in the course of the next decade.

Source: National Planning Association

Cost of Attaining
Our National Goals in 1975

Billions of 1962 Dollars

**Projected Total Cost
of the 16 Key Goals**

1,127

357 Needed to Raise Standards to Goals

770 Needed to Maintain 1962 Standards

1975

**Projected Potential GNP
Assuming a 1962-1975
Growth Rate of:**

4%

981

3%

810

GNP
Actual

650

1965

560

1962

Cost of Reaching Each of the National Goals*

Billions of 1962 Dollars

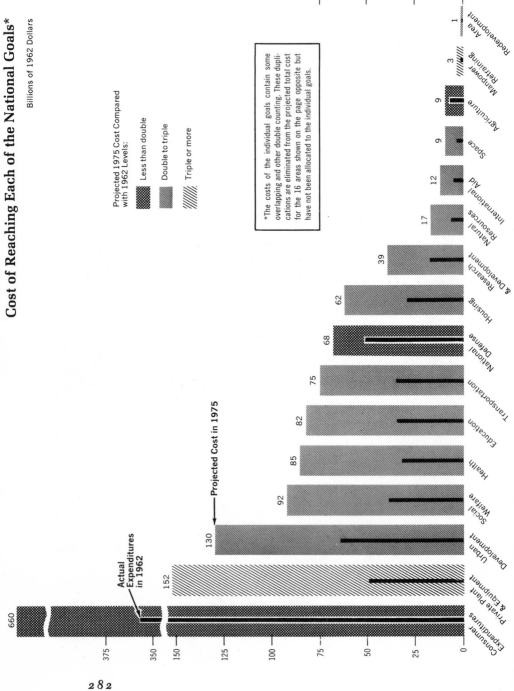

Projected 1975 Cost Compared
with 1962 Levels:

- ▓ Less than double
- ▒ Double to triple
- ▨ Triple or more

*The costs of the individual goals contain some overlapping and other double counting. These duplications are eliminated from the projected total cost for the 16 areas shown on the page opposite but have not been allocated to the individual goals.

Projected Cost in 1975

Actual Expenditures in 1962

660

152 — Private Plant & Equipment

130 — Urban Development

92 — Social Welfare

85 — Health

82 — Education

75 — Transportation

68 — National Defense

62 — Housing

39 — Research & Development

17 — Natural Resources

12 — International Aid

9 — Space

9 — Agriculture

3 — Manpower Retraining

1 — Area Redevelopment

Consumer Expenditures

375
350
150
125
100
75
50
25
0

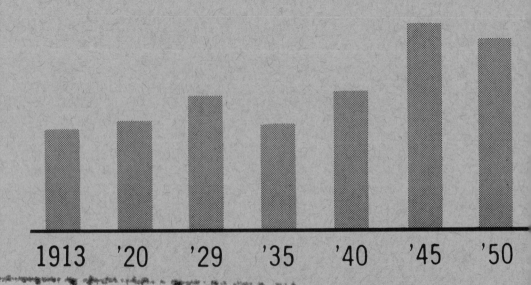

Thousands of Constant (1958) Dollars

1913 '20 '29 '35 '40 '45 '50